RICHARD
THE
LIONHEART

RICHARD
THE
LIONHEART

Antony Bridge

M. EVANS & COMPANY, INC.
New York

Published by arrangement with Grafton Books,
a Division of HarperCollins Publishing Group

Library of Congress Cataloging-in-Publication Data

Bridge, Antony,
    Richard the Lionheart / Antony Bridge.
      p.   cm.
    Includes bibliographical references and index.
    ISBN 0-87131-624-2 : $18.95
      1. Richard I, King of England, 1157-1199.   2. Great Britain—Kings
and rulers—Biography.   3. Great Britain—History—Richard I.
1189-1199.   I. Title.
DA207.B575   1990
942.03'2'092—dc20
    [B]   90-13819
                                                                    CIP

M. Evans and Company, Inc.
216 East 49th Street
New York, New York 10017

Manufactured in the United States of America
9 8 7 6 5 4 3 2 1

CONTENTS

PREFACE

Some years ago when I was writing a history of the Crusades, the extraordinary degree to which our attitude to them differs from that of our ancestors was brought home to me as I compared the works of modern historians with those of past scholars. Typical of our own attitude is the way in which we ask whether they were the last barbarian invasions of the civilized Graeco-Roman world, still very much alive under the Byzantine emperors, or the first movements in the vast expansion of western Europe which culminated in the nineteenth century. That they were examples of the worst kind of barbarous religious wars we have no doubt; and yet, at the same time, we have to admit grudgingly that they were inspired by the highest idealism and waged with astonishing courage, endurance and occasional acts of sublime chivalry. They also opened up that dark little corner of the Eurasian land-mass, later to be known as western Europe, to trade with the outside world and to a mass of ideas by which it has been greatly changed for the better. So our reactions to the Crusades are ambivalent.

In spite of the fact that most people know little about either the Crusades or crusaders – or perhaps because of this comparative ignorance – they seem to react in preconditioned and remarkably uniform ways to the names of the few crusaders, of whom they have heard: Saladin was a great and splendid man, noble and faultless, while Richard was a barbarian and a brute. Well, was he? Many modern historians have answered that question with a resounding 'Yes', but I was not sure, and I wanted to find out the truth about Richard. Hence this book.

In order to discover the true Richard, it was necessary to try to see him in the context of his own time and society with its very different beliefs and standards: different, that is to say, from those held by most people today, and not to view him distantly through the wrong end of a twentieth-century historical telescope. As a result, I tried to get inside the mind of his own time and society, viewing it as much as possible through its own eyes, and plainly this was difficult; but the difficulty of the task was nothing to its fascination. The people of the latter half of the twelfth century, their manners, beliefs and customs and their volatile, bubbling, richly creative – though often by our standards deeply schizoid – lives, fascinated me more and more as I got to know them. Similarly, the more I discovered about Richard himself, the more interesting I found him. Far from being little more than a bone-headed soldier – a brutal oaf good at nothing but killing his fellow men – he was a subtle, complex and many-sided man, quite impossible to describe in simple black-and-white terms. During his lifetime and for centuries after his death he was idolized by friend and foe alike as one of the great romantic heroes of all time –the *preux chevalier par excellence* with the heart of a lion – and there was truth in that picture: indeed, more truth than in the modern picture of him; but it was not the whole truth. My hope is that this book may help the reader to discover where, between those two extremes, the true Richard may be found.

But I cannot end this preface without confessing to one more thing which intrigued and fascinated me while writing Richard's biography. When searching for appropriate quotations to place at the head of the various chapters, again and again I found them in Shakespeare's *Richard II*, and at first I could not think why this should have been so. It could scarcely be written off as mere coincidence, and yet two hundred years separated the two Richards. In the end, I concluded that it could only be explained on the grounds that Shakespeare had a deeper understanding of the Middle Ages and of the problems and splendours of their kings than anyone else before or after his time; and perhaps, considering the breadth and depth of his genius, this is not surprising.

Finally, I must admit the obvious: this book is not meant for scholars. There are plenty of scholarly, comprehensive and detailed histories of the period, a few of which I have listed in the bibliography for those who wish to follow the subject up with further reading; but this book is aimed at the intelligent general reader, for whom I have great respect and affection. I dedicate this book to all members of that precious species individually and corporately, and I hope that they will enjoy it.

THE FAMILY OF HENRY II

HENRY II m. 1151 Eleanor of Aquitaine (1122-1204) (annul. 1151) m. 1137 Louis VII King of France (1121-80)

William (1153-6)

Henry (1155-83) m. Margaret, daughter of Louis VII of France

Matilda (1156-89) m. Henry Duke of Saxony
— Otto IV (c. 1182-1218) Holy Roman Emperor

RICHARD I (1157-99) m. Berengaria, daughter of King of Navarre

Geoffrey (1158-86) m. Constance of Brittany
— Arthur (d. 1204)
— Eleanor (d. 1241)

Eleanor (1162-1214) m. Alfonso King of Castile
— Blanche m. Louis VIII of France

Joan (1165-99) m. (1) William II of Sicily (2) Raymond, Count of Toulouse

JOHN (1167-1216) m. (1) Isabelle, daughter of Earl of Gloucester (2) Isabelle of Angoulême
— HENRY III (1207-72)
— Richard (1209-72)
— Joan (1210-38)
— Isabelle (1214-41)
— Eleanor (1215-75)

William Longsword, Earl of Salisbury

Geoffrey, Archbishop of York

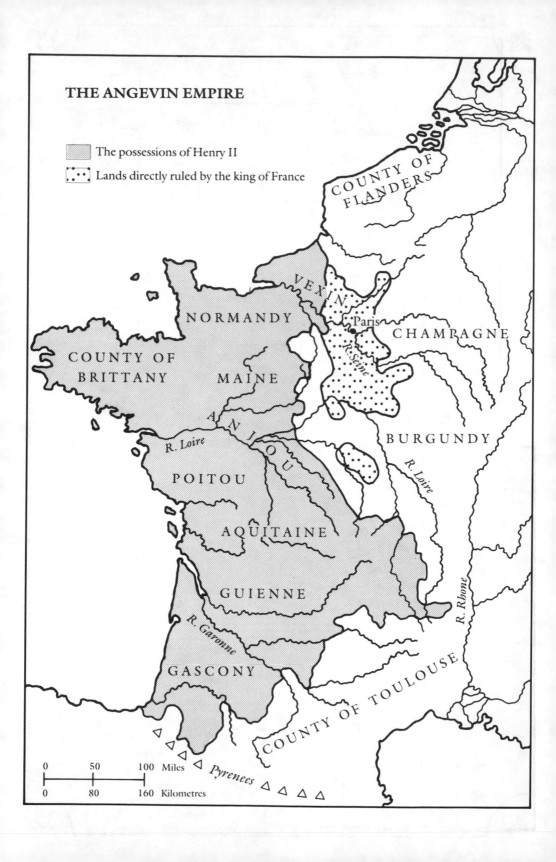

THE ANGEVIN EMPIRE

The possessions of Henry II

Lands directly ruled by the king of France

COUNTY OF FLANDERS

VEXIN

NORMANDY

Paris

CHAMPAGNE

R. Seine

COUNTY OF BRITTANY

MAINE

ANJOU

BURGUNDY

R. Loire

POITOU

R. Loire

AQUITAINE

GUIENNE

R. Rhone

R. Garonne

GASCONY

COUNTY OF TOULOUSE

Pyrenees

| 0 | 50 | 100 | Miles |
| 0 | 80 | 160 | Kilometres |

OUTREMER IN RICHARD'S TIME

Mediterranean

Tripoli

Sidon

Tyre

Acre

Damascus

Jaffa

Jericho

Ascalon

Jerusalem

Dead Sea

| 0 | 50 | Miles |

| 0 | 80 | Kilometres |

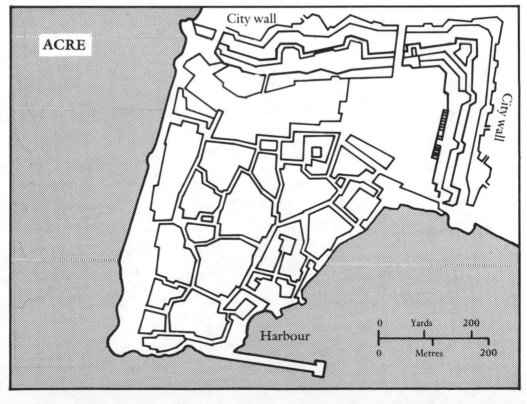

ACRE

City wall

City wall

Harbour

| 0 | Yards | 200 |

| 0 | Metres | 200 |

PART 1

*A Twelfth-century
Childhood*

I

This royal throne of kings, this sceptr'd isle.

Shakespeare, *King Richard II*

Richard was born at Oxford on 8 September 1157, the third child of Henry II of England and Eleanor of Aquitaine. That is a simple statement of fact, and it is a true one. Thus it would seem to be an appropriate and innocuous way in which to begin a biography of him; but biographies are funny things, and people should be warned in advance not to imagine for a moment that it is a simple task for their authors to give their readers a true picture of the lives of men and women in the past merely by studying the facts of their lives. The dangers of such a simplistic notion were well illustrated by the German church historian and theologian, Adolf Harnack, who set out to write a life of Christ shorn of all later, and so possibly legendary, accretions. When the book was published, it was reviewed by the French Catholic theologian, Alfred Loisy, who made the caustic comment that 'Herr Harnack, gazing down the long well of time and seeing at the bottom of it the pale reflection of a liberal, German, Protestant face, has cried "My Lord and my God!" ' It was not a kind remark, and Harnack is not the only man who has read the ideas, values and outlook of his own age back into the past while fondly imagining that he was being faithful to the facts; but it was a fair comment on his book, and it remains a salutary warning to all historians of the dangers implicit in their task.

So let us begin again with the statement that Richard was born at Oxford, the third child of Henry II and Eleanor of Aquitaine, even adding for good measure that he was probably born in

Beaumont Palace, and ask what dangers lurk unseen below the surface of that apparently harmless statement of bare facts. The answer is 'Legion!' For the pictures conjured up by it almost automatically in the heads of modern readers are likely to be about as wildly different from the historical reality as they very well could be: mental pictures of Oxford with its dreaming spires, its mellow honey-coloured medieval colleges and the peaceful water meadows of the Thames; of England's green and pleasant land with its patchwork of fields, its towns and villages, its population of staunchly patriotic, if socially varied, English men and women; of King Henry II and his wife Eleanor, members of our well-beloved royal family, an English king and his queen comfortably settled in Beaumont Palace, an early version of Windsor Castle or of today's royal residence in the heart of London: such notional pictures, assiduously fostered by the makers of romantic historical films and the writers of popular historical romances, bear little or no relation to the truth. So perhaps the first thing to do in trying to get a glimpse of Richard and his life is to look, however briefly, at the world into which he was born, and ask what it would have looked like to someone viewing it from inside a twelfth-century head.

First and foremost, it was a far bigger world than our own and a vastly more mysterious one, and it was flat; everyone knew that. There it was around them, stretching out like some infinitely extended plain, covered in parts by unexplored and unmeasured oceans and broken in others by mountains, to edges which no man had ever seen, but which everyone knew must exist somewhere in the mists of unknown lands and supported by the pillars mentioned in the Bible – 'for the pillars of the earth are the Lord's, and on them he has set the earth' (I Samuel 2:8). People living in the small villages and hamlets seldom saw a traveller, for their world was still a profoundly primitive one, in which they eked out an isolated and precarious existence not unlike that of some people today in the more remote and backward villages of a country like Ethiopia. It has been well described by the French historian, Georges Duby.

Unending emptiness extending so far west, north, east and south that it covers everything – fallow land, fens and wandering rivers, heaths, woods and pasture land, every conceivable type of forest – clearings here and there, wrested from the forest but still only half tamed; shallow pitiful furrows that wooden instruments drawn by scrawny oxen have scratched on the unyielding soil; within this food-producing area, large still-empty blotches – fields left fallow for one year, or two or three, sometimes even ten years so that the soil can rest and recover its fertility in nature's own way – huts of stone, mud, or branches, clustered in hamlets surrounded by thorn hedges and a belt of gardens.

These hovels were shared by men, women, children, domestic animals and cattle; there was no drainage, no ventilation; the stench of excreta and wood smoke vied for dominance of the air, while the forest nearby was still the home of deer of all kinds, wild boar and a few wolves. To people living in such conditions the concept of England as a country to which they owed some sort of respect or affection was as alien as the idea of it as a nation to which they somehow belonged. Apart from anything else, England was still an island inhabited by a number of people of very different racial origin, language and custom. The north of England was an outpost of the old Anglian settlements, though even here there were pockets of people of Scandinavian origin betrayed by some of the place names of the fells, the haughs and the thwaites. Modern Yorkshire with some of Westmorland and Cumberland was Danish in character, speech and custom, and so was the region of the Wash and East Anglia. People there enjoyed greater freedom than their English neighbours to the south and west, though the people of some southern areas such as Kent were more prosperous. On the fringes, the people of Cornwall were both racially and linguistically distinct, and remained so until relatively recently, as have the people of Wales. But whoever they were, and wherever they lived, the ordinary people of England seldom moved out of their villages; there they were born on the mud floor of their family hovel; there they grew up, mated and sooner or later – generally sooner – died, probably on the same mud floor upon which they had dropped from their mother's uterus. They would have heard of whatever town or city happened to be nearby – Worcester perhaps or Exeter, Canterbury or York – and they would have heard of Jerusalem and Bethlehem and perhaps even of Rome and London, but of other places they would almost certainly have lived their lives in splendid ignorance. The boundaries of the local world they carried around in their heads were very limited.

Life in the towns was not quite so basic, although there, too, usually it was precarious, uncomfortable and unhygienic. Oxford, where Richard was born, was not untypical. There had probably been a village there in Roman days, but no Roman road passed within three miles of it, and it does not appear in history until much later, when it acquired some importance in the tenth and early eleventh centuries as a frontier town between Mercia and Wessex. It was attacked by the Danes and burnt on three occasions, and it suffered badly at the time of the Norman Conquest. When the Domesday book was compiled, it boasted fewer than a thousand houses, and nearly half of them – four hundred and seventy-eight, to be precise – were in ruins. However, it grew slowly under the Normans, who built a castle and some churches there, and it had a regular market. Richard's grandfather, Henry I, built Beaumont Palace there in about 1130, but although there was an abbey at Osney and a monastery dedicated to the English abbess Frideswide in Oxford itself, where some theological lectures may have been given as early as Richard's time, Balliol, one of the earliest if not the earliest college, was not founded until over a century after Richard's birth. The history of other towns and cities was much the same as Oxford's in that many of them suffered at the time of the Conquest, but grew slowly in the twelfth century as trade increased. Few of them exceeded six thousand in population.

Even then, however, London was different, although the one and only thing to impress a foreign visitor to the city in the last years of the eleventh century was the alarming number of savage dogs, which lurked around St Paul's at night, terrorizing the citizens. But London, too, grew during the twelfth century. The *Oxford History of England, Domesday Book to Magna Carta*, records how

> *in 1135 it was described as the metropolis and queen of the whole kingdom; its citizens, like those of the Cinque Ports, were described as barons. It had been surrounded by a wall since Roman times, and it was now approached by seven gates. Besides the White Tower, two other strongholds were already standing, both on the western side, the castle of Montfichet and Baynard's castle, whose lords commanded the military forces of the city and controlled the Thames fishing as far as Staines bridge.*

Still its pretensions were modest; its houses were fragile structures, mostly of wood and thatched with straw. Fire and tempest wrought havoc in such conditions. William of Malmesbury gives a vivid description of a south-easterly gale in 1091 that destroyed six hundred houses in London; churches were heaped upon houses; roofs, rafters, and beams hurtled through the air. Another catastrophe occurred in the first years of Stephen's reign; a fire starting from London Bridge swept through the city, demolishing St Paul's and most of the rickety dwellings as far as St Clement Danes, some distance to the west and outside the city wall. A new city arose upon the ashes, and the wealthier citizens took the precaution to build their houses of stone and tiles. This was the London represented to us by William Fitz Stephen, who wrote his famous description somewhere about 1180. He was himself a Londoner and extremely proud of the city of his birth; but allowing for pardonable exaggeration, it was evidently a very fine and prosperous place with its thirteen monasteries and one hundred and twenty-six parish churches; with its schools and its streets cleansed by sewers and conduits . . . London was besides a city of pleasure with its carnivals and its horse-racing, with its opportunities for sport of every kind – bull-baiting, bear-baiting, archery, wrestling, and skating on ice.

But if the citizens of London, on the whole, lived their lives in less primitive conditions than most people, the feudal rulers of society formed a privileged class apart from other men, and enjoyed a way of life made possible by their wealth and consequent power; and here, too, was the greatest racial and linguistic division in twelfth-century society. For the rulers were nearly all Normans, still speaking French even in Richard's day nearly a century after the conquest, and still distrusting their English compatriots despite the efforts of successive kings to weld the two races together. In the year in which Richard was born, Richard de Lucy, the justiciar or chief political and judicial officer appointed by Henry II and one of the great barons of the land, could still speak of 'us Normans' and of the need for protection 'against the wiles of the English'; though in the later years of the twelfth century the division of the nation into foreign – that is to say Norman-French – rulers and English subjects gradually disappeared, and it became progressively difficult to tell whether someone was of Norman or English origin. Until then, however, inevitably the land was divided into two more or less hostile groups, and while Richard de Lucy warned his fellow Normans against the perfidious English, William of Malmesbury deplored the fact that the Normans were able to have everything their own way. The legend of Robin Hood, the noble English resistance fighter against the occupying Norman invaders, may be a legend, but it probably embodies a true memory of the divided state of the land in the century which followed the Conquest. It has been said that William the Conqueror was king of the Anglo-Normans; one hundred and thirty years later at the time of Magna Carta, John was king of England. It is one of the ironic facts of history that Richard, perhaps the least English of all the Norman kings, who spent only six months of his ten years' reign in England, and did little if anything to promote the unity of the two races living there, should later have become an almost legendary hero of the people he had so largely ignored during his lifetime.

If the rulers of that time were rich and powerful, and if this made it possible for them to enjoy a way of life denied to those over whom they ruled, that way of life was neither comfortable nor luxurious, if judged by later standards; indeed, by such standards it was abysmally spartan and materially limited. However rich and powerful some of the barons may have been, they lived in castles or fortified manors which were cold, draughty, damp, ill-lit, and smoke-filled in winter without being much more salubrious in summer; of privacy they enjoyed little or none, for they lived in the midst of a mob of supporters, military retainers, hangers-on, cooks, chamberlains, servants and serfs of all kinds; and indeed the higher their social position and rank, the more disagreeable became the implications of the phrase 'public life' whether at home or on the move. Even their food and drink would have been without much variety or attraction, especially in winter; it is easy to forget that potatoes, rice, maize, and many if not most of the green vegetables and fruit we take for granted were wholly unknown in the twelfth century, as were tea, coffee and chocolate, while the only alcoholic drinks readily available even to the rich were beer, cider and some wines.

Meanwhile, of course, the rich and powerful were as prone to disease and early death as anyone. In our own day, the medical profession has banished early death so successfully that we all live in the splendidly comfortable perspective of assured longevity. When a child or a young adult dies, everyone is deeply shocked, and even when a man dies of a stroke or a heart attack in his early to mid-fifties, his death is regarded as tragically premature. In the twelfth century, however, and indeed throughout history until the dawning of our own sanitary and surgical age, death was an everyday occurrence, an ever-present possibility, and most people died young; infant mortality was huge, and the gauntlet of lethal diseases run by growing children on their way to maturity was only too effective in thinning their ranks and keeping the population of the world within reasonable bounds. One pope, born into a family of twenty-two children in Italy, was one of only two to survive to the age of twenty, and this was not at all unusual; most children died. Those who survived to become adults were the lucky ones, but even then there was no way in which they could count on that luck continuing to favour their survival. Brawls, fights, duels, muggings and drunken murders were commonplace; mild infections could take a sudden turn for the worse and kill, while Henry I, as every schoolboy knows, died after eating too many lampreys, to which he seems to have been allergic, and against which he had been warned by his doctor; a fever, a colic, a quinsy, a burst appendix, an attack of dysentery, of measles, of smallpox, or one of a dozen different kinds of growth could, and often did, carry a man off after a few days' illness, while such regular scourges as leprosy and the plague were dreaded and appalling pests which killed millions of people from time to time. Famine, too, was a killer; when the crops failed because of two or three years' drought – or conversely floods – there were few reserves of food upon which to fall back; and although members of the ruling class escaped the worst horrors of the resulting dearth, country people died like flies, and in towns like London, where the death rate in normal times was anyway higher than in the country, the streets soon filled up with emaciated corpses.

If life in the twelfth century was always precarious and by later standards extremely uncomfortable, the politics of the day sometimes made it even more uncertain. Twenty-two years before Richard was born, when Henry I died on 1 December 1135, in his mid-sixties, the question as to who should succeed him was not an easy one to answer; he had fathered at least twenty-one children but only two had been born in lawful wedlock. William, his only legitimate son, had died at sea fifteen years before his father, and his only legitimate daughter, Matilda, was highly unpopular in England. She was an unpleasant woman, haughty, insolent and avaricious, who had been married twice, first to the German Emperor, and after his death to the Frenchman Geoffrey of Anjou, who was as much disliked by the Norman barons as she was herself; as an English chronicler said at the time, 'All the French and English thought ill of the marriage,' and few in England wanted to see Matilda seated on the vacant throne. So no one protested for long when one of the dead king's nephews, Stephen of Blois, crossed to England and with the help of his younger brother, Henry of Blois, who, by a happy coincidence, was bishop of Winchester at the time, seized first the treasury and then the throne; it had all happened *quasi in ictu oculi*, as one contemporary observer put it – as if in the twinkling of an eye – and a few weeks later he was recognized as the lawful king of England. But the unattractive Matilda and her even less endearing husband, Geoffrey of Anjou, were not the kind of people to sit back while their legal rights were usurped, and they had an ally in Matilda's half-brother, Robert, earl of Gloucester. This is not a history of Stephen's disastrous reign, and it must suffice to say that, although he seems to have been rather an amiable and attractive man, he was hopelessly indecisive, a characteristic which ill-fitted him for the part he had to play when Robert of Gloucester openly rebelled in favour of Matilda, and civil war followed as night follows day.

For nearly ten years conditions not unlike those which had prevailed during the worst years of the Dark Ages returned to England, while the fortunes respectively of the king and of his rebellious enemies swung from momentary triumph to sudden *débâcle* with exasperating impartiality, as battle followed battle and victory was succeeded by defeat. Many of the leading barons of the land changed sides with as little compunction as a man might feel about changing his shirt, using the chaos of the time to build themselves castles, from which they might emerge to terrify the country round about and extort by violence as much loot from all and sundry as the threat – and often enough the reality – of torture or death could procure. The notorious earl of Essex, Geoffrey de Mandeville, was typical of many others, changing sides whenever it suited him to do so, and constantly plotting to betray whichever side he happened to be supporting at the time; even when arrested and charged with treason, he escaped with the loss of one or two castles, and went off to Ely, which he used as a base from which to vent his violent rage on the wretched inhabitants of the fens. He seized the abbey of Ramsey, drove out the monks, turned it into a fortress and military headquarters for his gang of mercenaries, ruffians, cut-throats and thugs, emerging from it to plunder and ravage the country far and wide. Cities like Cambridge were sacked and burnt; religious houses with their reputation for hidden wealth were viciously attacked; anyone suspected of being a hostage worth a large ransom was subjected to every form of torture that the sadistic ingenuity of the appalling earl could devise, and neither women nor children were spared. Under this reign of terror, all work stopped; the fields were untilled; the crops uncut or destroyed. Over a stretch of thirty or more miles of country, not an ox or a plough was to be seen at work, for the peasants dared not emerge from their hovels in daylight; as a result, famine added to the already huge death-roll, and there was nothing anyone could do about it. When Stephen tried to bring justice to the land and retribution to the man responsible for the murderous anarchy under which it was suffering, Geoffrey de Mandeville merely withdrew into the heart of his swamps and fens, and defied anyone to come near him; and had he not been struck by an arrow and killed in August 1144, his reign of terror might have gone on indefinitely.

Of course, the anarchy of Stephen's reign was exceptional; most of the time law and order were preserved, and men could live and go about their business in peace: at least, they could do so in England, though in France things were rather different. The feudal system of government through a hierarchy of baronial land-owners, each owing allegiance to the one above him, until the king was reached at the top of the social and legal pyramid, although it had slowly but eventually rescued Europe from the endemic turmoil of the Dark Ages, was always liable to occasional outbreaks of violence; a baron might suddenly become more powerful than hitherto by marrying an heiress who brought with her as part of her dowry large estates, castles, revenues, and armed retainers, and this sudden access of power might tempt him to attack his neighbour or his liege lord; the latter would retaliate, and war would follow, turning the particular part of the country in which the antagonists lived into a shambles of burnt crops, sacked towns, ruined villages and unburied corpses. Personal jealousies could also lead to war, for while it was regarded as perfectly acceptable for a man to have a mistress – or, indeed, a bevy of mistresses – a wife might not stray from the path of conjugal fidelity under any circumstances; if she did so, her husband's reaction might be limited to personal violence against her lover, but it might also lead to war. A Flemish nobleman, Philip of Flanders, was content to hang his wife's lover upside down in a cess-pit until he was dead, but when the French viscount, Aimar of Limoges, suspected that his wife was having an affair with his uncle, he did not hesitate to go to war, attacking his amorous kinsman without warning and plunging the countryside around his home into darkness and desolation. France was particularly subject to such local outbreaks of violence, partly because it was much bigger than England; and while sporadic war was more or less endemic on the borders of Scotland and Wales, it was rarer elsewhere in England except in times of weak government like that of Stephen. The damage done during his disastrous reign was soon repaired by Henry II, Richard's father, who kept his English barons under iron control; but in France even Henry found it impossible to prevent occasional outbreaks of rebellion and petty violence by barons, who waited until he was conveniently far away in England to defy him, forcing him to cross the Channel and hurry south in order to bring them to heel again with all the attendant violence and destruction which that inevitably involved.

To twentieth-century eyes, the surprising thing, however, is that despite the sporadic violence of the times – and indeed partly because of it – the twelfth century was an age of astonishing, bubbling and creative intellectual endeavour and artistic life. People were conscious of living in a new age after centuries of darkness: an age in which doors that had been closed for centuries were opening again on almost forgotten and enormously exciting vistas of adventure and opportunity. Ever since the slow death of the Roman Empire in the west, western Europe had been sunk in barbarism and political chaos; when not being invaded by barbarians , it had been perpetually subject to civil war, and although every schoolboy knows this, it is almost impossible to imagine how hideous life must have been for almost everyone in the Dark Ages, or how exciting it must have been to begin emerging from them. Memories of what life had been like under the *pax romana*, where they survived at all, had become so dim as to seem unreal; but then in the middle of the eleventh century – a hundred years before Richard was born – the darkness had begun to give way to a glimmer of new light, and the glimmer had grown. Trade had become possible again, and with the growth of trade people had begun to travel, exploring new places, encountering new ideas, and rediscovering old ones from the golden ages of the Graeco-Roman past. A great longing for knowledge was born, and young men of ability flocked to the new schools in monasteries like Le Bec in Normandy, in cathedral cities like Chartres, and above all in Paris to sit at the feet of men such as Bernard of Chartres, Lanfranc, Anselm and Peter Abelard. Perhaps the excitement experienced by people in our own time, as they sat transfixed in front of their television sets while some of their fellow human beings stepped out of their space capsule on to the surface of the Moon, may give an idea of the excitement aroused in the breasts and minds of students in the twelfth century, as they began to discover what the golden age of Rome had really been like; to explore the works of such men as Cicero, Sallust, Suetonius, Seneca, the elder Pliny and Apuleius, let alone the works of Plato and Aristotle, even if they were available at that time only in Latin translations, was to wander wide-eyed through the sylvan landscapes of the ancient world, to discover the streets and squares of Rome, to enter into the minds and thoughts, the hopes and dreams, the loves and the sorrows of those long-dead men and women of old and to become guests in their homes.

The basis of all learning was Latin, and in the most celebrated of all the twelfth-century centres of intellectual life, Paris, the part of the city to which young men from all over Europe flocked to sit at the feet of masters such as Peter Abelard is still called the Latin Quarter. Elsewhere, Bernard of Chartres used his lessons in Latin grammar as an excuse to explore the works of the great classical writers, devoting the morning to reading, the afternoon to discussion and the evenings to philosophical discussion. John of Salisbury, one of the greatest intellects of the century, remarked on the fact that, after a year, only the most unimaginative and stupid students were unable to read and write Latin fluently and easily. But perhaps it was Abelard who best defined the nature and aim of this new intellectual adventure upon which some of the most able young men of the day had embarked with such excitement, when he said, 'By doubting we come to enquiry, and by enquiring we come to the truth.' Predictably, at first the church regarded such a doctrine with the deepest suspicion, and not surprisingly Abelard was excommunicated; but by the time Richard was born Abelard had been dead for fifteen years, and his doctrine had been accepted as the basis of all learning. Although it produced a few sceptics – Richard's brother, John, never missed an opportunity to mock the Church and all its doings, whatever he may have believed about God, and Gerald of Wales, a chronicler whose works are an invaluable source of contemporary information, may possibly have taken a similar view – the vast majority of people never doubted for a moment that the search for the truth must inevitably lead in the end to God, for God was the truth. Indeed, what made the search for truth so wildly exciting was precisely that it was a search for God.

This flowering of intellectual life in western Europe in the twelfth century was accompanied by a great blossoming of the arts. Some of the most marvellous cathedrals ever built – Durham, Lincoln, much of Canterbury and many more, not to mention the great Romanesque cathedrals and abbey churches of France – were raised at this time, covered outside in a wealth of extraordinarily exuberant and imaginative carvings and decorated inside with some equally splendid mural paintings, a few of which have survived; lit through windows filled with stained glass of unrivalled splendour and richness, when in use for worship they echoed to the sound of Gregorian chant and by Richard's time to that of early polyphonic choral singing by men and boys. As part of this blossoming of the arts, though on a more modest scale, many of the parish churches built throughout England and France at this time were carved and painted, if less profusely and sometimes more naively, with no less imaginative and creative vigour than that lavished on the great capitular buildings of the day, though few of them would have boasted a choir, and only the larger ones were elaborately carved or furnished with stained glass.

To a twentieth-century eye gazing back across the intervening centuries, one of the most surprising features of this intellectual and artistic renaissance was not only that it took place at a time when outbreaks of violence were, if not endemic, extremely frequent, but that it did so in part at least as a result of the wars and horrors of the day. Once again, the anarchy of Stephen's reign provides the best proof of this, for even in the parts of England which were worst affected by the civil war such as Oxfordshire, Wiltshire, Gloucestershire and Worcestershire, some of the finest monuments of Anglo-Norman architecture were being built irrespective of the smoke from burning cities and the stench of death hanging in the soft west country air; the abbey church of St Mary at Malmesbury with its superb arcades and some of the finest Romanesque sculpture in the country was begun at this time; the tower of Tewkesbury abbey was built, and the choir of Peterborough cathedral was finished while the war raged; and these are only the most splendid of the architectural achievements of the time. To most of us today, the coincidence of brutal civil war and the building of superb churches, of social anarchy and the production of artistic masterpieces, is as difficult to understand as the mentality of the average twelfth-century man who was responsible for both the one and the other; but perhaps the clue to both lies in the record of a little church, built by a certain Ralph of Worcester in the hamlet of Hailes near Winchcombe at the height of the war. Not much is known about him except that he had occupied by force nearly the whole county of Gloucester, fortified a castle and dominated the countryside from within its walls, and that he also built this little church at Hailes to make amends to God and his fellow west countrymen for the damage he had done to both of them during the war. It was an act of compensation, and it speaks volumes about the contents of a twelfth-century head.

For the one thing that was common to nearly everyone in God's twelfth-century world, whether he was a rich man, poor man, beggarman or mercenary, was the certainty that it was indeed God's and no one else's; there were a few who doubted the existence of God, but they were very few, and the vast majority never doubted it for a moment. Today, the ordinary world of living and loving, working and playing, doubting and eventually dying is the real world, the primary reality and probably the only world there is; a few religious people believe in God, but even many of them have only the vaguest idea of what the other world, as it is sometimes called, will be like when they reach it – if it exists and if they do so. In the twelfth century and indeed during most of the Middle Ages it was the other way round; this material world was an ephemeral, dangerous and deceitful place haunted by spirits and beset with pitfalls for the unwary; when people went to bed at night, they never knew whether they would wake up in the morning or die before the sun rose again; on a journey they might be struck by lightning or be thrown by a horse and killed or land in a flooded pot-hole and drown; and the area in which they happened to live, wherever it might be – the scrap of territory which they could claim to know fairly well – was surrounded by the huge, unknown world, out of which came stories of strange beasts and even stranger people. Some of the most highly educated men of the day, monks or priests like the remarkable John of Salisbury and the no less astonishing William of Conches, came near to agreeing with Plato that this material world was more a place of shadows than of hard reality, while the ordinary men and women in the streets of London or Winchester, Paris or Chartres, illiterate and less articulate than their fathers in God, still knew perfectly well that since, as Job said, 'man that is born of a woman hath but a short time to live; he cometh up, and is cut down like a flower; he fleeth as it were a shadow, and never continueth in one stay.' No one but a fool would regard this world as anything but a fleeting antechamber to the real world, of which the detailed geography and hierarchical structure was well known to everyone, and where God reigned supreme at the summit of the divine feudal pyramid of angels and archangels and all the company of heaven.

This is far the most difficult aspect of life and human consciousness in the twelfth century for us to understand; we can do so intellectually, but we cannot recreate in our imagination what it must have been like to live in a world overarched by the realm of God, haunted by unseen angelic messengers and the ever-present spirits of patron saints, and undermined by the devil and his hellish minions; and unwittingly we reveal our inability to grasp this primary fact about the daily consciousness of people alive at that time in a thousand little ways. For instance, in the volume of the *Oxford History of England*, already quoted, which covers the twelfth century, just under a quarter of a page is devoted to the subject. 'To the men of the twelfth century religion meant a very great deal,' wrote the author. 'It is not without significance that men great and small invested their capital in "pure and perpetual alms" for the safety of their souls; it was not merely for the love of adventure that men in their thousands embarked on the hazardous pilgrimage to the Holy Land; nor was it mere love of splendour that made them build the most magnificent churches that the architects of any age could conceive. It was because religion to them was fundamentally the most important, the most real thing. It was the vital force in their lives.' No one could possibly quarrel with that; but the significant thing about it is not its truth, but its length; it adds up to ten lines out of a total of some 16,500 or a little less than quarter of a page out of 486 pages in the entire book. Meanwhile, social and economic conditions are awarded just under a hundred pages, justice and finance receive just under forty, and even the early years of Oxford University get five pages to themselves, while the rest of the book tells the story of the time with its people, politics, and wars: a splendid if unconscious commentary upon the attitude of our own age to the proper place of religion in human life and history.

Perhaps the reason why we relegate the dominant and all-pervasive faith of the men and women of the twelfth century to a mere paragraph, while admitting in as few words as possible that it was indeed both dominant and all-pervasive in their lives, is that, while we are forced by the facts to admit its reality, it seems to be so full of what we, with our twentieth-century skulls full of twentieth-century ideas, regard as ludicrous contradictions, that we are baffled by it; and this is hardly a crime on our part, but it does make the understanding of history elusive. How could a man like Ralph of Worcester solemnly build the lovely little church at Hailes as an offering to God, while the entire county of Gloucester was black with his deeds of violence and his own hands red with the blood of those whom he had killed in the process of committing those deeds? And yet he was far from the only one during the anarchy of Stephen's reign to divide his time between crimes of murderous violence and acts of piety; many of his contemporaries plundered the land, and endowed monasteries with the proceeds; they built castles and at the same time churches, hospitals and leper houses. In much the same way, how could the overtly feudal status of the bishops of the church and their involvement in the brutal power politics of the day be consistent with faith in him who said that the meek are blessed and the poor citizens of God's kingdom? Henry of Blois, Bishop of Winchester, who has already been mentioned as Stephen's younger brother, owned six castles, and was as much at home at the head of his armed retainers fighting a battle as when presiding at Mass or chairing a church council. Another great churchman of much the same day, Bishop Roger of Salisbury, who had attracted the attention of Henry I by the speed with which he could say Mass, virtually controlled the entire administration of the country during Stephen's reign, while covertly influencing much else behind the scenes through his family connections; for his illegitimate son was the King's chancellor, his nephew bishop of the same diocese of Ely, and another nephew bishop of Lincoln. Meanwhile, he himself openly lived with his mistress, Matilda of Ramsbury, not even trying to conceal her from prying eyes. Of course, the twelfth century produced other very different bishops, of whom Anselm and Hugh of Lincoln were the most outstanding, but they were exceptions; and obviously, bishops were not the only churchmen or even the most typical churchmen of their age. The parish clergy, then as now, greatly outnumbered them, and most people would have judged the church by the quality and behaviour of these humbler and more typical exemplars of the priestly way of life, rather than by setting the virtues of a few bishops against the known vices of most others and then trying to draw up a kind of celestial balance sheet.

But here, too, the picture is unlikely to inspire a modern reader with much enthusiasm for the church. Gerald of Wales has left a splendidly vivid, if perhaps slightly satirical picture of the manners of the ordinary clergy of the day in his *Gemma Ecclesiastica*. The typical parish priest was virtually illiterate with hardly enough Latin to say Mass, repeat the offices or take the other church services correctly; he was so ill-paid that he was forced to take money for saying Masses for the dead and for the other spiritual services he rendered to the people in his care to augment his meagre and inadequate income; in nine cases out of ten, he was either married or at least kept a 'hearth-girl' or *'focaria'*, of whom Gerald of Wales said that 'she kindled his fire but extinguished his virtue . . . and kept his miserable house cluttered up with small infants, cradles, midwives, and nurses.' In the evening, perhaps in order to escape from this illegitimate domestic bliss, he repaired to the village gild or drinking house; most villages had at least one such place – Battle in Sussex had three – and there he got drunk with his friends; and no one, it seems, thought much the worse of him as a result.

So we are baffled. How could all these things – murderous barons building churches and hospitals, fornicating bishops riding to war at the head of private armies, and drunken parish priests living openly lecherous lives – how could all these things coexist with a deep and universal faith in God strong enough to inform men's lives almost from the moment of their births, and to send many of them to their deaths on Crusades to the Holy Land? Vice, of course, is always news, while virtue is boring, and there may well have been saintly bishops and sober, industrious parish priests of whom we hear nothing; but the fact remains that the Christian faith does not seem to have inspired the deeply believing man in the twelfth century to obey the kind of moral rules for which many of us look in such a person and by which we judge the sincerity of his faith; that is undeniable. Instead, however, it did three other things for him of enormous importance, providing him with three fundamental require-ments of a full and richly human life: requirements often conspicuously lacking in the tamer, if sometimes more conven-tionally moral, lives of many people in our own century. First and foremost, it gave transcendent meaning and significance to his life, however obscure, humble and short it might be in human terms, and however lowly he might be socially. The idea that his life might be meaningless never occurred to him; very, very few people in the twelfth century, if any, would ever have dreamed of crying with Macbeth that 'life's but a walking shadow, a poor player that struts and frets his hour upon the stage, and then is heard no more; it is a tale told by an idiot, full of sound and fury, signifying nothing.' On the contrary, if there was one thing of which he was certain, it was that he had been created by God for an eternal purpose, and redeemed by Christ for an eternal future, so that his every action, his every thought, his every instant of sleeping and waking, playing and praying, making love and making war was of infinite moment; though each was of different value in the perspectives of eternity and his future. Thus, whatever other anxiety might attack him, he never suffered from that most insidiously destructive and disabling suspicion that life was absurd: a suspicion which had made the author of the book *Ecclesiastes* cry in terminal despair, 'Vanity of vanity, saith the Preacher, all is vanity;' and this liberated him to lead an astoundingly full and richly varied life, even if it was often both tempestuous and bewilderingly volatile, as he lurched from moments of great nobility, courage and compassion to those of black treachery and barbarous brutality.

The second thing his faith did for him was to leave him in little or no doubt about the difference between black and white, right and wrong, sin and virtue. This provided him with the means of recognizing his own guilt when he sacked a village, murdered his mistress or someone else's, looted a monastery, burned his enemy's crops, or bullied and oppressed the peasants on his own estates; and at the same time it provided him with the means of off-loading that guilt and making reparation for his sins of commission and omission. There were almost no lengths to which he would not willingly go in order to free himself of their burden; it was this which moved the more powerful members of the twelfth century to build churches as well as castles and endow hospitals for the sick after slaughtering their neighbours; others would undertake pilgrimages to Rome or Santiago de Compostella to expiate their own particular sins, while perhaps the most compelling motive for going on one of the Crusades was the promise of general absolution from a lifetime of sinning held out to those who risked their lives on one of these holy enterprises. Such expedients may seem a little too convenient and much too easy to many of us alive today, but we might do well to reserve our most pungent criticisms until we have tried walking to Rome or Santiago de Compostella on twelfth-century roads, let alone to Antioch or Jerusalem through the forests of eastern Europe and the deserts of Asiatic Turkey, in the knowledge that we will probably be killed when we reach our destination. We may not agree with those who undertook such arduous tasks or with their naïve belief that they could free themselves of guilt in the process, but we can hardly deny their sincerity or that, being wholly sincere, subjectively at least, they probably succeeded in shedding their load of guilt and eventually dying in peace.

Indeed, freedom from anxiety over death was the third boon conferred on them by their Christian faith. All animals are frightened of being killed or dying, and when threatened with imminent death, their hearts beat, they sweat, tremble, evacuate their bowels and bladders to lighten themselves for flight, and relax only when the imminent danger to their lives has passed. As far as can be ascertained, however, only human beings sometimes lie awake at night, prevented from sleeping not by any immediate danger, but by a deep and terrifying awareness of how thin is the membrane which separates the small, warm, infinitely precious citadel of their sentient beings from the dark abyss of nothingness all round and underneath them. As any psychologist will affirm, this is a corrosive anxiety which can have devastatingly destructive effects on the lives of those who have no means of coping with it, driving some people to suicide, some to violence, and others to the relief provided briefly by alcohol or drugs. The average twelfth-century man, whether he happened to be a peasant, a townsman or a member of the ruling baronial class, might be deeply worried by the changes and chances of this mortal life, to which all men were liable – the failure of the crops, a fire which might destroy his home and business, a successful attack by a rival baron on his ancestral estates – but when it came to dying, he knew what to expect, and though he was often frightened, he does not seem to have been anxious about it. That 'fell sergeant death' might be strict in his arrest and unwelcome as a visitor, but no twelfth-century man would have cried, 'The rest is silence,' at the moment of death, as did Hamlet; death was not the gateway to silence, darkness and the unknown; it was the portal to eternal life, the conditions of which were well known to everyone and depicted in the lively mural paintings which covered the walls of many of the churches in which they gathered to hear Mass week by week and to feast on high days and holidays. Only a fool did not prepare himself for the moment of death, but when it came, as long as he had made his last confession and had been duly shriven, he had little to fear and much to look forward to.

Into such a world Richard was born, the son of Henry II of England and Eleanor of Aquitaine, the former wife of Louis VII of France. Both were remarkable people, and since they were to dominate his childhood years and form many of his attitudes to life, they too must be described before turning to Richard himself.

II

The childhood shows the man, as morning shows the day.

Milton, *Paradise Regained*

The most easily forgotten and yet the most salient fact about both Richard's parents is that they were French. Although Henry II was king of England for thirty-five years from his accession after the death of Stephen in 1154 until he himself died in 1189, he was born in France, he died in France, and he was buried in France; he did not even speak English but always French, and he married a French woman. Indeed, Eleanor was French to her elegant finger-tips, having been born in south-western France in the land of the troubadours and of the literature of courtly love, where, when her father died, she became the duchess of Aquitaine in her own right; at the age of fifteen – and by all accounts ravishingly beautiful – she married Louis VII of France a month before he was crowned king, and for fourteen years she reigned as his queen. Eventually, however, her marriage to him was annulled on the convenient though rather belated grounds of consanguinity, while the real reason for their separation was the failure of the marriage to produce a son and heir to the throne of France, although Eleanor had borne two daughters. Less than two months later, in what to a later age might well have seemed to be rather indecent haste, but was regarded at the time as a highly astute political move, she married Henry Plantagenet, Matilda's son, who was at that time count of Anjou and eleven years her junior, thus uniting the enormous Angevin estates with her own even larger domain in Aquitaine; and just over two years later she found herself queen of England, as Henry, her new husband, succeeded Stephen on the throne. That the failure to produce a son for King Louis was not her fault was very soon demonstrated, when she began to give birth to Henry's children; she bore him five sons and three daughters in almost as many years. If, as rumour had it, her first husband had had the temperament and habits of a monk, it was abundantly obvious that her second did not.

It is difficult to decide which of Richard's parents was the more formidable, for although they were people of very different temperaments and talents, each was a redoubtable character. So much is undisputed; but when it comes to assessing the kind of people they were, the task is not so easy. Henry in particular, like so many figures from the twelfth century, refuses to fit neatly into any of the accepted twentieth-century categories. He was half one thing and half another, and just as Thomas Becket – Thomas of London, as he was called at the time – could switch from being Henry's closest and most trusted friend, a layman, a courtier and as secular a man as could very well be imagined, to become almost overnight his bitterest enemy, an archbishop, religious zealot and sanctified martyr, so Henry could be a coarse brute of a man at one moment and a highly intelligent statesman and scholar at the next. Physically he was immensely strong, squarely built, stocky, and of medium height with red-gold hair, grey eyes and freckles: a tawny lion of a man, people said, who had enormous powers of endurance. On a horse, he could outride his exhausted courtiers, and make them wish that they had never been born, especially when he wanted to surprise some rebellious subject by the impossible speed with which he could travel from one place to another and administer retribution. Hunting was his passion, and here too he seemed inexhaustible, while everyone else dropped from fatigue. His court was always on the move, never staying more than a few days in any one place in some royal castle, abbey or hunting lodge before moving on again with its enormous paraphernalia of government – the royal treasure, business documents, chancellor and clerks – and the almost equally enormous domestic staff of stewards, chamberlains, butlers, constables, bearers of the king's bed, tailors, cooks, keepers of his hounds, others of his mews with its hawks and falcons, hunt servants, wolf hunters, cat hunters, men of the king's bodyguard and a dozen others including the man in charge of a pet bear which accompanied Henry everywhere. When provoked, his rage could be terrifying; his eyes became bloodshot, his face dark and suffused with blood, while he shook and trembled with fury, sometimes even falling to the ground and chewing the rushes – or so his enemies said – and if this were all that could be said of him, he could be classified easily enough as at best a mindless boor with no interests beyond blood sports and at worst a savage monster: a conclusion which would be hopelessly far of the mark, for there was an entirely different side to Henry.

Normally, he was cool, calm, patient, astute, calculating and perhaps the most able politician of his time. No violent and unbalanced lout could have ruled an empire that stretched from the Solway Firth to the borders of Provence and held it together for thirty-five years as successfully as Henry did. On the contrary, he was a man of quite exceptional ability, highly intelligent and well educated with some of the tastes of a scholar. 'With the king there is always conversation with learned men and discussion of learned problems,' said Peter of Blois, while others commented on his remarkable memory; he could speak half the current European languages – 'every language from France to the Jordan' – as fluently as his native French, though like nearly all his fellow Normans with the exception of a few senior clergy he did not bother with English, despising it as the language of serfs. That he could both speak and write Latin goes without saying, for it was the language of scholarship, law and the church, and anyone laying claim to even a modicum of education could do the same; but the fact that he could speak it better than Becket, who, when archbishop of Canterbury, was nervous of preaching in Latin for fear of making mistakes, speaks volumes for Henry's accomplishments as a linguist. The true judgement of him probably is that he was a typical child of his time, even if a notable one; for, as said already, to live in the twelfth century was to be constantly aware of the precariousness of existence and therefore of the need to live life to the full while it lasted. Henry was perpetually active, both mentally and physically, squeezing every last drop out of every passing moment: someone who today would be classed unhesitatingly and probably correctly as a workaholic; but life was too precious to be wasted in cautious indecision or wise procrastination. So men and women were volatile, decisive, impetuous, rash, courageous, running from one extreme to another at a moment's notice and 'blowing their tops' from time to time, but also becoming emperors, saints, adulterers, murderers, and even grandparents in their mid-thirties in case they died before reaching the age of forty, as most did. Henry was no exception except perhaps in the range of his physical and intellectual abilities, which was greater than that of most of his contemporaries.

But his abilities were no greater than those of his wife. Married to two kings and the mother of three, Eleanor of Aquitaine has fascinated and puzzled historians and biographers ever since her long and eventful life ended in 1204 at the age of eighty-two. She has fascinated them in much the same way as she fascinated people in her lifetime by her beauty, her intelligence, her lively independence of mind, her disregard of convention, when it suited her to disregard it, and by the web of romantic stories which has been woven round her name; but she has puzzled them too, partly because that web has tended to obscure her rather than reveal her, and partly because there are many fewer reliable descriptions of her than there are of Henry, her husband. We do not even know for sure what she looked like, although everyone is agreed that she was beautiful: so beautiful, in fact, that poets sang her praises, troubadours claimed her as queen of the courts of love, which they liked to celebrate at the time, even if they probably never existed except in their own literary imaginations, while gossip attributed a number of illicit love affairs to her, one of which gained some credence with her first husband, Louis. With typical courage and independence, she went on Crusade with him to the Holy Land – an undertaking which he bungled, as he bungled most things – and on arrival she became so friendly with Raymond of Poitiers, prince of Antioch, that Louis began to suspect something more than friendship might be involved in their relationship, even though Raymond was her uncle – albeit a very young uncle. But despite all this rumour and gossip, no one has ever suggested that any of Eleanor's many children were illegitimate, and although she may well have found her first husband's ascetic, religious and near-celibate ways increasingly intolerable as the years of their marriage went by, she seems to have solved that problem, not by taking lovers, by whom she would inevitably have had children in the days before contraceptive devices were available even to queens, but by marrying Henry, eleven years her junior and very far from monastic in his habits. A dozen years later, the fact that Henry was a good deal younger may have contributed to his love affair with Rosamund de Clifford and, if gossip is to be trusted, a number of other mistresses; but once again she seems to have solved the problem posed by Henry's infidelity, not so much by taking lovers, as by withdrawing to Aquitaine. By this time she was in her fifties, and after bearing children almost annually for years, the urge to amorous adventure may well have become less than irresistible; in all probability, too, fewer lusty and importunate suitors would have been laying siege to the citadel of her virtue at this time than when she had been the slender and vivacious incarnation of Aphrodite she seems to have been in her late teens and early twenties. So, while the old saying that 'there is no smoke without fire' may be the distillation of centuries of well-tried cynicism and wise enough in its own disillusioned way, we may with some confidence give Eleanor the benefit of the doubt and acquit her of the accusations brought against her by the gossips of her time.

Certainly, after her marriage to Henry, Eleanor bore him child after child in an almost unbroken succession. William, her first-born, perished before reaching his third birthday, dying just after the birth of her second son, Henry; a daughter, Matilda, followed, and then Richard, Geoffrey, Eleanor, Joan and John in that order. There seems little doubt that Richard was her favourite, and that he adored his mother, but whether this mutual fondness began during Richard's infancy or later it is impossible to say, for little is known about his early years save the fact that he was handed over at birth to a wet-nurse named Hodierna, who brought him up together with her own son, Alexander, at least for a year or two. However abhorrent such a custom may seem to some people today, it was virtually universal amongst the nobility and the ruling families of the day; no one who was anyone dreamed of suckling and caring for their own children, but handed them over to nurses as a matter of course. From the point of view of later historians, this is tiresome; for nurtured as we all are by psychologists to search the records of a man's childhood for the seeds of his later achievements and aberrations – for his kinship to Oedipus, for example, or some other sexually deviant type-figure – the absence of specific information about the early years of the children of the nobility in the twelfth century poses a problem, while their early separation from their mothers provides the imaginative analyst with a splendid means of explaining, if not justifying, most of their more horrendous later crimes. But if Wordsworth was right to anticipate today's psychological dogma by affirming that 'the Child is Father to the Man', how can anyone write intelligently about the Man, with or without a capital M, if he can discover little or nothing about the child? In Richard's case, however, things are happily not as bad as all that, for, if there are few records of his earliest years, much can be inferred about his experience at this time from the facts known about the contemporary treatment of children in general and eminent children in particular.

First, then, he was born one of eight children, and like them handed over into the care of nurses while his parents went about their regal business, though it is known that he saw more of his mother than of his father. His birthplace, Beaumont Palace in Oxford, sounds both splendid and luxurious, but by modern standards was neither, and indeed it was not raised to the status of a palace until much later; at the time of Richard's birth it was known simply as 'The King's House'. Even that is misleading, for it was not a single mansion; it was a group of buildings, some of wood, some of stone and all of massive construction and daunting discomfort, extensive enough to have needed forty thousand oak shingles when they were re-roofed in 1171, and it was sur-rounded by a defensive wall. There was a great chamber in which the king held court when occasion arose, a great hall decorated with mural paintings, two chapels, one of which was probably dedicated to St Nicholas, a cloister and other rooms reserved for the use of the queen, the royal chaplains and other court functionaries; and of course there were huge kitchens, larders and other domestic offices of the usual kinds. It must have been dank and dark at all times, even in summer, and draughty, damp, and icy cold in winter except in the immediate vicinity of one of the great log fires which would have partly warmed some of the rooms, while filling them with smoke when the wind was in the wrong direction. In Richard's day, few if any of the windows would have been glazed – the great hall was partly glazed and wainscotted nearly a hundred years later in the 1240s – and the floors would have been of the most primitive variety, and most people from the king and queen down to the host of servants would probably have had to resort to the medieval equivalent of those malodorous receptacles, politely known later as *pots de chambre*, when they were in need of physical relief. The word 'bath' would scarcely have featured in anyone's twelfth-century vocabulary, if one is to judge by a revealing little passage in a record of an itinerary taken by Richard's youngest brother, John, fifty years after their childhood together in Oxford, when he had become king; there it is recorded with evident amazement that between 29 January 1209 and 17 June of the same year, the king had a bath on eight different occasions at eight different places in the course of his travels: bathing, that is to say, with the unheard-of frequency of once every three weeks. He even owned a dressing-gown. That such an excess of cleanliness provoked astonishment half a century after Richard's infancy speaks volumes for the conditions in which he was raised, and remembering the way in which all children, crawling happily about on all fours, are liable to pick up and taste almost anything which comes into their grubby little hands, the huge rate of infant mortality in medieval days is not surprising.

Even so it is very difficult to kill a baby; small human beings are remarkably tenacious of life, as their survival for days in the rubble left behind by earthquakes is sufficient proof, and only one of these royal children died in infancy. Moreover, if it is difficult to kill babies, it is almost equally difficult not to become fond of them, as they begin to respond to the approaches of their parents and nurses, gurgling, kicking, crowing and smiling from ear to ear with evident pleasure as they are tickled or kissed. We know that Richard loved Hodierna, for later, when he was king, he gave her a pension large enough for her to live at ease in the country, presumably somewhere in the parish of West Knoyle in Wiltshire, which is also named after her and known as Knoyle Odierne. Richard seems to have been brought up largely by Hodierna and other nurses for about the first five years of his life, either in Oxford, which was considered safer for the royal children than France at the time, or wherever Eleanor, his mother, occasionally chose to take him.

However, at the age of five or thereabouts, Richard was partly handed over into the hands of men appointed by his parents to begin his education, and he may also have been travelling more often with one or other of his parents, as he continued to grow up; certainly, he and his elder sister Matilda went to Normandy with their mother when Richard was only seven and Matilda was nine, and two years later he was in Anjou with his father. Into whose hands his education was entrusted we do not know, though we do know that his youngest brother John was instructed in his youth by the great lawyer Ranulf Granville, amongst others, and doubtless Richard, too, would have had tutors of comparable eminence and intellectual distinction. They would have been churchmen, for education was a monopoly of the church; so theology would have come high on the list of subjects to be learnt, as would Latin; but grammar, rhetoric and dialectic – the so-called *trivium* – would certainly have been included in any self-respecting syllabus. To most twentieth-century ears, this sounds staggeringly dull: almost the quintessence of dullness indeed, but something has already been said about the enormously exciting vistas opened up in the minds of those learning such subjects as Latin and theology, and it need not be repeated here. In addition to this basic training, Richard would also have been taught something about music, arithmetic, geometry and astronomy, four subjects known as the *quadrivium*, and it seems highly likely that he enjoyed them greatly, for later in life he showed himself to be extremely talented and knowledgeable musically, composing songs and vying with the troubadours of southern France for recognition as a poet in his own right, and a man of wide interests and a lively mind. But when all this has been said, it is also true that, though the training of his mind would have been regarded by his parents as of great importance, Richard's education, like that of all the sons of the ruling class in medieval days, would not have been exclusively concerned with intellectual or artistic achievements, but also – and indeed perhaps above all – with various physical sports of one kind or another, which were essentially preparations for war; fencing, wrestling, running, jumping, and throwing the javelin were among his everyday pursuits, while he learned to ride a horse almost as soon as he could walk, eventually becoming a superb horseman. Today such an accomplishment is seldom a matter of life or death, but in the twelfth century it could be just that; for to wield a lance almost the size of a telegraph pole effectively on horseback, either in a tournament or in battle, was an extremely difficult art, and on its mastery a man's life might depend. As one expert has put it, a knight in combat often had to swerve at the last moment to avoid a head-on collision with his opponent, while at the same time he had to grasp his lance, that heavy unwieldy weapon, as tightly as possible to his side under his arm, so that the lance blow was struck with all the weight and momentum of both horse and rider behind it; if in swerving aside he moved his hand or used his arm to thrust at his enemy, the blow would have almost no effect at all. To deliver an effective blow with the whole weight of both horse and rider behind it required split-second timing and horsemanship of the highest order, let alone immensely highly trained horses, which became fantastically valuable in consequence; and Richard mastered these military arts early in life, laying the foundation for his unparalleled prowess later on.

Richard was raised in a feudal society, as everyone knows; but perhaps it is more difficult to put flesh and blood on to that bald statement, and to re-create in the imagination what it must have been like to grow up from infancy knowing that you were destined to play a vital role in maintaining the precarious balance of the social parts of the feudal pyramid in which medieval society was arranged, culminating as they did in the person of the monarch at the summit. Yet this must have been Richard's experience from the moment he became conscious of what it meant to be his father's son: not his eldest son, but nevertheless a prince of the realm with the certain destiny of eventually inheriting an enormous domain and a comparably huge respon- sibility. If little boys today are vulnerable, as they so often are in their alarming masculinity, to an infallible conviction of their own inadequacy, as they are encouraged by their god-like elders to be brave and manly like their fathers, it seems highly probable that Richard and his brothers suffered much the same pangs of self-doubt, accompanied again, as they so often are, by an intimidating cocktail of emotions: excitement, pride, bravado, fear, and something rather like anger at a world full of people who ought to know better than to subject small boys like oneself to such traumas. Of course, this is speculation; but history was made by people with hopes and dreams, fears and foibles, weaknesses and strengths, and as he grew up at Oxford and travelled abroad from time to time with his parents, Richard would not have been human if he had not reacted to the world and the people around him with at least some of the emotions experienced by the ordinary adolescent boy. Moreover, with a formidable father like Henry II some of those emotions must have been sharp, for in some ways Richard and his father were perhaps too alike to get on easily with each other; certainly, later in life their relationship was often seriously strained.

But to return for a moment to the social system into which Richard and the other royal children were born, and in which they would have known from the earliest age that they were going to have to play their parts, viewed retrospectively from the vantage point of our own century, it looks antique, undemocratic, oppressive and often barbarous, and so it was. Something has already been said about the chaos and civil war which engulfed much of England in Stephen's reign; but even though the medieval system of government broke down completely from time to time, and was seldom free of small disturbances and occasionally of larger ones, from a twelfth-century viewpoint it was a great and civilized improvement on what had gone before. It had evolved slowly and painfully out of the total and almost unimaginable chaos and barbarism of the Dark Ages which had followed the collapse of Roman rule and society in western Europe: and folk memories were long. People may not have remembered the horror of it all in detail – the way in which the cities had fallen into ruin, how they had been damaged by fires and by wars, how their inhabitants had been massacred or wiped out by disease until previously thriving towns and villages had become the haunt of owls with tiny reduced populations of a few half-starving, frightened people – but they would have been aware that life for their grandparents and great-grandparents had been much harder and more precarious than it was in their own day, and they would have given credit where credit was due, namely, to the feudal system. For with all its faults and shortcomings, it succeeded much of the time in controlling and containing those two most deeply seated aggressive instincts in the breast of the human male, the territorial imperative and the mating drive. As everyone knows nowadays from the study of other animals including our evolutionary first cousins, the primates, these two basic drives are kept under control, especially in groups of social animals, by a pyramidal system of dominance in which the most dominant male is at the apex with his mate or mates beside him. With its pyramidal hierarchy established by law, maintained by force if necessary, and well understood by everybody, if not always passively accepted, the feudal system, with the king as the dominant male at the summit of the pyramid, was just such a method of organization, and it did much to banish the old chaos of the Dark Ages, when there had rarely been a central authority strong enough to control, let alone put an end to, the eternal and murderous feuds of the petty lords, descendants of the various barbarians who had conquered the Roman world and who had dominated its shattered fragments for so long. The system ensured, too, that land passed from one owner to the next according to strict rules of inheritance and descent; as a result, both marriages and the children they produced became part of the elaborate power game of maintaining the *status quo*; land, titles and power were passed from one generation to another, and the fabric of society was maintained in peace.

Maintained, at least, unless and until two more or less equally dominant males came into competition, as did Louis VII of France and Henry II of England in his capacity as feudal lord of parts of France that were larger in area than those which owed direct allegiance to Louis. Later, their respective sons, Philip Augustus of France and Richard I of England, came into conflict with each other for the same reasons. The system also broke down when the dominant male in any given society proved to be insufficiently dominant or decisive to maintain control, because he lacked the necessary ruthlessness and determination. The example of Stephen's reign was so fresh in everyone's memory that Henry II and Eleanor must surely have reminded their growing sons again and again that the quality of greatness in princes was not very different from what was sometimes called ruthlessness in other men. If Richard learnt that lesson at his mother's knee, he can hardly be blamed for taking it to heart, and perhaps some of his actions may be more easily understood and sympathetically regarded than might otherwise be the case.

But knowledge of the future demands which the social system would inevitably make upon anyone born into Richard's position would not have been the only political reality of the day to shape and form him as he grew up; for behind the immediate exigencies of the domestic politics of England and France, infinitely remote geographically but ever present morally and romantically, the existence of the Crusader kingdoms and principalities in the Holy Land – in Outremer, as it was called – where Christ had lived and died, and their demands upon a man's attention, generosity and self- offering must have exercised an enormous influence upon the imagination of a growing boy. Europe had been fascinated for nearly a century by the idea of rescuing and then defending Jerusalem from the clutches of the 'godless spawn of Hagar, sons of dogs, slanderers of the *Logos* of God, disciples of the false prophet, who eat the flesh of camels,' as the Byzantine Emperor Nicephorus Phocas picturesquely described its Moslem conquerors; and many people made little distinction in their minds between the real geographical city and the New Jerusalem of Christian apocalyptic hope. To Richard and his brothers and sisters, whose mother Eleanor had actually been to Outremer, and who would surely have told them stories of her journey and her time there, the idea of going there on a Crusade and becoming at one fell swoop a soldier of Christ, a pilgrim into the unknown, and a knight errant riding to the aid of their beleaguered fellow Christians must have held enormous excitement. If it is true that every generation needs a star to follow, an ideal to set them alight, a transcendent goal to beckon them on through the boring plains and over the difficult rocky passes of everyday life, there is little doubt that the Crusading ideal, which inspired so many people for so many years in medieval days, could hardly have failed to affect Richard and influence him deeply as he grew to maturity. He could not have avoided such a conditioning, whether we approve of what it did to him or not.

Similarly, he could not have escaped the influence of family tradition, and some historians have made much of this – too much, perhaps, especially of one ancestral story, which Richard is said to have mentioned to a friend in jest on one particular occasion. According to this family legend, he was descended on the Angevin side of his family from a lady of questionable nature, more devilish than human, and of unearthly beauty. Her name was Mélusine, and she was married to a count of Anjou, to whom she bore four children. She was a perfect wife and mother and much loved by everyone, but there was one very odd and disquieting thing about her: she hated going into churches, and she flatly refused to be present during Mass at the consecration of the Host. Inevitably, people gossiped, and this worried her husband, who determined to put an end to speculation about the reason for this peculiar behaviour once and for all. He insisted on her accompanying him to Mass one day, and when she started to leave just before the moment of consecration, he ordered four armed men to seize her; she became deathly pale, shook off her cloak, by which the men were holding her and, wrapping two of her children in her arms, floated out of an open window and disappeared for ever, leaving her husband and her other children aghast and trembling. So ran the family legend. The Lusignan family was also said to be descended from the same lady, but in their case she turned into a serpent from the waist downwards every Saturday night, a fate from which she was promised escape only if she could find a husband who would promise never to see her on Saturdays. When eventually she found such a man, all went well until he succumbed to temptation and spied on her in her bath one Saturday evening, whereupon, still half-serpent, she flew away through the bathroom window never to return again. Whether anyone at the time took these legends seriously seems doubtful, and it is even more unlikely that Richard would have used the story of his diabolical ancestress to excuse the faults of his own nature to himself, as has been romantically suggested. The story of Mélusine was related at length by Jean d'Arras in his *Chronique de la Princesse*, written years later for the amusement of the duke of Berry and his sister, Marie of France, in 1387, and though Richard, too, may well have been amused by it, it is hard to believe that it worried him very much. It is far more probable that his descent from the Plantagenets of Anjou on his father's side and from the dukes of Aquitaine on that of his mother, and through his paternal grandmother from Henry I of England, would have helped him form his own idea of himself rather more than did the legend of Mélusine; and unless human nature has changed more radically and more rapidly than seems to be the case, from his earliest years he would almost certainly have been treated by his nurses and everyone with whom he came into any sort of childish contact, with much the same mixture of deference, affection and delight as is accorded to today's children of royalty whenever they appear in public. Far from growing up worried by some terrible hypothetical taint inherited from his improbable forebear, Mélusine, Richard would have grown up conscious of the royal blood in his veins and in all probability half proud of his birthright and half intimidated by all that his illustrious heritage was likely to involve as the years passed; and not many of those years were to pass before he did, indeed, become deeply involved in that heritage.

PART 2

Duke of Aquitaine

III

Not yet old enough for a man, nor young enough for a boy; as a squash is before 'tis a peascod, or a codling when 'tis almost an apple, 'tis with him in standing water, between boy and man.

Shakespeare, *Twelfth Night*

Although a few hard facts about Richard's earliest years, such as his place of birth, his nurse's name and his various visits to France with one or other of his parents have already been mentioned, it was not until later that he began to emerge from the obscurity of his childhood into the full light of history, and almost the first occasion on which he did so was that of his betrothal to Alice, one of the daughters of Louis VII of France and sister to his son and heir, Philip Augustus, the belated child of the French king's third wife, Adela of Champagne. Richard was eleven years old at the time, and was thus spared the diplomatic charade endured by his elder brother, Henry, who had actually been married to another of Louis' daughters when he was five years old and his bride was three. In fact, Richard had only just escaped a similar fate, for he had been betrothed once before at the age of two to the infant daughter of the count of Barcelona and his spouse, the queen of Aragon; but nothing had come of this arrangement. However, three years after his betrothal to Alice, when he was fourteen on 11 June 1172, the octave of Whitsunday, he was publicly installed as duke of Aquitaine by the archbishop of Bordeaux and the bishop of Poitiers in the abbey church of St Hilary in Poitiers; there seated in the abbot's stall, he was given the sacred lance and banner, the insignia of his ducal office; he then moved to Limoges where the ring of St Valeria, a much revered Aquitainian martyr whose corpse was in the proud possession of St Martial's abbey in the town, was placed on his finger to signify that he was made duke with the approval of the saints of the land and of the church as well as that of his feudal superiors. From this moment onwards, information about him and his movements becomes increasingly abundant, as he began to play his allotted part in the political dramas of the time.

Richard's political début as boy-duke of Aquitaine was only made possible by two things: first, his father, Henry II, wanted to involve his sons in the business of governing his empire as soon as possible, partly to lighten the load on his own shoulders and partly to train them for the task of government; and secondly Richard had first to do homage to Louis VII of France as his feudal overlord in that country before he could become duke of any part of it. Henry's desire for help was understandable, for his domain was enormous. It had been extensive enough when he had become duke of Normandy at the age of twenty and count of Anjou a year later on the death of his father; but it was vastly enlarged a year later when he married Eleanor, who brought the duchy of Aquitaine with her and, when he succeeded Stephen on the throne of England a year later still, his dominion stretched from the borders of Scotland in the north to the Pyrenees in the south and took in over half of France. To rule such a huge area, peopled as it was with numerous quarrelsome barons accustomed to a certain amount of local autonomy in which to live their hideously bellicose lives, would have been difficult at any time, but it was made doubly difficult by the appalling state of the roads. In twelfth-century England, the means of communication were bad enough, but distances were not as great there as they were across the Channel, and it did not take Henry long to impose the rule of law and keep the peace in England after the shambles of Stephen's reign. In France, however, it was not only the roads – or, rather, the lack of them – which made his task a formidable one; understandably, the French king was both alarmed by the sudden explosion of power in the hands of one of his nominal subjects, and also deeply resentful and angry that that same subject should have married his ex-wife, Eleanor, so soon after his own marriage to her had been annulled. As a result, he did everything in his power, both by fair means and sometimes by means bordering on the foul, to clip Henry's over-mighty wings and to foster opposition to him. Moreover, Louis was not the only Frenchman to be resentful of this Angevin upstart who had become the most powerful man in Europe almost overnight, and some of the more turbulent and jealous of the French barons took every opportunity offered to them by Henry's absences in England to cast off their feudal allegiance and revolt against him. With his apparently tireless ability to move from one place to another without rest or respite, exhausting his camp followers and making his own thighs so sore from long hours in the saddle that he sometimes found walking painful, Henry succeeded in keeping order in his vast realm better than most other men could have done; but even so revolts and rebellions broke out, and he badly needed the help of his sons as soon as they became old enough to assist him in the task of governing so huge an area. So, the eldest son, young Henry, as he was called, was crowned king to share his father's throne, doing homage to Louis VII of France for the duchy of Normandy and the county of Poitou; Richard was made duke of Aquitaine; and Geoffrey, his third son, was betrothed to Constance, the heiress of Brittany, and thus destined to become duke there in due course.

In doing homage to the French king, however, as inevitably all three young English princes were bound to do, Henry's sons were placed in an odd situation; for by the letter of feudal law their homage to Louis gave him a higher claim upon their allegiance than that of their father, and Louis had every intention of reminding them of this highly convenient fact whenever possible. His opportunity came even sooner than he could have hoped. Richard's elder brother, the young King Henry, was just eighteen, Richard not yet sixteen, and Geoffrey a year younger, when their father made a mistake. Worried over the future of his youngest son, John, who was not only his favourite but the only one of his sons to whom he had not been able to assign a position comparable to those given to his brothers – a fact which had resulted in the boy's being nicknamed John Lackland – he decided to endow him with some of the land which he had already handed over to his eldest son, the young King Henry, and which included the three important castles of Chinon, Loudun and Mirebeau, while betrothing him to the infant daughter of the count of Maurienne. This was too much for young Henry, who was already irritated by the fact that, even though he had been made duke of Normandy and count of Poitou, his father continued to act as though he himself was still the true ruler of these lands and his son only nominally so. Richard and Geoffrey had been treated in much the same way, and were equally aggravated; it is difficult to imagine any arrangement more likely to foster ill-will between a father and his sons than one in which a number of ambitious but still callow youths are apparently given great power and wealth only to discover that they have merely the shadow and not the reality. Even so, all might have been well, if Eleanor had not taken a hand: a hand which she may well have been preparing to play for some time.

By this time her marriage to Henry was on the rocks, though precisely why is difficult to determine for sure; historians have argued over the reasons for its breakdown. Eleanor was an unconventional woman with a mind and a will of her own, and she may well have chafed at the years of domestic and political subordination to her husband which she had had to endure; but it has also been suggested that another factor leading to the shipwreck of their relationship may have been Henry's tactless disregard of her feelings and those of the people of Aquitaine when he made the count of Toulouse do homage for his county to young King Henry and not to Richard as duke of Aquitaine, to whom Toulouse had always owed immediate feudal allegiance. However this may have been, there can be little doubt that one of the chief reasons for their estrangement was her bitter resentment of his open affair with Rosamund de Clifford, the fair Rosamund of historical romance, whom he seems genuinely to have adored, and by whom he had two illegitimate sons, William, who became earl of Salisbury, and Geoffrey, whom he made his chancellor and who eventually became archbishop of York. At all events, so estranged from her husband was she that for some time Eleanor had lived in France, seeing as little of Henry as possible, and when her eldest son ran to her in a rage over his father's attempt to give some of his lands and castles to his youngest brother, John, without so much as having the courtesy to consult him over the matter, Eleanor advised him to defy his father and seek the help of his father-in-law and feudal superior, the French king.

Raymond of Toulouse had warned Henry II that his wife and sons were hatching some sort of plot against him, but he does not seem to have been much worried by the news; after all the boys were still very young, and he could hardly take a threat posed by three lads of eighteen, fifteen and fourteen very seriously, even if they were aided and abetted by their mother, which probably seemed to him far from certain. Henry must have known of Eleanor's bitterness against him, but the idea of a wife openly rebelling against her husband was virtually unthinkable at the time, so Henry did little about the warning he had received. But when young King Henry slipped away from him one night when he was asleep in Chinon castle, and fled to the court of King Louis, he was forced to act and issued orders to make all the necessary preparations for war. A few days later he was told that his other two sons, Richard and Geoffrey, who had been with their mother in Aquitaine, had joined their brother at the court of King Louis, and that his wife was on her way there. What Louis thought about the prospect of Eleanor's arrival we shall never know, but he must have experienced a strange medley of conflicting emotions at the thought of welcoming his ex-wife as she prepared to make war on the man for whom she had left him twenty years earlier. In the event, however, she never arrived; although she travelled in disguise, she was arrested in Poitou and sent to Henry in Rouen; there he shut her up in a well-guarded castle where she could make no more mischief.

Apportioning blame is always a difficult and invidious business. The young King Henry was a feckless and ineffectual youth, handsome, boastful, and arrogant, but he was only just eighteen and he cannot bear the whole blame; as for Richard and Geoffrey, it would be stupid to lay much blame on them, although Geoffrey was later to become a most unpleasant and unsavoury person, who was described by Gerald of Wales as being 'overflowing with words, smooth as oil, possessed by his syrupy and persuasive eloquence of the power of dissolving the apparently indissoluble, able to corrupt two kingdoms with his tongue, of tireless endeavour and a hypocrite in everything.' Eleanor would there-fore appear to be the main candidate for blame; but, even so, it seems unlikely that she would have been able to push her children into rebellion against their father unless their relationship with him had already been extremely bad, and although she cannot be acquitted of all responsibility for their revolt, the fact that Henry had been a difficult and dominant father by virtue of the sheer weight of his personality, and more often than not an absentee from home during the most impressionable and formative years of their childhood, must have played its part in preparing them for the moment of rebellion. Perhaps the chief culprit, however, was the feudal system, in which they were all born to play leading parts, whether they liked it or not; for while it was admirable in intention and often admirably effective in practice in controlling men's most aggressive instincts, it inevitably involved them all in a power game of checks and balances, bluffs and counter bluffs, threats and retaliatory menaces, which was bound every now and again to result in civil disturbance and war instead of achieving its purpose of peace.

Wherever blame should be laid, one man was delighted by the rebellion of the young princes. The French king welcomed them to his court with open arms, told them how right they had been to cast off the shackles of their youth and stand up to their oppressive and unjust father, and assured them that he would give them every possible support, both moral and military. For such an openly – indeed, almost ostentatiously – pious a man as Louis, celebrated for the depth of his Christian faith, almost monastic in his habits and greatly influenced in all his decisions by the bishops and other leading clergy of the church in France, to encourage and support the patricidal intentions of green and callow youths may seem out of character and oddly anachronistic; one would expect him to have heard of the fifth commandment, 'Honour thy father and mother that thy days may be long upon the land which the Lord thy God giveth thee'; but it seems to have slipped from his memory at this time in what one must charitably hope was a fit of temporary, if convenient, amnesia. But once again, it is easy to cast stones only if one forgets the history of Louis' relationship with Henry II, who had not only humiliated him by taking the wife with whom he had failed to beget a son and heir and proceeded to keep her almost perpetually pregnant for the next decade or so, but who had also risen in a few vertiginous years from the comparatively humble status of lord of one local county among many others in France to become the largest and most powerful feudal lord in the country and king of England to boot. He would have had to be as saintly as his great-grandson and namesake, Louis IX, not to have rejoiced at such an opportunity to turn the tables on Henry, and in the spring of 1173 he persuaded the three young princes to swear an oath not to make peace with their father without his consent and that of the barons of France.

In the end, it did him little good. Rather surprisingly, most of Henry's feudatory barons remained loyal to him, and refused to take part in the revolt, though some of the barons of Poitou and Anjou sided with Eleanor and the young princes. Even so, when news of the revolt first reached Henry, things must have looked very black indeed; at that time he did not know who would side with his wife and sons and who remain loyal, and as news of the defection of such of his own men as William of Angoulême, Guy of Lusignan, Geoffrey his brother and other leading barons in the heartland of his empire began to come in, he would hardly have been human if he had not been angry, alarmed and depressed. His prospects looked even bleaker when it became known that the counts of Flanders, Boulogne and Blois had taken up arms against him, and that King William of Scotland, whose hostility might have been predicted, but whose enmity was nonetheless depressing for being foreseeable, was preparing to invade the north of England. But if Henry was alarmed, he gave no sign of it; on the contrary, he remained cool, baffling his enemies by his inaction as he waited to see what they would do, and demonstrating once again those qualities of imperturbability and judgement, coolness and courage, which made him by far the greatest statesman in western Europe at that time. Meanwhile, he used his very considerable resources to hire a large army of Brabançons, or Brabantines, as they were called, in readiness for whatever was to come.

Brabançons were mercenaries, soldiers of fortune ready to serve anyone who hired them, and if justice were to be done, they would be recognized as the true makers of history in the Middle Ages. Kings, dukes, counts and lesser baronial fry, together with popes, archbishops, bishops, abbots and a rare peppering of saints might hold the centre of the historical stage, planning this move and that, strutting from here to there, rising and falling as their fortunes ebbed and flowed, saying prayers and making dynastic marriages in infancy, besieging one another's castles and making war over one another's lands, but it was the Brabançons who did the fighting, deciding the outcome of those wars, killing or being killed or dying in agony of wounds, unnoticed and unmourned by their lordly employers. Those employers almost invariably survived to fight another day, because they were too valuable to be killed; instead, they were locked up in castles by their captors, and released on payment of large sums of money in ransom. Despite their name, the Brabançons did not come from Brabant, and no one seems to know how they came to be so called or exactly who they were; they were the nameless and faceless by-products of the pressure of population on the resources of medieval society, landless peasants, unemployed townsmen, refugees from parts stricken by famine, where drought or floods or war had ruined the crops, the outcasts of society whom nobody loved. As a result, they loved no one in return and did not hesitate to pillage the lands over which they fought, burning and looting towns and villages, raping the women and the girls and murdering any men foolish enough to resist them. It would be fascinating to know what went on in their heads, how they saw the world which had rejected them, what they believed, hoped for, and feared; but we do not even know their names, except those of a very few of their leaders. They were born, lived, breathed, loved, hated, fought, killed and died; but they left no records, and we shall never know what their world was like.

During the early summer of 1173, while his enemies made their preparations, Henry was at Rouen, spending most of his time hunting as though nothing untoward was afoot. He gathered his mercenaries, alerted those barons who remained loyal to him, and waited on events. In July, the count of Flanders, accompanied by the young King Henry, invaded Normandy from the north-east and took a number of small towns before laying siege to Drincourt, while Louis marched through the country to the west of Paris known as the Vexin, and attacked Verneuil, which shut its gates against him. On hearing the news, Henry crossed to England, set its defences in order, and returned at once to France, leaving others to deal with William of Scotland, and arriving in Rouen again before his enemies realized that he had been away. On arrival, he was told that Philip of Flanders had withdrawn from the war; his brother Matthew, the count of Boulogne, had been wounded in the thigh by an arrow on St James's day during the siege of Drincourt; the wound had turned septic, and he had died. Matthew was not a particularly amiable character; he had obtained his county by marriage, but shortly before his death he had sent his wife back to the convent from which he had plucked her in the first place, managing somehow to have their marriage declared null and void; whereupon he had promptly married the rich widow of the count of Nevers. His brother, Philip of Flanders, was upset by his death, not so much because of any affection he might have felt for his brother, but because they had both sworn fealty to Henry II exactly a year previously on St James's day; his brother's death as the result of a wound incurred on the precise anniversary of their oath of loyalty was such an evident indication of God's displeasure that he felt that he had no choice but to withdraw from the war or face a similar fate. So he took his troops home to Flanders, leaving King Louis ineffectively besieging Verneuil away to the south-west.

Nothing could have suited Henry better. With a massive force of mercenaries around a core of loyal barons, all of whom were hardened fighting men, Henry marched on Verneuil; town after town opened their gates to him on the way, and a castle belonging to Robert, the hump-backed earl of Leicester who had sided with the French king, was taken and burnt. Alarmed by his approach, Louis sent emissaries who suggested that the two kings should meet and attempt to settle their differences by discussion rather than by arms. Meanwhile, the city of Verneuil, which was near to famine, on hearing that a conference was to take place agreed to a truce and opened its gates to its besiegers. With calculated and unsavoury duplicity, Louis set the place on fire, and promptly fled; it seems he never had the smallest intention of meeting Henry there; instead, he left it in flames with many of its citizens dead in the streets as he himself led his army in retreat towards Paris. Indignant at such perfidy, Henry chased him, cutting down many stragglers from the French army and capturing its baggage.

The two original attacks on Normandy having thus collapsed, Henry was free to turn his attention elsewhere, and it was high time that he did so; for the revolt had spread to Brittany, where some of the leading nobles together with a few Normans and malcontents from England, including the earl of Chester, had taken up arms against him. With Henry busy elsewhere, things had gone pretty well for them; they had captured Dol and Cambour, more of the local barons had joined them, and they were in confident mood; but they had counted without Henry's ability to move from one place to another with amazing rapidity, and while they were still elated and basking in the euphoria of success, he bore down on them with a large army and utterly defeated them, recapturing Dol on 23 August with much treasure and most of the rebel barons, including the earl of Chester. Meanwhile, in England things were going equally badly for the rebels; the hump-backed earl of Leicester, having taken the revolt home to his own county when he was chased from France, had been besieged in the city of Leicester, and although he had escaped and fled back to France, his castle had been captured, while in the north King William of Scotland had been ignominiously defeated and chased back over the border into his own country. In fact, the revolt, hopelessly mismanaged and almost entirely unco-ordinated, had been virtually crushed in less than three months, and the rebels were dismayed and depressed by their failure; Louis in particular was deeply alarmed by the ease with which his over-mighty subject had been so universally successful in spite of the defection of his wife and sons. It was time to sue for peace, and the French king asked the papal legate to invite Henry to the conference table.

In his own day, Henry II was most admired for his brilliance as a soldier and his skill as a ruler, and indeed these were great; but what appeals most to modern eyes is his astonishingly generous – his unfailingly and in the end suicidally generous – treatment of his sons, and it was on this occasion, when he met the French king near Gisors on the borders of Normandy and France, that that generosity first showed itself clearly and unequivocally despite the fact that three of those sons sat beside Louis on the other side of the conference table: a fact which might well have aroused almost any emotion other than generosity in the breasts of most fathers without incurring the world's censure. As king of England, Henry was accompanied by a number of bishops, archbishops, counts and barons, as befitted his position, and Louis came with most of the principal members of his court and the three young English princes, Henry, Richard and Geoffrey. It is impossible to know how each side felt as it faced its opponents, but it seems highly probable that Louis and his adherents would have felt on the defensive and at a disadvantage as they faced Henry and his men; after all, he had defeated every initiative on their part, both in France and in England, without once being defeated himself. It must therefore have come as a most unexpected and welcome surprise to discover that he was prepared to offer his sons remarkably generous terms of settlement; to young Henry he offered half the revenues of England or half those of Normandy and some castles, to Richard much the same in Aquitaine, and to Geoffrey the whole of Brittany upon his marriage to Constance, the rightful heiress, reserving to himself only the final right of sovereignty and the administration of justice in all three areas. It was generosity taken to the point of munificence, and it is difficult to believe that his sons had any part in deciding to turn down their father's offer, yet Louis persuaded them to do so. He must have mistaken Henry's generosity for weakness, while behind the scenes he used the time spent at the conference to win support from some of his barons for the idea of continuing the war, and the meeting broke up in disorder.

It did not do so, however, before the earl of Leicester, arriving hotfoot from his defeat in England and the humiliating loss of his castle, had to be physically restrained from drawing his sword and attacking Henry in a fury. But even in the twelfth century, such personal violence at a peace conference was not tolerated, and Henry left the room unharmed. The phrenetic earl rushed back to England with a force of Flemish mercenaries, landed in Norfolk, and was once again roundly defeated by two of Henry's most staunch supporters, Humphrey de Bohun and Richard de Lucy, ably assisted by the earls of Cornwall, Gloucester, and Arundel and a large mob of local farmers and peasants armed with flails and pitchforks. It is likely that they had not enjoyed anything so much for years, as they set about the Flemish soldiers and chased them from the battlefield. The bellicose hunchback was sent under escort to Henry, who put him in irons at Falaise with the earl of Chester for company; his fate should have been a signal to the other rebels to come to terms with reality, to recognize Henry's superiority, both in men and strategy, and to admit defeat; but it had no such effect, and the rebellion dragged drearily on with Richard harrying his father's supporters in Aquitaine, and Philip of Flanders freed once more from his previous fears and scruples, together with the young Henry preparing yet another invasion of England. To counter this last threat, King Henry decided to return home.

He sailed from Barfleur on 7 July 1174, and after an appallingly rough crossing landed at Southampton. He had taken the wise precaution of bringing his most important prisoners with him, Eleanor his wife, and the earls of Chester and Leicester, whom he safely locked up and lodged where they could cause no more trouble. He had also brought the little girls, Alice and Constance, to whom Richard and Geoffrey respectively were betrothed, to England with him for safe keeping, and when they, too, had been safely stowed away, he put the war and politics behind him in order to do something he had long planned. However strange and difficult some people may find his actions during the next few days, they were magnificently typical of the twelfth century, and it would be a great mistake to regard them as insincere; indeed, a failure to appreciate Henry's sincerity and the importance to him of the actions he was about to take, symbolic as they were but at the same time creative of the reality symbolized, would be a failure to get into the soul of medieval man or to plumb the depth of his understanding of what it was to be a human: an understanding more profound in some ways than that of twentieth-century man. C. P. R. James, a learned early Victorian historian, writing in 1840 or thereabouts, prefaced his account of Henry's actions at this time with the premise that 'even admitting to the fullest extent Henry's tendency to superstition' it was scarcely possible to suppose that what he was about to do was anything but an elaborate charade – a piece of histrionic chicanery – but if he really did believe that it might have some efficacy, one had no option but to attribute to him 'a prostration of mind which could only stamp a fool, or duplicity of conduct, which could only characterize a knave'. This is such a magisterial condemnation of the twelfth century – let alone such a masterful misunderstanding of the human mind – that it is difficult to imagine how any serious student of the time could have misjudged either the one or the other so completely.

What Henry did was to set out to Canterbury on a personal pilgrimage of repentance for the murder of Becket, though whether he had ever intended to have him killed is far from certain; indeed, no one was more appalled by the deed than Henry, bitterly regretting the impatient words he had uttered in a moment of anger which had encouraged four of his knights to murder the archbishop. The story of Becket is well known, but in some ways it is so typical of the twelfth century that it is worth recalling briefly. Thomas was born in London on 21 December 1118 of middle class Norman stock. His father was a merchant from Rouen, who had settled in London, where at one time he held the office of sheriff, and his mother was a native of Caen. Their son was educated at Merton priory and later at one of the city's grammar schools, where he proved to be extremely able, though he never became a great academic scholar: a failure which meant that later in life as archbishop he was always nervous when he had to preach or speak in Latin. After leaving school, he received a business training from a kinsman, Osbert Huitdeniers, a wealthy city magnate who was justiciar of London in 1141, while during his school holidays he was taught to love such field sports as hunting and falconry by a family friend, Richer de Laigle. After leaving school, it was not long before he was introduced to the household of the Archbishop Theobald of Canterbury, where he took minor orders, and was soon marked out for advancement. Benefices, provostships and several prebends were bestowed upon him, providing him with a more than adequate income, but it was as a comparatively minor official at Henry's court that he began to rise to fame, eventually becoming chancellor and the king's closest friend. As such, in true twelfth-century style he lived the part assigned to him to the full, acting it out with such complete sincerity and gusto, dressing in such a splendidly secular and courtly manner, and behaving in such a magnificently unecclesiastical way that it would have taken a clairvoyant to have guessed that he was a man in holy orders. Henry both liked and trusted him, and in May 1162, a little more than a year after the death of Theobald, he pressed him to become archbishop in Theobald's place. The papal legate, Henry of Pisa, added his voice to that of the king, urging Thomas to accept the appointment; but Becket was not easily persuaded to agree, foreseeing the inevitable breach which would result. In the end, however, he was induced to give his assent, and he was consecrated by the bishop of Winchester on 3 June, the Sunday after Whitsunday: a day which was later to be dedicated to the Holy and Undivided Trinity and which became especially popular in England partly because Thomas had been consecrated archbishop on that particular Sunday.

Henry's motive in promoting Thomas to the See of Canterbury was plain; the power of the church had grown enormously during the chaos of Stephen's reign, and the king wanted to reduce it, particularly the power and the scope of the ecclesiastical courts. But just as Thomas had thrown himself wholeheartedly into the role of courtier and chancellor, now he resigned his chancellorship and threw himself without reservation and with complete sincerity into the role of churchman and man of God. He adopted an extremely austere way of life and devoted his entire energy and considerable administrative talents to the interests of the church, opposing every move made by the king to limit its power and jurisdiction. As a result, in less than a year after his consecration, Thomas and Henry were at loggerheads. In the same volume of the *Oxford History of England*, already quoted, it is said that 'it is unquestionable that Becket's conduct was gratuitously aggressive at this time; he opposed the king at every turn, even on issues of purely temporal concern'. He resisted all royal attempts to interfere with the privileges of the ecclesiastical courts, even when Henry had good cause to complain of their workings. There was a case of manslaughter by a priest in the diocese of Salisbury, another of rape followed by the killing of the injured girl's father in Worcestershire, and the murder of a knight by a canon of Bedford who, after having been acquitted by the bishop of Lincoln's court, was brought before the lay court, where he not only refused to plead, but insulted the royal justice, Simon Fitz Peter. When the matter was referred to the king, Becket countered Henry's vigorous complaints with a refusal to admit that there was anything wrong with the workings of the ecclesiastical courts, even defending the homicidal canon of Bedford and his right to refuse to appear before a lay court. This was so evidently unjust that one of the archbishop's own clergy, William, canon of Newburgh, was forced to admit that Thomas and the bishops supporting him brought upon themselves the great contest with the crown which followed; 'they were more intent upon defending the liberties and rights of the clergy,' he remarked, 'than on correcting and restraining their vices.'

That contest lasted for nearly eight years with ever-increasing bitterness between Thomas and the king, though there were times when attempts were made to reconcile the two men. This is not the place to describe it in detail; instead it must suffice to say that just after Christmas 1170, matters came to a head when Henry uttered a few unguarded words in a moment of ungovernable and understandable anger: words which were taken as an invitation to murder by four of Henry's knights, whose names have gone down in the annals of infamy: Hugh de Morville, William Tracy, Reginald Fitz-Urse, and Richard Le Breton. That they have been thus condemned by history is not entirely fair, for in their somewhat brutal, not too intelligent, bellicose way they were as typical of one section of twelfth-century society at its least attractive as, for instance, Eleanor of Aquitaine and such men as St Hugh of Lincoln were typical of other aspects of it at its best. As everyone knows, they rode to Canterbury where they stabbed the archbishop to death in his own cathedral on 29 December to the horror of the whole of Europe. However dubious a life a man may have lived, martyrdom was a passport to sanctity throughout the early Christian centuries, and even some who never became martyrs for their faith were sometimes canonized despite having lived lives of a far from saintly nature. For instance, Vladimir of Kiev, a man who was said to have had 800 concubines and who was described at the time as a fornicator *immensus et crudelis*, was later canonized for having forced his Russian subjects to choose between becoming Christian or being beheaded, thus giving birth to Holy Mother Russia. It is therefore not very surprising that when a number of miracles were recorded at Thomas's tomb in Canterbury Cathedral, his fame spread, pilgrims began to come in increasing numbers to pray for his favours, something very like a cult developed, and on 21 February 1173 he was canonized.

Whether it was his canonization which finally determined Henry to make a pilgrimage of repentance to the tomb of his old friend and enemy will never be known; in the event, he set out, eating nothing but bread and drinking nothing but water, and riding so hard that he covered the 120 miles between Southampton and Canterbury in less than four days. On arrival, he dismounted outside the west gate of the city, and removing his shoes, donned the grey and shapeless habit of a pilgrim before walking barefoot through the narrow cobbled streets to the cathedral, where he threw himself on to the stone floor of the crypt beside Becket's tomb in a torment of penitence and prayer, confessing his sins and craving the forgiveness of God and the church. Having received absolution, he bared his back, while still kneeling and gazing at the sarcophagus containing the mortal remains of Thomas, and he was formally scourged by the assembled bishops and clergy, each delivering a few symbolic strokes as they shuffled past the crouching figure of the king. For nearly twenty-four hours Henry stayed there in prayer, neither eating nor drinking; he joined the monks at midnight as they said the office of Lauds, but returned once again to the crypt until the morning, when he joined them once more for Mass. Then and only then, when Mass had been said, did he put on his own clothes again, attend to the by now pressing needs of his physical nature, have a meal, and set off, radiant with relief and the joy of his newly cleared conscience, for London.

On arrival in the capital, he was told that William the Lion of Scotland, thirsty for revenge on those who had driven him back into his own country so ignominiously after his last excursion into Henry's kingdom, had invaded the border country again, and was looting what little there was to loot and burning everything else, leaving behind him a trail of black and smoking fields, burning villages, and a sprinkling of unburied corpses for the crows to squabble over and the dogs to tear to pieces with their teeth; but Henry had been in London for no more than a day or two, when he heard that the Scottish king had been captured and locked up in Richmond castle. It was not much longer before the king's mere presence in England once again so over-awed the few remaining barons supporting the rebel cause that they returned to their former allegiance and reaffirmed their loyalty to him, thus extinguishing the last flicker of revolt. But if his presence in England had been enough to restore peace there, his absence from France had encouraged Louis and young Henry with the count of Flanders to besiege Rouen, while Richard was busy attacking anyone in Aquitaine who had remained loyal to his father. With his usual ineptitude Louis failed to take Rouen by siege; its citizens shut the gates against him and beat off his various attacks, and when, with his almost equally usual duplicity, he attacked it under cover of a truce, once again the citizens manned the walls in time to defeat his discreditable manoeuvre. Disheartened at last by this failure, Louis decided to make peace with Henry and end the war between them.

The two men met on 8 September 1174, at Gisors once again. It was Richard's seventeenth birthday, but Richard was not there; in marked and painful contrast to the blatant military incompetence of the French king, hc was pursuing the war in Poitou and Aquitaine with a vigour, relentlessness and flair which would have been remarkable in anyone, but was extraordinary in a boy of his age, and his absence from the conference table cast a shadow over the proceedings. Neither Henry nor Louis felt that they could agree upon the terms of a peace treaty while Richard was still making war in his father's dominion, and this created a problem for both of them. They solved it by agreeing to a truce, during which Henry would march south and bring his son to heel. History does not record Richard's reaction when he heard that his father was bearing down on him with a large force, and that the French king and his brothers had agreed to this new move, abandoning him to whatever fate Henry might devise for him, but it must have been bitter. In the event, he was not prepared to make war on his father in person; instead, he retreated before him, allowing city after city and castle after castle to fall into his hands without a struggle, until the moment came when he decided to beg his father's forgiveness for what he had done. If father and son differed in some ways, they also had some things in common, and as Richard threw himself upon Henry's mercy without making any conditions or leaving any hostages for his safety, so Henry forgave him without either condition or recrimination. Instead, he raised him to his feet, embraced him, and kissed him. The rebellion was over.

IV

With a monarch's voice
Cry, 'Havoc!' and let slip the dogs of war.

Shakespeare, *Julius Caesar*

After the reconciliation with his father, Richard spent a year in England with his family. At the age of eighteen, he was tall, long-limbed, athletic and strong; and with a mass of reddish-golden hair, blue eyes and finely formed features, even his enemies admitted that he was handsome. He was endowed, too, with a certain natural dignity so that more than one observer described his manner as that of one 'worthy to occupy a place of high command'. He was no dandy, but unlike his father he dressed with care, and he had a great sense of occasion; when he considered that the event warranted it, he enjoyed dressing up and cutting something of a dash to enhance the impact of the moment. But if there were traces of the exhibitionist in him, his manner was quiet, and he never courted popularity; on the contrary, there were times when his determination to do whatever he deemed to be necessary and right, however unpopular his chosen course might be, made lifelong enemies of people whom lesser men – or perhaps less straightforward men – would not have dared to offend. But although at the time this kind of behaviour made enemies, on the whole in his own day even his enemies admired him for it, whereas many latter-day critics have described him as ruthless, counting his ruthlessness as a vice. By the standards of our own day, Richard was indeed ruthless from time to time, but this characteristic was seen in a very different light by his contemporaries as part of what they called Richard's 'constancy', a quality universally admired in medieval times. 'Among the virtues in which he excels,' wrote Gerald of Wales when Richard was in his mid-twenties, 'three especially distinguish him: supereminent valour and daring; unbounded liberality and bountifulness; and steadfast constancy in holding to his purpose and his word.' This constancy and steadfastness of purpose, this determination not to allow anyone or anything to deflect him from the course which he had chosen, when he considered it to be right, was to show itself in action when, at the end of his year in England, Henry sent him back to Aquitaine to restore order there. He told him, too, to restore the lands and castles of those barons who had lost them by remaining loyal to the king during the recent rebellion, and to dispossess the rebels of any gains they might have made as a result of it. It was a formidable challenge for a young man of not yet twenty years of age, and Richard had need of all the constancy with which nature had endowed him, and even a touch of ruthlessness in order to accomplish it successfully.

On arrival, he found most of the barons of Aquitaine in arms against him: a fact which should surprise no one, and certainly did not surprise Richard, for they were notoriously belligerent. Joan Evans in her book, *Life in Medieval France*, described them as living 'in a perpetual state of private war . . . so that war seemed to spring from the soil itself.' Like their predecessors in the Dark Ages, there was nothing they enjoyed more than making war; the celebrated troubadour and poet, Bertrand de Born, spoke for them all when, on hearing of Richard's approach with a large army of feudal levies and Brabantine mercenaries, he cried out in delight at the prospect of the coming conflict:

> We shall see axes and swords battering coloured haumes and hacking through shields at entering *mêlée*; and many vassals smiting together, whence run freed the horses of the dead and wrecked. And when each man of prowess shall be come into the fray, he thinks no more of breaking heads and arms, for a dead man is worth more than one taken alive. I tell you I find no such savour in eating butter or sleeping, as when I hear cried, 'On them!' and from both sides hear horses neighing through their head-guards, and hear shouted, 'To aid! To aid!', and see the dead with their truncheons, the pennants still on them, piercing their sides.

These were the men whom Richard was ordered to suppress and control.

In the event – or rather the series of events – which followed, both Bertrand de Born and the nobles of Aquitaine were to discover that making war against Richard was no enjoyable game, while the knights who had rallied to his banner, partly because he was the rightful duke to whom they owed allegiance, but also partly because he had been so well provided with funds by his father that he was able to pay them all generously, soon discovered, too, that to fight under Richard's leadership was certainly not to play at making war but to be led from victory to victory by someone who never swerved from his purpose of defeating the enemy.

It would be tedious to describe the next few years too minutely, tedious and in part impossible, for while much of the political manoeuvring, the squabbles for possession of little orphaned heiresses as wards and therefore as valuable pawns in the political game, the battles, the sieges, the marches, the counter-marches and the fluctuations of military fortune are recorded by the chroniclers of the time in loving and often impenetrably boring detail, there are large gaps in their accounts when we have no idea what Richard was doing between the various campaigns and battles so punctiliously recounted. But the general outline of events must be described, for, after his childhood, this time of his life must have been both crucially influential and formative. It would be fascinating to be able to look out at the world with his eyes, seeing it as he saw it, and evaluating it in the light of what it did to him during these years of his earliest manhood, and indeed in the light of what it forced him to do in reply; but since this is impossible, there is no alternative but to look at the course of events over these years, picking out the highlights and trying to assess their impact on Richard. We know his overall aim at this time; at least we do if Gerald of Wales is to be trusted, for he set it out clearly in his chronicle, *Concerning the Instruction of Princes*. It was to restore the ducal authority in Aquitaine, 'that hitherto untamed country . . . that he might quell the insubordination of an unruly people, and make innocence secure amongst evil-doers.' Even Richard's severest critics could hardly find fault with that, and that that was indeed his intention is borne out by the fact that at one point he waged a campaign against the people of Navarre and the Basque country in order to stop them robbing and attacking pilgrims on their way to pray at the tomb of St James the Apostle at Compostella in northern Spain, there to ask God's merciful forgiveness for their manifold sins and wickedness.

At the outset of his task, he arrived to find that one of the principal barons, Vulgrin the count of Angoulême, had preceded him with bellicose intent, marching into Poitou with an army of mercenaries; however, this invasion had already been checked by the bishop of Poitiers, who had temporarily stepped down from his episcopal throne in the cathedral church of St Peter there in order to mount a war-horse and lead his own private army against the belligerent invader from Anjou. This prelatical pugnacity would have raised very few priestly eyebrows in the twelfth century, so accustomed were all men in holy orders to seeing their fathers in God engaged in holy warfare. But in this case, although the militant bishop had checked Vulgrin, he had not utterly defeated him. Richard, however, did so in a battle near Cognac, before leading his troops, elated by this early success, into the Limousin, where another local baron, Aimar of Limoges, was in revolt; but he, too, was utterly defeated, losing both his castle at Aixe and the city of Limoges after a brief siege of a few days only.

So far, things could hardly have gone better for Richard and, encouraged by the news of these early victories – or perhaps slightly jealous of his younger brother's success – the young King Henry now joined Richard, and marched south with him to lay siege to the city of Châteauneuf, which surrendered after a fortnight. But the young king had no stomach for the serious business of war, far preferring a life of royal fun and games, and he did not stay long after the fall of Châteauneuf. In *The Lives of the Troubadours* his conduct was contemptuously described with little or no attempt to hide the author's scorn: 'And the young king departed and went into Lombardy, and gave his days to tourneys and vain pleasures, leaving all the barons at war with Lord Richard; and Lord Richard laid siege to castles and to towns, and destroyed them, and took lands and burnt and laid them waste; and the young king held tourneys, and lived at ease, and slept, and disported himself.'

After the fall of Châteauneuf and his brother's departure, Richard turned towards Angoulême, where Vulgrin had taken refuge after his defeat at Cognac together with his father, Count William, as well as some of the other leading rebels; Aimar of Limoges and the viscounts of Chabanais and Ventadour were there, and the chance to capture all five of them at one fell swoop was too good to miss. They evidently felt secure enough in their fortified city, but they counted without Richard's growing reputation, which had been positively burgeoning as success followed success, so that now his mere approach struck terror into those opposed to him. Angoulême surrendered after a siege of only six days. Vulgrin and his father, Aimar of Limoges and the two viscounts were sent under guard to Winchester, there to explain themselves to Henry II and to make their peace with him as best they could. In fact, with his usual generosity, Henry readily forgave them, not even depriving them of their lands.

But it was by his defeat of yet another of the great barons of Aquitaine, Geoffrey of Rancon, that Richard's growing reputation for military prowess was confirmed once and for all. Geoffrey was the owner of two formidable castles, one at Pons not far from Jonzac and the other at Taillebourg overlooking the Charente five miles downstream from the old Roman city of Saintes, with its cathedral of St Peter, its celebrated abbey full of nuns and its bridge across the river on the pilgrim route to Santiago. Early in 1179, Richard invested Pons; but the place was immensely strong, and although he had a large army under his command, the siege did not go well, and it soon became evident that it would take a long time to persuade its defenders to surrender. Richard had already gained such a reputation as a military prodigy that a defeat or a serious set-back at this time might well have shattered the growing myth of his martial infallibility, and it seems that he realized this; he decided to leave enough of his troops behind to continue the siege of Pons, while he led the remainder of his men away to besiege and capture a number of minor castles belonging to Geoffrey of Rancon at such places as Richemont, Genzac, Marcillac, Grouville and Anville. They all duly fell to him without much trouble, reinforcing his reputation for invincibility and spreading dismay amongst his enemies, while the rumour of these new conquests reached Pons and greatly disheartened its defenders, who awaited his return with increased nervousness.

But Richard did not return there. Instead, in May he led his men north to besiege the impregnable little town and castle of Taillebourg: impregnable, that is to say, hitherto, for no one had ever yet dared to attack it. In an immensely strong natural position on the summit of a rocky pinnacle, it was defended on three sides by sheer cliffs, crowned at the top by triple walls with fortified towers at intervals along their length, and on the fourth side by massive fortifications, triple walls and a triple ditch to guard the only gate into the place. On hearing of his approach, the people in the villages and farms in the surrounding countryside had taken refuge in the little town, bringing some supplies with them, but considerably increasing the number of mouths to be fed in the event of a prolonged siege, and thus adding to the worries of the townsfolk and the garrison troops left there by Geoffrey of Rancon to defend the citadel against just such a possible attack. But it seems that, on the whole, the mood of the people of Taillebourg and their defenders spoke of over-confidence rather than of despair or defeatism; Richard might be a prodigy, but no one had ever had the temerity to assault their unassailable little fortress home before, and they felt confident that this Plantagenet paragon was about to be taught an overdue lesson in humility. So they were not unduly worried when he and his men camped below their walls on the one accessible side of the place, bringing up a battery of siege engines with which to bombard the gate into the little town; but when they also saw smoke rising from the surrounding countryside, as parties of Richard's men laid it waste, they became angry. His camp lay invitingly close to the town gate, and the garrison decided – or, perhaps, were persuaded by the refugees from the countryside, as they watched their fields and homes go up in flames – to launch an attack on the besiegers and drive them away. It was just what Richard wanted, and as the defenders of Taillebourg sallied forth from the town and attacked him, he counter-attacked with his usual vigour, driving them back to the gate, where a fierce hand-to-hand struggle ended with Richard's men forcing their way into the town before the gate could be closed against them. Most of the garrison managed to reach the safety of the citadel, but with many of their supplies now in Richard's hands, and the town at the mercy of his victorious troops, further resistance was doomed to failure, and rather than prolong their agony, the garrison soon surrendered. The whole operation had lasted three days, and the impregnable fortress of Taillebourg could call itself impregnable no longer. The shock to the barons of Aquitaine was enormous, and Geoffrey of Rancon surrendered Pons without further resistance, while his ally, Vulgrin of Angoulême, followed suit a few weeks later, surrendering his capital city and his castle at Montignac. The result, as Roger of Howden, another contemporary chronicler, said in his *Gesta Henrici II et Ricardi I*, was that when Richard sailed for England, 'he left all things settled according to his will' in Aquitaine. It was a remarkable achievement.

This peaceful state of affairs lasted for two years, and since there were no wars for them to record and little else seemed worthy of their notice, the medieval chroniclers of the time fell silent, and we have no idea what Richard was doing during this period. But just over a year after the fall of Taillebourg, an event took place which was destined to have a lasting influence on his whole life: Louis VII of France died at the age of fifty-nine on 18 September 1180, and his son Philip Augustus, who had celebrated his fifteenth birthday just a month before his father's death, succeeded him on the throne. Louis had been one of the least impressive kings ever to rule France, while as a man, although obsessionally religious, he had proved to be shifty and untrustworthy on more than one occasion. In marked contrast, Philip Augustus was destined to become one of the most successful of French kings, if success and greatness are to be measured by the greatness with which he succeeded in endowing the land over which he ruled; for when he came to the throne, France was a deeply divided country dominated by the Angevin empire, whereas when Philip died forty-three years later, he had virtually destroyed that empire and restored France to something like the glory it had enjoyed in the days of Charlemagne. As a man, however, he was far from endearing, being cunning, deceitful and sly, and showing himself again and again to be almost completely devoid of moral scruples of any kind. However, before judging him too harshly, it is as well to take into account the circumstances of his world and the challenges which faced him.

Both Richard and Philip were destined by the accident of royal birth to be thrust into positions of great power and equally great responsibility at a tender age, and although as men they could scarcely have differed more in temperament and talents, they shared one thing: determination to achieve their ends. As men at the summit of the social pyramid, they could have chosen to take their duties and obligations as lightly as possible, escaping into a life of 'vain pleasures', as did young King Henry, or one of religious devotion, as did Louis VII, to be judged by history as an irresponsible playboy on the one hand and a religious freak on the other. However, historical hindsight gives the people under its critical microscope little say in their fate; so Richard, taking seriously the responsibilities thrust on him by his position of great power, is accused of cruelty and ruthlessness, while Philip Augustus, equally determined to achieve his political ends but on the whole eschewing war when he could do so in favour of what is often euphemistically referred to as diplomacy, is accused of being treacherous, crafty, false, slippery and a liar.

In physique, too, Philip Augustus was very different from Richard. What he looked like as a boy of fifteen, when he inherited the throne from his father, we are not told, but later in life he was described as being well enough built, though a bit ungainly, with a shock of untidy brown hair; his dress was slovenly and dull, and his tastes almost equally so; he had lost the sight of one eye, and he took no interest in sport or games of any kind; courage was not one of his virtues, and intellectual pursuits bored him as did the arts; he was ill-educated, self-indulgent and at times bad-tempered, though he learned to control his irascible disposition as the years passed. On the credit side, however, what he lacked in charm and other virtues, he made up for in patience, shrewdness, and dogged persistence in carrying out his royal duties in what he believed to be the best interests of his country; and while he was niggardly and mean to his friends, rather surprisingly he could be generous to the poorest of his people, championing them against those who oppressed or exploited them.

Most of these characteristics became evident only as he grew from a boy into a man and tried to cope with the difficult task he had inherited from his ineffective father. His immediate problems would have been daunting enough to have dismayed a much older and more experienced man than he could possibly have been at fifteen; the comparatively small portion of France which constituted the royal domain – a small strip of land running roughly north–south through Paris – was hemmed in by the Angevin empire in the west and the kingdom of Arles to the south-east. As we have seen, Henry II controlled a far greater part of France than Philip did himself, and he was also overshadowed by the power of his uncles, William, archbishop of Rheims, Henry, count of Champagne, and Theobald, count of Blois and Chartres, none of whom did he trust. Thus the task before him of consolidating his position on the throne was a formidable one, and he would hardly have been human if he had not also felt that for a king of France to be in such a position was deeply humiliating; indeed, it may well have been that his lifelong determination to re-create the power and dignity of France and her kings was born at this time. However that may have been, his first move in the game of power politics which he was destined to play until the day he died was both typical and astute: he invited his most powerful and dangerous rivals, Henry II and his sons, to help him. With his usual generosity, Henry immediately responded, promising that he and his whole family would do anything they could to assist Philip to establish his authority: a promise which he must have come bitterly to regret during the remaining years of his life.

For the time being, however, all went well between Henry and the boy king of France, and as Richard and his other sons joined Henry for Christmas 1182 at Caen, the family seemed once again to be at peace, and Henry must have felt reasonably free of political troubles for the first time for many years; but the surface amity hid some nasty undercurrents, and one or two of the king's guests were busily, if quietly, stirring up trouble behind the scenes. One of them was the troubadour, Bertrand de Born, whom Richard had brought with him, though it is impossible to say whether he had done so out of friendship and admiration for his poetry – he was a lover of poetry all his life – or out of a conviction that the man was such a born troublemaker that it would be better to keep him under his own eye rather than to leave him behind in Aquitaine where he had played a leading part in the recent rebellion.

In the event, it would probably have been better if he had left him behind to stir up what trouble he could in his own territory rather than giving him the chance, which he took with great alacrity, of acting as a snake in the grass in the rich pastures of Henry's court. For under the amiable surface of family unity and affection, the tensions between Henry and his sons and also between the sons themselves were considerable and kept under fragile control only for the sake of peace and goodwill at Christmas. To make things worse, Bertrand de Born was bored, complaining that although it was Christmas, there was 'no gab or laughter and no giving of presents' at Henry's court to make it worthy of the name. The party was only redeemed for him by the presence of Richard's sister, Matilda, to whom despite the presence of her young husband, Henry the Lion, duke of Saxony and Bavaria, he addressed an amorous poem in which he indulged in a little lascivious speculation upon the imagined loveliness of the lady naked; but the fact that she gave these poetic advances an icy reception did nothing to make his Christmas happier.

The middle-aged troubadour was not the only one in a bad mood. The young Henry was not bubbling over with enthusiasm for peace on earth and goodwill towards men either; indeed, he had been feeling progressively disgruntled for some time, and one must have some sympathy for him. Since he was his father's heir, and had already been crowned king to reign jointly with him, he might have expected to find himself in a better position than that of his younger brothers; but where Richard enjoyed a very real measure of power and independence as duke of Aquitaine, as did Geoffrey to a lesser degree as duke of Brittany, he had to content himself with a purely nominal role in the affairs of government under the dominant shadow of his father. It could not have been much fun living in such a completely subordinate position under old Henry's watchful eye, and his discontent was made no easier to bear by hearing more and more talk of Richard's growing renown as a soldier. Whether or not he knew of his own burgeoning reputation as a playboy we have no means of knowing, but it seems highly likely that he must have had some idea that most people regarded himself and Richard very differently; and this could not have pleased him. Unfortunately for him, he had neither the maturity nor the sense to realize that time was on his side; he had only to wait for power and independence to fall into his lap in an abundance that none of his brothers would ever know; but patience was not one of his virtues, and he spent Christmas planning ways of asserting himself. One of these ways was secretly to encourage Richard's enemies in Aquitaine to rebel yet again against this over-imperious and over-talented brother. Thus he would teach Richard who was king.

Young Henry had already made contact with some of the discontented barons of Aquitaine before joining the family for Christmas at Caen, and it seems almost certain that while he was there he took the opportunity to approach Bertrand de Born on the subject, knowing how enthusiastically the bellicose old versifier had encouraged those involved in the recent rebellion with his political ballads; but it was not until the new year that he made his first move. Richard had unwittingly given him a splendid excuse by building a castle at Clairvaux on a site which was not technically within the boundaries of his duchy, and young Henry complained to his father that thereby Richard was trespassing on Angevin territory which he himself would eventually inherit as king. As a result, he said, he had pledged himself to support the barons of Aquitaine against his brother. When old King Henry summoned Richard and taxed him with his brother's accusation, at first Richard refused to give up the castle, but after a little persuasion he agreed to hand it over to his father for him 'to dispose of it according to his good pleasure.'

As far as old King Henry was concerned, that was the end of the matter, but it did not satisfy young Henry, who now demanded that his brothers should pay him homage, and thus show him the proper respect which Richard had so manifestly failed to show by building the castle at Clairvaux in the first place; at least, this seems to have been what happened, though it has been suggested that old Henry, worried by these quarrels between his sons and determined to ensure a peaceful succession in the event of his own death, summoned Richard and Geoffrey and bade them pay homage to their elder brother. Whatever is the truth of the matter, Geoffrey agreed readily enough to pay his elder brother homage for Brittany, but Richard refused. Aquitaine was not subordinate to the Angevin empire, he said; he had inherited the dukedom from his mother, Eleanor, and thus he held it independently of his brother, who was in any case no more nobly born than he was himself. After a time, however, once again his father persuaded Richard to change his mind, but he did so only on the understanding that it should be clearly recognized that he and his heirs were the sole lords of Aquitaine by right for ever; and this immediately proved unacceptable to his brother Henry on the ground that it would not be accepted by those Aquitainian barons whose cause he pledged himself to support. So, to the intense irritation of the old King Henry, stalemate seemed to have been reached.

In an attempt to break out of this impasse, old Henry called his three sons together, this time to Angers, and suggested that they should sign a pact of perpetual peace, and that once signed, the malcontent barons of Aquitaine should be invited to join them in order to air their grievances and then sign a similar pact. All three agreed to this plan, and Geoffrey was sent to the Limousin, there to summon the malcontent barons of Aquitaine to Mirebeau, where the proposed oath of peace was to be signed. But when Geoffrey met the discontented barons of Aquitaine, instead of summoning them to a peace conference, he joined them. Meanwhile, immediately after Geoffrey's departure, young Henry, who almost certainly had a good idea of what Geoffrey was doing, announced that he would only accept Richard's homage to him if it was accompanied by an oath of fealty sworn upon some holy relics. This was too much for Richard; implicitly it cast doubts on his word and his honour, and he flew into a rage, stormed out and rode angrily to Poitou, where he put his various castles and fortified towns in readiness for war. The young King Henry, adopting an air of injured innocence, asked his father's permission to join his brother Geoffrey in his mission of peace, and promptly rode off to the Limousin without a thought of peace in his head to do what Geoffrey had already done: namely, to join the insurgents against his brother Richard.

Of course, the barons of Aquitaine were greatly encouraged by this sudden access of fraternal royal support for their cause, and Geoffrey and Henry were greeted with enthusiasm. In anticipation of their coming, some of the leaders of the last revolt against

Richard, Aimar of Limoges and others, had already raised a large
force of Gascon mercenaries and Brabançons, and Geoffrey had
summoned others together with some of his own knights
from Brittany to join the growing army arrayed against Richard,
which soon amounted to a formidable instrument of war. Not
everyone, however, in the Limousin was on the side of the rebels;
there were still men like the abbot of St Martial's abbey, a
passionate protagonist of peace and enemy of those who made
war, who had rejoiced at Richard's attempt to bring peace and the
rule of law to his dukedom, and these men kept him informed of
what his brothers were doing. On the whole, Richard had come
extremely well out of the whole messy, underhand, scheming
complex of malodorous events at Christmas; he had behaved
openly, straightforwardly and honestly, not even trying to hide
his eventual anger at the duplicity of his brothers under an
unctuous cloak of filial obedience, but storming out of his father's
presence without disguising his loss of patience with what he
doubtless thought of as his whole damned family or the appropriate twelfth-century equivalent term. Now, when he was told of
the growing build-up of forces against him under his brothers'
command, his reaction was equally straightforward and
uncomplicated: he seized the initiative, launching an attack on
his brother Geoffrey's mercenaries before they even realized that
he knew of their existence, hunting them down like animals,
killing many, executing those who fell into his hands as prisoners,
and taking the war into Geoffrey's camp by launching raids into
Brittany. It was entirely typical of him, and it has been one of his
many actions to which those who accuse him of ruthlessness
have pointed in support of their charge; and their indictment of
him does not stop there. For once again he took the initiative, and
on about 10 February, at the head of a small force of cavalry, he
rode virtually without stopping for two days and two nights to fall
like the wrath of God on Aimar's mercenaries as they attacked a
church a few miles outside Limoges, still fondly believing him to
be fifty miles away in Poitou. Aimar escaped, and Richard's horses
were too tired to pursue him, but the captain of the mercenaries
was killed, and most of his men were carried off by Richard to be
drowned in the river Vienne, slain by the sword or blinded.
Undoubtedly, this was a ruthless operation by any standards, but

it was one against people who would today be called the worst kind of terrorists: paid killers who made their living by hiring themselves out to slaughter people whom they had never seen, and against whom they had no quarrel, to rape them, rob them, burn their churches, their villages and their crops, and leave the few survivors and their terrified children to starve to death in the resulting desolation. Many of Richard's contemporaries, especially churchmen who longed and prayed for peace, regarded Richard's so-called ruthlessness as the vengeance of God on the enemies of the poor, and it is not difficult to see why they did so.

And it was not only the very poor – the peasants and the villeins in the country and those near to destitution in the towns – who prayed for Richard's success; so did all those engaged in trade: the merchants and small businessmen in the towns, whose livelihood depended on being able to move about the country in reasonable safety. As long as the wars of the time remained strictly local, they could continue to make a living by avoiding the areas of conflict, but once the fighting spread, it became almost impossible for them to carry on business of any kind. If they ventured out on the roads, the chances of running into a band of mercenaries were far from remote; in such an encounter, the best that a merchant could expect was the loss of his merchandise, while the worst and more probable result of such a meeting was the loss of both his goods and his life. Thus trade suffered badly during times of war and, as trade suffered, so did the general prosperity of the realm; in its turn this affected the yield from taxation, and the warring parties were forced to raise the money to pay their mercenary troops by other means. Tenants could be penalized for not paying their rents and other taxes by seizing their goods in lieu of monetary payment, but since both rents and taxes were often levied and collected in kind rather than money, this did not help very much.

As an illustration of this form of taxation partly in kind and partly in cash, in 1175 the Count of Troyes issued a proclamation to the citizens of one of the so-called New Towns – the *Villes Neuves* – in his domain, in which he told them of their obligations to him as their landlord. 'Know all men,' he began, 'that I, Henry Count of Troyes, having established the customs defined below for the inhabitants of my *Ville Neuve* near Pont-sur-Seine between the highways of the bridges of Pugny; every man dwelling in the said town shall pay each year twelve deniers and a measure of barley for the price of his domicile; and if he wishes to have an allotment of land or meadow, he shall pay four deniers an acre as rent.' That the Count should have collected so much of the rents in cash and so little in kind was proof of the modernity of his methods, for other landlords, less up-to-date than the Count, still collected more in kind than in cash. Such arrangements were all right in time of peace, but since much of the warfare of the day consisted of laying siege to your enemy's towns, burning his crops, and seeing your own crops burnt in return, in times of war often enough there was little or nothing left either in kind or in cash for the greedy hands of the landlord or the tax man to seize. Thus, in order to balance their bellicose books the high contending parties had to resort to other means; they seldom found these difficult to discover, as long as they ignored any residual moral sense, from which they might still improbably suffer from time to time. The claims of practical necessity were so much more persuasive than the still small voice of conscience that it was easy enough even for such a devout and princely Catholic churchman as young King Henry to decide that, however deplorable it might be, he had no alternative but to attack and rob any wealthy monasteries unfortunate enough to be within reach of his mercenaries.

In the worst affected areas, where the burning of crops, the cutting down of fruit trees, and the slaughter of domestic animals by the contending armies often led to famine, another source of income presented itself in the form of savage fines imposed on anyone who was driven by his own hunger and that of his family to poach in the royal forests or the woods reserved for the use of the local grandee: anyone, that is to say, who was unfortunate enough to get caught while doing so. But probably the most profitable source of income in wartime was provided by holding those captured in battle to ransom; the richer and more important the captive, the greater the sum of money which could be demanded for his ransom.

Thus life for the ordinary men and women of the land, whether in the country or in one of the many small towns attacked and pillaged or even burnt by one or other of the warring armies, was reduced to the barest essentials and rendered miserable in the extreme while the fighting lasted even for those lucky enough to survive; many did not, either dying of hunger or being casually slaughtered by passing mercenary soldiers. But while it is true that life for many people was turned into a kind of hell on earth by the warring princes, it would be wrong to conclude that therefore Richard and his brothers, together with the whole feudal system which they epitomized, should be condemned as equally guilty. It must never be forgotten that both in historical fact and in the aspirations of people alive at the time, the feudal system was designed to save the ordinary peasant and the poor townsman from the worst horrors of the unceasing wars and brutal chaos of the Dark Ages. In a celebrated poem *Miserere*, written just after Richard's time at the beginning of the thirteenth century, the ideal basis upon which feudal society was built was made clear:

> *Labours de clerc est Dieu prier*
> *Et justice de chevalier.*
> *Pain lor truevent li laborier.*
> *Chil paist, chil prie, et chil deffent.*
> *Au camp, a le vile, au moustier*
> *S'entreaident de lor mestier*
> *Chil troi par bel ordenement.*

'It is the work of a clerk to pray to God, of a knight to do justice, and the labourer gets their bread. This man labours, this prays, and that defends. In field, in town, and in church these three help one another in a beautiful dispensation.' Thus, at its best, the feudal system tried to bring men together in a bond of mutual interdependence, the weak depending on the protection of the strong, the strong on the labour of the weak, and both depending on the grace and protection of God through the prayers of the church. As a result, the author of the *Chanson de Guillaume* could say that *'gent senz seigneur sunt malement bailli'* – 'men without a lord are ill provided for.' This medieval view of the necessity of the social contract provided by the feudal system was well illustrated a little later in the *Coutume de Bayonne*, where it was laid down that 'the people come before the lords. It is the lesser folk, more numerous than the others, who, wishing to live in peace, create lords to restrain and defeat the strong and to maintain each man in his rights, so that each may live according to his condition, the poor with their poverty and the rich with their wealth. And to assure this in perpetuity, the populace has submitted itself to a lord, has given him what he holds, and has kept what the people hold for themselves. It is in witness of this that the lord should take the oath to his people before the people take it to their lord; and this oath taken by the people to their lord is only binding as long as the lord keeps his oath'.

Nothing could be much fairer than that in theory, even if it did not always work out like that in practice; but which social system devised by man has ever turned out to be perfect in practice? If the feudal system was therefore not guilty of causing the wars of the time, the blame must be put on the men who started them; and plainly some were more guilty than others, for some were defenders of the peace, while others were aggressors. Because Richard was more often involved in waging war than his brothers, the tendency has been to blame him more than them; but this is entirely unfair. As the rightful duke of Aquitaine, inevitably Richard was cast in the role of defender of the peace, of law and order, and the countering of aggression whenever that peace was broken by an aggressor: a fact not always recognized by his critics. It is therefore not surprising that so many of his contemporaries prayed for his success. He did not always succeed in protecting them from the horrors of war, but at least he tried, as for instance when his brothers attacked him and carried the war deep into his domain; and many of his more humble subjects gave him credit for that.

Even so, looking back down the centuries it is a little difficult to understand why the people at large did not rise up in righteous wrath against the entire princely Plantagenet clan – or brood of devils, as they must have seemed to be. The answer probably is that the ordinary men and women of France in the twelfth century – and those of Aquitaine in particular – were so well accustomed to living under the shadow of a barbarous and bellicose nobility that enduring the horrors of war seemed to them to be the normal human lot; for while Henry II had restored peace and established the rule of law in England after the chaos of Stephen's reign, he had been less successful in France, where distances were much greater, and where war was still the

favourite outdoor sport of the local landed gentry, who still liked
to behave as they had always behaved during the Dark Ages. It
had been barely a century since the Church had tried to limit
private warfare by commanding all Christians to observe a 'Truce
of God' on Sundays and holy days; later still an attempt had been
made to extend this Truce and to limit war to three days a week,
but as Runciman remarked in his *History of the Crusades*, 'movements for peace are seldom as impressive in fact as in theory', and
the barons of Aquitaine had taken little notice. So although the
war between Richard and his brothers made life hideous for
many people in Aquitaine, they were used to such conditions,
and even the country folk and the inhabitants of the small towns
– the most vulnerable sections of the community – had learned by
bitter experience how to survive most of the time, while praying
for the success of their rightful feudal lord.

Meanwhile it is difficult to generalize when trying to assess the
impact of the wars of the day on the people of the bigger towns
and cities. Plainly, it must have varied, but even the worst affected
would not have suffered as much as the small towns, let alone the
isolated hamlets and farmsteads. Of course, Paris was unique
even in the twelfth century, and it remained uninvolved in the
fighting; but it was not so different from the other great cities of
France as to bear no comparison with them, and it is instructive to
look, however briefly, at the way of life and the spirit of the
people there during this period. Fortunately, in the same year as
Henry of Troyes drew up the charter for his *Ville Neuve* near Pont-
sur-Seine, namely 1175, a certain Guy of Bazoches described
what life was like in the capital.

> I am in Paris [he wrote] in that royal city where abundance of natural
> wealth not only holds those who live there, but also attracts those from
> afar. Just as the moon outshines the stars in brilliance, so does this city, the
> seat of monarchy, lift her proud head above the rest. She lies in the
> embrace of an enchanting valley, surrounded by a crown of hills which
> Ceres and Bacchus make fruitful. The Seine, proud river of the East, runs
> there a brimming stream, and holds in its arms an island which is the
> head, the heart, the marrow of the whole city. Two suburbs extend to right
> and left, of which the lesser alone rivals many cities. Each of these suburbs
> communicates with the island with two bridges of stone; the Grand Pont
> towards the north, on the side of the English Channel, and the Petit Pont
> towards the Loire. The first – great, rich, trading – is the scene of seething

activity; innumerable ships surround it, filled with merchandise and riches. The Petit Pont belongs to dialecticians, who walk there deep in argument. In the island, by the side of the King's palace that dominates the whole city, is seen the palace of philosophy, where study reigns as sole sovereign in a citadel of light and immortality.

This Paris does not sound like a city which would ever despair of itself, even when shortages in time of war reduced its 'great, rich, trading' activity. On the contrary, it sounds like what in fact it was: namely, a city exhilarated by the knowledge that the world of which it was a part was moving out of a long and appalling time of darkness and brutality into an immensely exciting time of growth and intellectual adventure; and though the other great cities of France were lesser places than Paris, they were inhabited by the same kind of twelfth-century people – resourceful, resilient, abounding in curiosity, hope and optimism, and as tough as old boots. Presumably, what was true of the towns' folk of the day was also to some degree true of the peasants and country folk. Obviously enough, they did not spend time savouring the delights of dialectical discussion and philosophical speculation, but their toughness cannot be doubted, nor their resilience. They suffered much more severely than their urban compatriots, as has already been said, and if they had not been both remarkably tough and resilient, they could hardly have survived as well as in fact they did despite their grievous losses. Moreover, even in the country districts, there was a great flowering of the arts at this time. Romanesque churches were built; inside they were decorated with lively and inventive mural paintings, while outside they were enriched by carved doorways, and their west fronts were covered with ebullient carvings of Christ in glory, the Blessed Virgin and a creative splendour of saints. Stained glass was less commonly seen in the small parish churches of the day than in the great cathedrals and abbey churches, but it was not unknown, and it is impossible to believe that all this sprang out of a despairing, deeply depressed populace who had lost all hope as a result of their sufferings under the wars of their feudal overlords. On the contrary once again, although they could not have enjoyed those wars, they too must have been buoyed up by the knowledge that the worst of the darkness of the past was giving way to new light and new hope, and that ultimately beyond disaster God was in charge to save and to re-create.

But to return to the narrative. By this time news of the war between his sons had reached Henry II, and he had set out with a few supporters to ride to the Limousin in order to bring this fratricidal strife to an end. Whether he blamed Richard for the war or not, he was soon to change his mind, for as he rode up to the walls of Limoges, where he knew the young Henry to be, his little party of horsemen was violently attacked by a number of armed men from the city. One of his household was killed, and he himself had a narrow escape, before one of his attackers belatedly recognized his royal banner, and the attack was called off. By this time, Henry was both shocked and angry, and he refused to enter the city; turning away, he rode to the fortified city of Aixe, where he and his little party took refuge. The young Henry visited him there that evening, but though he did his best to explain and excuse what had happened, his father was in no mood to listen to his specious self-justification, and he was forced to ride back to Limoges and his fellow conspirators having failed to persuade the old man of his total innocence in the whole affair. It seems that, at last, it had dawned on Henry that Richard was not the aggressor but the injured party, and he immediately set about joining and supporting him.

It was not before time. By now, not only had all those who had bitterly resented being kept in order by Richard, and who longed for a more malleable overlord whom they could ignore with impunity, rallied to the young King Henry's banner, seeing in him the perfect answer to every anarchically minded baron's prayer, but such men as Raymond of Toulouse and Hugh, duke of Burgundy, who resented the new-found power of the Angevin family, had joined the young king and for much the same reason as that which had motivated the Aquitainian barons: namely, that he was obviously an amiable nonentity, whom they could either ignore or manipulate as they pleased. Finally, Philip Augustus, the young French king, conveniently ignoring Henry's generosity to him barely three years previously, when he had been most in need of help, sent a large force of Brabançons to support the young king, his brother-in-law, though he did so for reasons which had little to do with kinship; on the contrary, what he wanted most in the world was to weaken and destroy the whole Plantagenet clan, and he saw a golden opportunity of at least starting to do just that by encouraging them to destroy one another. If this says little for Philip's trustworthiness, loyalty or sense of gratitude, it says a lot for his political astuteness, and it was destined to be his first move in a lifelong battle of arms and wits waged against old Henry and his princely brood from Anjou.

When the old king joined Richard, he had with him only a small party of supporters, whom he had brought as his personal bodyguard on the journey from Normandy, but by the beginning of March he had summoned his feudal levies to his side, and with his main army beside him, he and Richard were greatly strengthened and no longer so vulnerable to a sudden attack as they had been hitherto. By now, however, the various bands of mercenaries hired by the young king and his allies had also arrived, and the last vestiges of civilized order in France were giving way to chaos, as violence spread throughout the whole region like fire through dry grass in summer. The behaviour of the particular band of hired thugs sent by Philip Augustus was typical of the rest; they stormed the little fortified town of St Leonard-de-Noblat in what is now Haute Vienne, and after raping many of the women, massacred the inhabitants before sweeping on past Limoges, leaving its streets littered with corpses, to subject Brantôme to the same atrocities. Farther south, other bands of mercenaries —*routiers* as these particular bands of thugs were called — were committing much the same sort of crimes on behalf of their lordly employers, while Bertrand de Born welcomed the opportunity provided by the splendid havoc of the times to attack his brother in the family castle at Hautefort, and everyone cast in the same mould rejoiced that Richard's iron rule was over, and that the good old days of freedom to wage war, when and as one wished, had returned at last: everyone, that is to say, except the ordinary people of the land, who were forced to watch helplessly as their cattle were stolen, their towns and villages were sacked and burnt, their wives were ravished, and their children were murdered, before they themselves were killed in their turn by the hired assassins of their noble lords and masters. For them, the little people of Aquitaine, Richard's iron rule had been the greatest blessing they had ever known in their short and precarious lives.

The old king and Richard made no attempt to chase and destroy these marauding bands of mercenaries, whether Brabançons or *routiers*, partly because it would have been as endless a task as swatting a host of dispersed mosquitoes, but also because they knew that in the long run they would become a cause of weakness rather than strength to their employers; mercenaries had to be paid, and the young king was soon forced to resort to such desperate measures as the sacking of monasteries and the pillaging of churches to find their wages, bringing down the wrath and condemnation of the church on his head and thus risking the even worse fate of incurring the wrath of God himself. None of this made his cause any the more popular with even his staunchest supporters, who were as fearful of divine displeasure as anyone else; and so the longer the mercenaries plundered in order to raise the money to pay themselves, the more support the young king lost. So Henry and Richard let them be, and invested the city of Limoges, beginning a siege which was destined to last until the summer under the old king's supervision, while Richard took a party of troops west into Anjou, where he drove his brother's men out of some of the major cities there. Indeed, he harassed the young king's supporters with such vigour that he won the grudging admiration of Bertrand de Born, who wrote of Richard: 'hunted and wounded wild boar saw we never more furious than he is, yet he never swerves from his course.'

The fighting in Anjou and the siege of Limoges might have gone on for months, as the young king sacked more monasteries for their treasure and even pillaged the holiest shrine in the whole of Aquitaine at Rocamadour and stripped it of its riches, if an entirely unexpected event had not changed the course of the war. Late in May, young Henry contracted dysentery, and although he refused to take to his bed, he grew gradually weaker, and in early June, while out with his troops, he collapsed. He was carried to a blacksmith's shop in the little town of Martel a couple of miles north of the Dordogne valley, where it soon became evident that he was very ill indeed. Alarmed by his condition, he sent a message to his father, begging him to come to him; but Henry no longer trusted him and, suspecting a trap, he refused. The young king was barely twenty-eight years old. Having promised at one time to go on Crusade, he asked to be laid under his cloak with its crusader badge, at the same time instructing William Marshal, one of his closest lieutenants, to see that it was carried to the Holy Land after his death. Surrounded by this time by courtiers and clergy, at his own request his clothes were removed, and he was dressed in a hair shirt; a rope was tied loosely round his neck, and he was carried out of bed to be laid on a symbolic bed of ashes with his head resting on a stone pillow. Here, he made his final confession, received the last sacraments and, having kissed his father's ring, he died.

He was widely and deeply mourned. Looking back over the centuries which separate us from his time, it is not easy to see why he inspired such affection and admiration, but there can be no doubt that he did so. One contemporary wrote of him that even though he deceived an endlessly forgiving and indulgent father, committing treason against him and waging war against his own brother, chivalry blossomed in him as it had not been seen to flower for years, and the world was a richer place for his example. In similar vein, Bertrand de Born mourned his death in one of his most moving poems, 'Lament for the Young English King', which was splendidly rendered into English by Ida Farnell.

> If all the pain and misery and woe,
> The tears, the losses with misfortune fraught
> That in this dark life man can ever know,
> Were heaped together – all would seem as naught
> Against the death of the young English king;
> For by it youth and worth are sunk in gloom.
> And the world dark and dreary as the tomb,
> Reft of all joy, and full of grief and sadness . . .
> Bloodthirsty death, that bring'st us bitter woe!
> Well may'st thou boast, since that earth's noblest peer
> To thy dark realm a prisoner must go.

Yet another of the young king's contemporaries, writing in the year of his death, described him rather differently as 'rich, noble, lovable, eloquent, handsome, gallant, every way attractive, a little lower than the angels . . . all these gifts he turned to the wrong side . . . a prodigy of unfaith, a lovely palace of sin.'

His death meant the end of the war. Without him to replace Richard and his iron rule over the pugnacious barons of Aquitaine with their never-ending squabbles, there was no point in continuing the fight. Raymond of Toulouse and the duke of Burgundy went home to their own domains, leaving the lesser fry to their fate. Most of them had totally lost heart on hearing of the young king's death, although a few fought on in dispirited fashion, until Richard hunted them down one by one and forced them to surrender. By the end of June it was all over.

V

———

Within the hollow crown
That rounds the mortal temples of a king
Keeps Death his court, and there the antick sits,
Scoffing his state and grinning at his pomp;
Allowing him a breath, a little scene,
To monarchize, be fear'd, and kill with looks,
Infusing him with self and vain conceit
As if this flesh which walls about our life
Were brass impregnable; and humour'd thus
Comes at the last, and with a little pin
Bores through his castle wall, and farewell king!

Shakespeare, *King Richard II*

Richard was not quite twenty-six years old when his brother died in 1183 and he became heir apparent to the throne of England and the headship of the houses of Normandy and Anjou. When old King Henry heard of the young man's death, despite the fact that he was at war with him at the time, in his usual, large, warm-hearted, uncomplicated way he burst into tears of genuine grief; but we do not know how Richard reacted to the news. He had little enough reason to be fond of his elder brother, but again and again throughout his life he was to show himself astonishingly generous to those who had injured him, and he may well have forgiven the various attempted injuries done to him by young Henry. His behaviour to Bertrand de Born after the war in Aquitaine ended was typical; the old poet had been a principal agitator against him, had abused his hospitality at Christmas by plotting with young Henry, and had played a leading part in the subsequent war; yet after he had been forced to surrender to Richard, on pleading for mercy and promising that, if he was forgiven, he would be as true as steel in the future, Richard immediately forgave him and gave him the kiss of peace. The belligerent old troubadour was as good as his word, though whether from honourable motives or, as has been rather cattily suggested, because he realized that his talents for fighting might be exercised not less actively and a good deal more safely in Richard's service than in that of his enemies, it is difficult to say.

We are equally uninformed about Richard's reaction to suddenly finding himself his father's heir. He would hardly have been human if he had not been excited, but contemporary chroniclers are silent on the subject. Henry's reaction, on the other hand, was plain enough; first and foremost, he had no intention of repeating the mistake he had made by having young Henry crowned king, nominally to rule jointly with him but actually to be denied all real power and to be driven by frustration into the kind of intrigue, plotting and revolt which had occupied him during the last years of his life. Secondly, since the death of his eldest son had left the heartlands of the Angevin dominions without an heir, all he had to do to provide his youngest son, John, with an inheritance worthy of his rank as a prince of the blood royal was to move Richard out of Aquitaine into the positions and estates left vacant by young Henry's death, and John need no longer be dubbed 'Lackland'; he would become the duke of Aquitaine instead.

Since John was not yet seventeen years old and totally untried in a position of responsibility, Henry could hardly have intended to put him in immediate charge of the most rumbustious and ungovernable province of the Angevin empire; that might well have been a recipe for disaster. Indeed, two years later, when Henry sent him across to Ireland as governor, John behaved so irresponsibly and insolently that he did not last long; he mocked the Irish lords because of their unfamiliar clothes, pulled their beards, and laughed at their native manners, even robbing some of them of their land, while he and his young friends spent their time feasting and amusing themselves. But Henry's aim in putting John into Richard's place was to provide him with a properly endowed future, not an immediate position of responsibility, for which he was wholly unready. John had always been his father's darling. It is difficult to understand why Henry doted on him so much or to see what he found so attractive about him. John was a little man, five feet five inches in height and a bit on the fat side, and he was subject to sudden and unpredictable changes of mood; according to the *Oxford History of England*, he was 'made up of inconsistencies . . . cruel and ruthless, violent and passionate, greedy and self-indulgent, genial and repellent, arbitrary and judicious, clever and capable, original and inquisitive.' But however hard it may be to understand Henry's doting partiality, it is easy enough to understand his desire to put his youngest son in Richard's place in Aquitaine while moving Richard into positions of even greater responsibility and power. It must have seemed a simple and reasonable solution to the old problem of John's landlessness.

But it seemed neither simple nor reasonable to Richard. He had done homage to Louis VII for the duchy of Aquitaine, and he had been installed and invested by the archbishop of Bordeaux and the bishop of Poitiers, and no one could undo what the king of France and the representatives of God and the church had so solemnly done nearly ten years previously. Moreover, since then he had spent his life working and fighting to establish peace and order throughout his duchy, and he was not prepared lightly to hand it over to a boy of sixteen, even if that boy happened to be his brother. So, on being told of his father's intention, he waited until nightfall, saddled his horse, and rode south to Poitou, where on arrival he sent a message to his father to say that he would never allow John or anyone else to take his place as the rightful duke of Aquitaine, and the family row which was destined to do more than any other single factor to destroy the power and position of the Angevin dynasty in France – indeed the power and position of the kings of England in France – had begun.

Richard spent Christmas at Talmont. It was one of his favourite country resorts near La Rochelle, where he often spent a week or two hunting in the great oak forests with which it was surrounded in those days. There he entertained many of his friends and vassals as though he had not a care in the world, showing himself particularly generous to those who had remained loyal to him during the recent civil war. It was his way of saying 'thank you' and at the same time reinforcing their loyalty with a little well-timed generosity and ducal camaraderie at a suitably festive time of year. One of his guests was the leader of one of the many bands of *routiers*, a man named Mercadier, who first appears in Richard's service at this time, and who was to serve him faithfully until the day he died. He was one of many who found themselves unemployed after young Henry's death and the end of the civil war in France, which left most of them in desperate straits with no alternative but to turn to indiscriminate pillage and rapine in order to keep themselves alive. They spread such terror throughout the country that bands of self-styled 'peacemakers' sprang up all over France, dedicated brotherhoods of ordinary citizens sworn to resist and destroy these marauding gangs of murderers. One such mercenary gang under the command of a man named Curburan was almost wiped out by a band of peacemakers at Châteaudun in the Loire valley, most being killed in battle, while those who were captured were promptly hanged. These mercenaries were responsible for such appalling crimes that it is difficult to waste much sympathy on them, but it is only fair to remember that, if such men as the barons of Aquitaine had not employed them in their favourite pursuit of making private war on their neighbours, they would not have come into existence in the first place, the law of supply and demand being as applicable to them as to anything else. Once freed from the exigencies of the precarious and barbarous daily life of a mercenary soldier, many of them would probably have been no better and no worse than most other men, as Mercadier was to prove by his loyal and courageous life of devoted service from this time until Richard's death at Châlus sixteen years later.

Meanwhile, in Normandy Henry was having trouble with Philip Augustus of France, who was worried about his two sisters, Margaret and Alice. Margaret, the older of the two, had been married to young King Henry in infancy, and now that he had died without having produced an heir, Philip wanted her back again together with the dowry which she had brought to the marriage, namely a bit of land known as the Norman Vexin which formed a kind of buffer zone between Henry's own domain and that of the king of France; but in the end Philip agreed that old King Henry should keep it, as long as he paid Margaret a large annual pension. The problem posed by Alice was not so easily resolved; she had been reserved as Richard's future wife for fourteen years, and since it was customary at the time for children to be married for dynastic reasons while still absurdly young, Philip could not understand why their marriage had been postponed for so long. That he should have been puzzled is not surprising, and historians are almost as puzzled today as he was then; for while it was clear that Richard did not want to marry her – he made no bones of his aversion to the idea – no one knows for sure what caused that aversion. It has been suggested that he was homosexually inclined, and more must be said on that subject as the story of his life proceeds; but even if that were the case, and he had the same sexual tastes as his great-great-uncle, William Rufus, sexual desire and falling in love had so little to do with marriage in twelfth-century baronial society that Richard would hardly have been deterred from dutifully accompanying Alice to the altar simply because she did not arouse him erotically. Marriages were not about sexual satisfaction; they were about politics and power and international relations. Another possible, if somewhat unsavoury, explanation of Richard's reluctance to marry the French princess is that Henry, abusing his position of trust as her future father-in-law, had seduced her, making Alice his mistress, and that Richard did not care for the idea of marrying his father's 'whore', as he is said to have called her on one occasion. In view of Henry's lack of enthusiasm for setting a date for Richard's long-planned marriage to Alice, in marked contrast to the almost indecent haste with which he had arranged the marriage of his eldest son at the age of five to little princess Margaret of France before she was out of the cradle, this second solution is marginally more likely to be true than the first, especially since, like his grandfather Henry I, Henry II was known to be randy by nature. It may be, however, that Henry's procrastination after young Henry's death was because he had not decided whether Richard or John should become his principal heir, and was reserving Alice to be John's wife instead of Richard's. He doted on John to such an extent that he may have been thinking along such lines; he certainly gave Philip Augustus the impression that this was a distinct possibility, and Philip accepted this explanation.

Having thus temporarily satisfied the French king, Henry renewed his efforts to persuade Richard to give up the duchy of Aquitaine to John, but as the winter of 1183 dragged on, and the new year dawned without any sign of Richard's changing his mind, the old man began to lose patience, and in a moment of angry frustration he seems to have said something which John took to be permission to invade his brother's domain and take it by force. That John had been trying to provoke his father into something of the sort for some time seems likely, but he was still only sixteen years old, and it seems even more likely that he was being egged on by his brother Geoffrey, acting as *agent provocateur* in the background; for Geoffrey was a born mischief maker. Of all Henry's sons, he was by far the most undesirable; young King Henry might have been ineffectual, petty minded and dishonest from time to time but at least he had some compensating virtues including great charm, if charm may be counted as a virtue, while John, though not as bad as he has sometimes been painted, had some nasty characteristics, and Richard, the best of the bunch, was far from faultless; but it is difficult to find any redeeming feature in Geoffrey. One of his contemporaries described him as 'that son of perdition', while Gerald of Wales, also his contemporary, depicted him as 'overflowing with words, as smooth as oil, possessed by his syrupy eloquence of the power of dissolving the apparently indissoluble, able to corrupt two kingdoms with his tongue, of tireless endeavour and a hypocrite in everything'. He spent his life making trouble, and now that he and John had been granted permission – or what they took to be their father's permission – to attack Richard, they waited only long enough for the old man to return to England before launching a large force of Brabançons against Aquitaine in the early summer of 1184. Richard retaliated immediately by raiding Geoffrey's lands farther north, and once again much of France was subjected to suffering as war engulfed many of its little towns and villages. But even in the twelfth century, there were limits to what was regarded as tolerable, and when Henry heard of the fighting he was furious; he summoned his three sons to England with peremptory orders to stop fighting and, somewhat surprisingly, they all obeyed him. By this time, however, it was already autumn, and it was not until December that Richard, on the one hand, and Geoffrey and young John, on the other, were publicly reconciled at Westminster in the presence of Eleanor their mother, who had been released from prison by Henry specifically in order to help pacify her sons.

During the next few years, much the same pattern of family quarrels interspersed with intervals of peace repeated itself, but in August 1186 yet another entirely unexpected event changed the whole political scene. King Henry had at last told Philip Augustus that he would arrange for Richard to marry Alice in the near future; he could not do so immediately, for Richard was at war with Raymond of Toulouse: a fact well known to Philip already, for Raymond had begged him to come to his assistance against Richard, who was devastating his lands and even beginning to threaten his capital city, Toulouse itself. Such wars between the dukes of Aquitaine and the counts of Toulouse had become almost a matter of tradition, and the kings of France had often been called in to keep the balance between the conflicting parties, but on this occasion Philip had not responded to Raymond's plea for help, for he did not want to fall out with Henry at this particular juncture, since he and Geoffrey were quietly making other plans. Like everything else undertaken by Geoffrey, these plans were secret, devious and treacherous; unable to get his own way with his father, he had deserted his court and sought refuge with the French king, who had welcomed him with delight at the prospect provided by his arrival of sowing even greater dissension in the ranks of the Angevin family than was already at work there. As the weeks and the months had gone by, the two men had become inseparable, apparently becoming the closest of friends; Philip even made Geoffrey seneschal of France, a title traditionally associated with the lords of Anjou, and thus possibly a clue to the nature of his intrigues with the French king that he should take Richard's place as his father's heir. Fate, however, had other plans for him. In early August he took part in a tournament at Paris, was thrown from his horse, and before anyone could come to his assistance, he was trampled to death. He was buried with royal honours in Notre Dame, and Philip was so distressed by the loss of his friend that he had to be restrained from throwing himself alive into the vault with him.

Geoffrey's death transfigured the face of politics in France. He had had two children by his wife, Constance, and when Philip had recovered sufficiently to take political stock of the new situation created by his death, as feudal overlord of Brittany he immediately laid claim to the custody of Constance and her children. If Henry had agreed to this, Brittany would have been lost to him, and Philip would have won a considerable victory in his attempt to break up the Angevin empire. Needless to say, however, Henry did not agree, and since he had also failed to fix a date for Alice's wedding in spite of frequent promises that he would do so, Philip's patience at last ran out. Early in 1187, he began to mobilize his army at Bourges, and in early summer he marched into Berry, where he was stopped only by Richard's presence with a large force in the ancient fortified city of Châteauroux on the banks of the river Indre. Henry, who had waited until he knew where the French king would strike, marched to Richard's assistance with his main army of feudal levies and hired *routiers*, and on 23 June he and Richard drew up their combined forces in battle array just outside Châteauroux in full view of the French army. A pitched battle now seemed inevitable.

In our own day, battles between contending armies have become more and more impersonal and waged at longer and longer range: the range of a musket, a rifle, a machine-gun, a piece of heavy artillery, or a ballistic missile; as a result, a modern soldier seldom sees the people he kills, or those who are striving to kill him. In the twelfth century, a pitched battle might begin while the armies were separated by the length of a bowshot, but it was never long before the combatants were fighting eyeball to eyeball at arm's length in a huge, savage and largely uncontrollable *mêlée*, the outcome of which was largely unpredictable. As a result, the gamble of a pitched battle was highly unpopular and avoided whenever possible; warfare was waged by laying siege to your enemy's castles, by destroying his wealth-producing towns, villages and estates, and by chasing small forces with larger ones, during which some people were killed and others captured and held to profitable ransom. Very occasionally, however, opposing armies found themselves confronting each other, and when neither side was prepared to back down, a pitched battle followed with all its concomitant horror of suffering and violent death.

Such encounters have been glamorized by poets and historians alike, but in the bloody event they were never in the least glamorous, and the men drawn up in the fields outside Châteauroux on that June morning in 1187, facing each other on the eve of St John the Baptist's day, knew it very well. They did not in the least want to slaughter one another. As the two sides waited, uncertain as to whether there was to be a battle or not, the tension must have grown until everyone's nerves were as tight as the strings on their archer's bows. There were Frenchmen from Normandy, Anjou and Aquitaine fighting for Henry who knew that on the other side under Philip's banner were friends from Burgundy and Champagne whom they had known all their lives, and with whom they had often gone hunting, feasted or got gloriously drunk; the last thing they wanted was to kill them. The same was true of many men on the French side, who had brothers-in-law or jousting companions over there in the English ranks, where they could see steel helmets glinting in the sun and pennons fluttering in the breeze, as the sound of horses neighing drifted across on the warm, scented summer air. On both sides, men made their confessions, clustered round to hear the priests say Mass as the early morning sun rose above the horizon, ate the food provided at the camp kitchens, attended to the calls of nature, and did what they could to kill time, while they wondered who would be alive next morning and who dead. It was not an enjoyable time.

They might have been a little happier had they known that moves were afoot to avoid the final disaster of a battle. A legate had arrived from Pope Urban, charged with the task of making peace between the warring sides, and chiding them for fighting each other while their fellow Christians in the Holy Land were in desperate need of their help; instead of making war amongst themselves, they should all take the Cross and fight against the enemies of Christ in a new Crusade. It was an opportune message, and a number of high-ranking men on both sides, including Richard on the English side and the count of Flanders on that of the French king, met secretly and began to explore the possibility of making peace. Whether Henry was privy to these clandestine plans is not certain, for there are conflicting accounts by Gervase of Canterbury and Gerald of Wales; but what certainly happened is that Richard was led through the French lines by the count of Flanders, and had a long discussion with the French king on the prospects of peace, during which Philip made it clear that while he was not prepared to purchase peace at the cost of meekly submitting to Henry, he might agree to a truce. Henry may have known of this meeting or he may not; it is possible that he heard of it only after the event; but however it may have been, he became deeply suspicious of what had passed between his son and the French king. Instead of talking peace, had they been secretly talking about the succession after his own death? Plainly, it was in Richard's interest to be on as good terms as possible with Philip Augustus, and he might have seen a golden opportunity of cementing their relationship by making peace with him at his father's expense. Such thoughts may well have plagued Henry, as he waited, tense and anxious, on the eve of a pitched battle; but whether they did so or not, when Richard told him that Philip would agree to a truce if he would do likewise, Henry peremptorily refused. On hearing this, Philip ordered an attack at daybreak the next morning and, short of a miracle, war now seemed inevitable.

It was not a miracle, however, which saved the two armies from a senseless and savage blood-bath but a last-minute change of mind on Henry's part. He was not informed of the French preparations for an attack until the early hours of the morning, whereupon he became alarmed, sent for Richard, and asked him to make one last effort to stave off disaster by going to the French king and agreeing to a truce after all. Understandably, Richard did not like the idea; it would be humiliating to go to Philip at the very last minute, asking for his favour, but in the end he agreed to do so. He found the French king already armed for battle and, kneeling before him bare-headed, he offered him his sword, and begged him for a truce, promising that if Henry should break it, he would personally surrender to Philip's judgement in Paris. It was probably one of the bravest things Richard ever did, though he is unlikely to have seen it that way at the time; it must certainly have been one of the hardest for him to stomach, and it does not seem to have increased his affection for his father. For when Philip reluctantly agreed to a truce, which was to last for two years, and made ready to return to Paris with his army, Richard went with him.

In some ways it was an extraordinary thing to do. Why should Richard have stood shoulder to shoulder with his father outside the walls of Châteauroux if he intended to ride off to Paris a few days later with their common enemy? It has been suggested that the count of Flanders may have played some part in persuading Richard to such a course, perhaps speaking on behalf of the French king who had everything to gain by making trouble between him and his father; but it seems even more probable that both Richard and Henry had found the last few days together both tense and difficult. Ever since young Henry's death their relationship had become increasingly strained as King Henry stubbornly refused to confirm or deny that Richard was now his heir, and during his recent negotiations with Philip Augustus Richard could hardly have failed to notice that his father was becoming more and more suspicious of him. As he went back and forth to the French camp, the atmosphere between them would almost certainly have become thick with mutual distrust and exasperation, the air more and more loaded with angry unsaid words and stifled accusations, as overstretched nerves came near to breaking poiont; and then suddenly it all ended in anticlimax: a truce and no battle. The human reaction to such moments of explosive release from tension is often mixed: huge relief followed by a sense of flatness, exhaustion, and a longing to get drunk and sleep for a week. It would not be surprising if part of Richard's reaction to the events of the past few days was one of angry resentment against his father and a determination to have no more truck with him and his suspicions.

When Henry heard that Richard had gone to Paris with the French king he was worried and upset. He became more and more disturbed as the weeks went by and news of Richard's growing friendship with Philip reached him; it was even said that he was on such close terms with him that they shared the same bed and not surprisingly this has been seized on by some people as virtually conclusive evidence of Richard's homosexuality. This whole topic is discussed further in Chapter VIII, but in passing it must be said that the mere fact that he shared a bed with Philip is not in itself evidence of homosexuality; to imagine otherwise is to look back at the twelfth century through spectacles manufactured and tinted in the twentieth. It was not uncommon in the

Middle Ages for many people to share a bed; whole families often did so, and so did friends of the same sex. For instance, Henry II shared his bed with his adviser and his son Henry's tutor William Marshal from time to time, and anyone less homosexually inclined than Henry – or indeed, than William Marshal – it is difficult to imagine. But perhaps the most conclusive evidence that for men to share the same bed was not considered indicative of their sexual desire for one another is to be found, rather improbably, in Canterbury cathedral; there, in a window dating from the first quarter of the thirteenth century, just after Richard's time, the three wise men of St Matthew's Gospel – the Magi – are portrayed in bed together as an angel warns them to avoid Herod on their way home, and it is inconceivable that they should have been depicted in such a situation if it could have been regarded as even remotely compromising. At the time, as we might offer a friend a bed for the night, so the men of the twelfth century might offer to share their bed for the night with a friend without having the smallest sexual designs upon his person or his virtue. But it was precisely Richard's and Philip's friendship and its political implications which worried Henry, who 'marvelled what this might be . . . till he should know the outcome of this sudden friendship.' In fact, he need not have worried too much, for although Richard might become exasperated every now and again by his father, especially as Henry became more and more obstinate, touchy and difficult in his old age, at heart he was loyal to him, and after a time with Philip in Paris he simmered down enough to respond to Henry's repeated pleas to him to return to the fold. In the words of Gerald of Wales, 'he came and submitted to his father in all things, and was penitent for having consented to the evil counsels of those who strove to sow discord among them. So they came together to Angers, and there the son became his father's obedient man.'

Early in November, Richard was at Tours, when news of an event which had occurred two thousand miles away and four months previously changed the whole course of his life with its hopes and aspirations. Not long after Henry and the French king had signed the truce at Châteauroux, almost the entire Christian army in the Holy Land of Outremer had been wiped out by their Moslem enemies in a battle on a rocky hill known as the Horns of

Hattin in the desert country overlooking the Sea of Galilee. It was a shattering disaster. The King of Jerusalem, the irresolute Guy of Lusignan, had been captured, as had many other Christian knights and soldiers; hundreds of others had been killed, and the victors had gone on to take most of the great cities of the land including Jerusalem itself. Worst of all was the loss of the most sacred relic in all Christendom, a part of the true Cross, which had fallen into the hands of the unbelievers. The Moslem host had been commanded by a man named Salah ed-Din Yusuf, whom Richard was destined to get to know as Saladin, and of whom he may have heard for the first time as news of the disaster reached him. His reaction was swift and typical; early the next morning he met the archbishop of Tours in the cathedral there, and took the Cross.

Like Richard, the people of Europe were shocked by the news from Outremer. As itinerant preachers travelled round the country, people were swept along on an emotional tide of hatred for the Moslem desecrators of the holy places of the Christian faith as they listened to stories of Moslem atrocities. Some of these were even accompanied by visual aids; one of Saladin's knights was portrayed sitting on his horse, laughing with delight as it urinated on Christ's tomb, while another was depicted striking Christ in the face. It was heady stuff, and as crowds of credulous folk listened to such stories, they were horrified; calls from the pope and other senior clergy to avenge these insults to God and his church found a ready response. Rather as pacifists in 1914 were contemptuously handed white feathers as signs of cowardice, so those who did not volunteer to give up everything and go on a new Crusade were given little bits of wool, signs that they were no better than cowardly women at work on their distaffs, in contrast to the crosses of red cloth given to the Crusaders to be worn on their surcoats, from which the ceremony of 'taking the Cross' got its name. Those who did not volunteer were not only cowards, they were fools; for by failing to take the Cross, they were failing to take up the marvellous offer of a plenary indulgence for all their sins, and thus an assured place in heaven after death.

But if either Richard or the crowds who took the Cross imagined that they would be leaving for the Holy Land as soon as shipping could be found for them, they were soon to be disillusioned. They might be eager to be about God's business, but their feudal lords were not. When Henry heard the news of Richard's action, he was furious. Richard had neither consulted nor informed him of his intention, but now that he had actually taken the Cross, it was going to be extremely difficult for Henry himself not to follow suit; he had been promising for years that he would do so 'one day', and yet the last thing he wanted to do at this particular moment was to commit himself to an uncertain adventure two thousand miles away. Philip Augustus, too, was far from pleased by Richard's precipitate action; he had no intention of allowing him to leave France without first making a firm commitment to marry Alice, so once again he began to mobilize his army. Alarmed by the French king's belligerence, Henry met him near Gisors early in the new year of 1188 in order to talk things over, but instead of discussing Richard's marriage the two kings found themselves subjected to a rousing and persuasive sermon by Archbishop Josias of Tyre, which left them little option but to follow Richard's example and take the Cross with as good a grace as they could muster. Disguising their reluctance, they duly pledged themselves to go to the assistance of their fellow Christians in the Holy Land as soon as possible, while making mental reservations as to precisely when that might be; 'as soon as possible' was a useful phrase potentially covering a multitude of hesitations and reasons for delay. Henry was also determined to delay Richard's departure as well as his own, and set about thinking of ways of doing so.

As it happened, this did not prove to be difficult, for at the beginning of February another revolt had broken out in Poitou, and Richard found himself too fully occupied coping with the barons of Aquitaine to make any preparations to leave France. This new insurrection came at such a convenient time from Henry's point of view that he may have had a hand in encouraging or even instigating it, but there is no evidence of this; true or false, however, the uprising suited Henry perfectly, and it was several months before Richard once again succeeded in forcing his rebellious liegemen to sue for peace, granting their request only on condition that they all took the Cross: a sensible precaution which meant that, when Richard eventually left for the Holy Land, the most troublesome barons of Aquitaine would have to accompany him instead of staying at home and making mischief in his absence. It also increased the number of men pledged to sail east when the time came, but it brought that time no nearer; for the revolt in Aquitaine had scarcely been settled when war broke out again between Richard and the count of Toulouse over the arrest of some Aquitainian merchants and the detention of some knights returning from a pilgrimage to Compostella through the count's land. Some of the merchants had been blinded, some castrated, others killed, and although the knights had merely been imprisoned, their incarceration was entirely illegal, since the immunity of pilgrims from molestation of any sort was universally acknowledged to be absolute and inviolable. With his usual combination of military skill and well-timed ferocity, Richard invaded the count's land, sweeping all before him, capturing castle after castle, and eventually washing up against the walls of Toulouse itself. Deeply alarmed, Raymond of Toulouse appealed to the king of France for help, and Philip invaded Aquitaine from the north.

At first Henry made no attempt to come to his son's assistance as Richard hurried north to meet Philip's invasion of Berry, but as the French king went from strength to strength, Henry raised a large army in England and hastily crossed the Channel in an appalling storm, landing in Normandy in early July. This threat from Henry forced Philip to withdraw in order to defend his frontier with Normandy, by which time Richard had arrived, and the war dragged drearily on until the late autumn without much prospect of either side winning. As Runciman remarked in his *History of the Crusades*, 'This endless fighting horrified most good Christians,' and he might have added that even those who normally enjoyed nothing more than a little pleasurable anarchy from time to time were getting tired of it. As a result, in early October Philip and Henry accompanied by Richard met at Châtillon on the border between Berry and Touraine in an attempt to make peace; but little came of their efforts, which were hag-ridden by mutual distrust, and they broke up with nothing achieved.

With peace as far away as ever, the prospect of launching the Crusade receded once again into the dim and misty future, and this distressed Richard. The failure to reach any kind of agreement at Châtillon was a disaster, and he decided to approach the king of France directly in an attempt to break the deadlock; to go on fighting amongst themselves when they were so desperately needed by their fellow Christians in the Holy Land was not only utterly wrong but openly condemned by most of their subjects, and there is no reason to doubt that his motive in approaching Philip Augustus was to bring this to an end, as he later claimed; but there is equally little reason to doubt that it was not his only motive. By this time, he did not trust his father at all, and he may well have calculated that both his own personal interests and the interests of the beleaguered Christians in Outremer would be better served if he and the king of France came to terms with each other rather than if all three continued to fight. He may even have decided that should such an approach lay him open to a charge of abandoning his filial duty, so be it. Henry's behaviour as a father had not been beyond reproach in recent months, and the deadlock had to be broken somehow. So Richard met Philip Augustus, and offered to submit his quarrel with Raymond of Toulouse to the judgement of the French court in Paris; if the court decided that he should return his conquests to Raymond, he would abide by their decision as long as it ensured peace. Of course, Philip was delighted. By coming to him and offering to submit the outcome of the war with Raymond of Toulouse to his arbitration, Richard was not only openly acknowledging his authority as overlord of Toulouse and his own duchy of Aquitaine, but giving him a splendid opportunity of continuing to set him against his father.

It was an opportunity which he took with both hands at his next meeting with Henry. It took place at Bonmoulins on 18 November in an atmosphere of wary distrust. Philip and Richard arrived together to Henry's obvious discomfiture, and for three days they talked without getting very far. They spoke of an exchange of conquests, but could not agree on the details; and then on the third day, when tempers had become so frayed that once or twice the attendant knights had reached for their swords, Philip offered to return everything which he had conquered during the recent fighting on condition that Henry agreed to Alice and Richard's marriage, and made his barons, French and English alike, swear fealty to Richard as his heir. Henry complained that this was blackmail, and refused to act under pressure. Now it was Richard's turn, and he asked his father bluntly whether he would recognize him as his heir. Henry remained stonily silent. 'At last,' said Richard, 'I have no choice but to believe the impossible to be true,' and ungirding his sword, he turned and, kneeling before the French king, he did homage to him for the whole continental dominions of the Angevin house – Normandy, Aquitaine, Anjou, Maine, and Berry – swearing allegiance to him save only for the fealty he owed his father. Henry was too stunned to speak, let alone to comment, and after signing a truce which was to last until January, the conference broke up, no doubt in stilted and embarrassed silence.

Worn out by a life of unremitting activity which he had lived to the full with magnificent prodigality and twelfth-century zest, Henry was now old beyond his fifty-six years: old, tired, and sad. He spent a lonely and embittered Christmas at Saumur with a mere handful of his retainers, and there he fell ill. The truce with the king of France was due to expire half way through January, but when the time came to meet again and renew it, Henry was too ill to travel. He sent a messenger to beg the French king and Richard to extend the truce until he should have recovered sufficiently to meet them, but neither of them believed that he was sick; on the contrary, they were convinced that he was procrastinating as usual, and that his illness was a sham. So the war began again, and although Henry sent messenger after messenger to Richard begging him to come back, Richard did not even answer. He no longer trusted his father, or believed a word he said. By Easter, Henry was a little better, but it was not until Whitsun that he was well enough to meet Richard and the French king at La Ferté-Bernard on the road from Le Mans to Chartres. A papal legate, John of Anagni, together with the archbishops of Rheims, Rouen, Bourges and Canterbury, had arranged the meeting, but in spite of the pacific presence of these men of God, both sides came fully armed. Philip took the initiative, laying down three conditions for peace: Alice should marry Richard, Henry should publicly acknowledge Richard as his heir, and John should take the Cross. Before Henry could reply, Richard told him that he would 'in no wise go to Jerusalem, unless John went with him'. But Henry refused to accept these terms, suggesting instead that Alice should marry John, thus confirming with his own lips Richard's worst suspicions. At this point, John of Anagni threatened to lay the whole of France under an interdict if Philip did not come to terms with Henry; but Philip was unimpressed by this papal thunder, merely remarking that no doubt the legate's coffers were full of English gold, and the meeting broke up in hopeless discord.

In her biography of Richard written in the early years of this century, Kate Norgate remarked that 'if ever a father set at nought the precept, "Provoke not your children to wrath," Henry had done so by his conduct towards Richard, not merely on one or two occasions, but persistently through a course of years.' It is important to remember this, for Henry was such a splendid human being, larger than life, generous to a fault, and appealing even at his passionate worst, that his plight during the last few months of his life makes it impossible not to feel sorry for him, while at the same time blaming Richard for the miseries which beset him in his old age; but Richard was not to blame for them; Henry had brought them on himself by his obsessional infatuation with his youngest son, John: a fact which he was to recognize before he died, but too late to repair the damage it had done over the years. In the face of repeated provocation, Richard had been remarkably loyal, even if he had lost his temper from time to time, invariably coming back to his father's side and apologizing for his momentary lapse from filial duty. He would have had to be superhuman after what had passed at La Ferté-Bernard not at last to give up hope of a reconciliation with Henry, and to turn instead to looking after his own interests; and this is what he did.

While Henry rode back to Le Mans, where the bulk of his forces were gathered, Richard and Philip attacked the castle at La Ferté itself, captured it, and went on to attack four or five more castles in the area, all of which fell to them with little or no opposition. On 11 June, a thick fog reduced visibility in the valley of the Sarthe to a few yards, and under its cover Richard and the French moved quietly up to the walls of Le Mans without being heard or seen; as the sun came up the next day and the fog lifted, Henry suddenly saw the French tents pitched along the edge of the wood a few yards away on the other side of the river. He was so shocked that William Marshal had to lead him back into the town, dazed and shaky, while the alarm was sounded, and the garrison scrambled to man the walls of the city. Richard, of course, knew the place well, where the river could be forded, and where the walls were at their most vulnerable; but although Henry expected an attack at any moment, a day and a night passed without a sign of movement in the French camp, and he began to believe that Richard and Philip would never attack him in person. With his confidence restored, early the next morning he went to Mass, and then strolled out unarmed on to the city walls, as though he had nothing in the world to fear; but already Richard's men could be seen sounding the river with their lances, and there was fighting on the one and only bridge across the river. Moments later, flames could be seen rising from burning houses as the French fired the suburbs to the east, and as the fire spread, the wind blew the flames over the walls into the city itself, which was soon ablaze. Henry's knights on the bridge were greatly outnumbered by their attackers, and it was obvious that they would not be able to hold out against them for long; but just when things looked so black that it even seemed doubtful whether Henry would have time to escape from the city before it fell, the bridge over the river partly collapsed under the weight of the men fighting on it, and the attackers were momentarily delayed. Urged by William Marshal not to waste a moment, Henry fled by the north gate with a handful of friends and retainers.

But Richard had seen him go. So far he had taken no part in the assault, but now, even though he was totally unarmed, clad only in a doublet and not even carrying a lance, he gave immediate chase. Since no one in his senses, let alone anyone as experienced as Richard, would have dreamt of riding off thus attired if he was expecting to fight anyone, Richard's motive must have been to capture his father before anyone could do him any harm, and he very nearly succeeded in doing so; but when he had almost caught up with the old king, some of his men outstripped him, and he shouted to them to come back. William Marshal, recognizing his voice, wheeled his horse, and galloped straight for him with his lance levelled for the attack. Suddenly seeing the danger he was in, Richard shouted at the top of his voice, 'God's feet, man, kill me not! I am unarmed.' 'Let the devil kill you,' cried Marshal, 'for I will not;' and he plunged his lance into Richard's horse, which fell dead, throwing its rider to the ground. When a number of knights and men-at-arms crowded anxiously round him, Richard struggled to his feet almost in tears with frustration, and told them to stop the chase.

Henry's main strength was in Normandy, and there was nothing to stop him riding there, but he was tired, old and ill. With no more than a small personal escort, he rode to Chinon, and took to his bed, while Richard and Philip overran the surrounding country virtually unopposed. On 3 July, after a siege lasting only two days, the city of Tours at the very heart of the Angevin empire fell, and the French king summoned Henry to Colombières. The old king was in such pain from an ulcer that he could hardly sit on his horse, and he had a high fever. When Philip saw him, ashen faced and obviously in great pain, he offered to spread a cloak on the ground for him, but Henry refused. The terms of surrender were then read to him: first, he was to do homage to Philip for all his French lands, whereupon they would be granted back to him; Alice was to be surrendered to a guardian nominated by Richard, who would marry her on return from the Holy Land; Henry's subjects both in England and in France were to swear fealty to Richard as his father's heir; and Henry would pay Philip a fine of twenty thousand marks. Henry had no option but to agree, and he did so, stiff lipped and with a face like death. The meeting then ended with Richard receiving a formal kiss of peace; but as his father leant close to kiss him, it is said that he muttered in his son's ear, 'God grant that I may not die, until I have had my revenge on you.'

God did not grant his wish. As the conference broke up, he was too weak and ill to remount his horse, and he was carried back to Chinon on a litter, where once again he took to his bed. There, fate had reserved for him the cruellest blow of all; for when he asked to see a list of the names of those who had deserted him and joined his enemies, he was told gently that it included the name of his son John. After that, nothing much mattered, and three days later he died. William Marshal and a few knights who had remained faithful to him carried his body on their shoulders to the abbey at Fontevraud, where he lay in state before the high altar, while a few old nuns said psalms and mumbled prayers for his soul. When Richard came to pay his last respects to his father, except for a momentary shudder as he looked down at the dead face, he showed no sign of emotion; for a long time he stood in silence without moving. Then he knelt for a moment in prayer, rose to his feet, turned, and left the church.

PART 3

King and Crusader

VI

*For there shall be a day, that the watchmen upon the hills of Zion shall cry,
Arise ye, and let us go up to Zion. . . Behold, I will bring them from the
north country, and gather them from the uttermost parts of the earth.*

Jeremiah 31:6,8

Richard had barely left the abbey church in which his father's
body was lying, when he called William Marshal to him. They had
not met since their recent encounter near Le Mans and the killing
of Richard's horse, and Marshal's friends were understandably
nervous about Richard's intention towards him. They need not
have worried. 'So, Marshal,' Richard greeted him, 'you would
have killed me the other day, if I had not turned your lance aside.'
But Marshal was not to be intimidated. 'Sir,' he replied, 'if I had
meant to kill you, I could have done so; I killed your horse.' 'You
are forgiven,' said Richard smiling at him. 'I bear you no malice;'
and he was as good as his word. When Marshal told him that
Henry had promised him the hand of Isobel de Clare in marriage,
Richard immediately agreed that Marshal should marry her, and
since the lady was not only heiress to the county of Striguil in the
Welsh marches and to the Welsh county of Pembroke, but also to
the lordship of Leinster in Ireland, this was tantamount to making
him a very rich man. In the event, William was so eager not to
miss this opportunity that, in his haste to get back to England and
marry the lady, he fell off the gangplank into the sea in Dieppe, an
accident which soaked him physically but failed to dampen his
ardour for the countess.

In itself, Richard's treatment of William Marshal was a minor matter, but since it was symptomatic of his whole attitude to those who had been loyal to his father and hostile to his own cause at the time, it has its importance; far from resenting their opposition, he admired and rewarded their fidelity to old Henry, and thus won their allegiance to himself in a way which less generous treatment would never have done. He displayed the same attitude to Baldwin of Béthune, another of the dead king's most faithful supporters, who has not figured in the story so far, but who will play an important part in it at a later stage. Henry had promised Baldwin a large estate in France as a reward for his loyal service over the years, and although Richard could not grant him the exact estate promised by his father, for it had already been given to someone else, he arranged a marriage between Baldwin and a wealthy widow through whom he became the count of Aumâle in Normandy and a rich man. Once again, it was a comparatively small thing, but it was also a timely gesture which was destined to have considerable consequences. Only one man who had held high office under Henry incurred Richard's wrath: Stephen, the seneschal of Anjou and treasurer to the late king, was chained hand and foot and thrown into prison, though no one seems to know the exact cause of his offence. Whatever he may have done, Richard soon forgave him, releasing him after a month or two and restoring him to favour. But when it came to those who had deserted Henry to support him against his father, Richard told them firmly that he did not approve of treachery under any circumstances, and that by rights they should be treated as traitors; his words were harsher than his deeds, however, and none of them received anything worse than a verbal reminder of the paramount importance of loyalty.

He made an exception for one man only, his brother John, who had flagrantly deserted his doting father and had brought the old man's head down to the grave in misery and despair: yet unlike the other recreants from Henry's cause, he was 'received with honour and kindly comforted' by Richard. Indeed, he was singled out for very special treatment; the counties of Cornwall, Devon, Dorset and Somerset in the south-west with Nottingham and Derby in the Midlands were settled on John in order to produce an income of some four thousand pounds a year for him, and also to remove the stigma implicit in the name Lackland from him once and for all. But although this generosity on Richard's part would have met with his father's warm approval, he has been criticized for treating John in this way. It was a most dangerous act, rash, foolish and asking for trouble to give any subject such power: or so Richard's critics have said. More recently, however, at least one historian, John Gillingham, has defended Richard in his admirable biography of him, pointing out that John was not just another subject, but his brother and a prince of the blood royal, who had every right by the standards of the day to some such recognition as he now received at long last. After all, Henry's eldest son had been crowned co-king with his father at an early age, Richard had become duke of Aquitaine while still in his teens, and the odious Geoffrey had married the heiress of Brittany while equally juvenile; so why should John expect less? Moreover, at this particular juncture, John must have posed a specially difficult problem for Richard, as he prepared to go on Crusade. If he had insisted on John's coming with him in order to keep him out of mischief while he himself was out of the country, there would have been no adult male member of the Angevin family left in Europe to defend its interests in the event of a revolt, while if he had left him behind without first treating him generously and settling lands upon him, his own absence in the Holy Land would have given John the best possible opportunity to vent his spleen by seizing what he could while the going was good, and even perhaps organizing a full-scale rebellion against the absent king. Some such thoughts must surely have passed through Richard's mind at this time, when wondering what to do about John, and it seems highly probable that Richard, who both adored and respected his mother, would also have consulted her about the whole matter, and that she would have reminded him that, although he was going away on Crusade, she was not; let him settle enough land and money on John to keep him quiet, and she would make sure that he remained so. Thus, far from being a rash and foolish act on Richard's part, his treatment of John was probably quite sensible under the circumstances. That it did not have the desired effect is another matter.

A few days later, Richard moved to Normandy, where he was greeted by the archbishops of Rouen and Canterbury who absolved him from the sentence of excommunication imposed on him by the irate papal legate at La Ferté-Bernard when he and the French king had failed to make peace with Henry. On 20 July, he was invested with the ducal sword and banner of Normandy before the high altar in Rouen Cathedral, and received the fealty of the Norman clergy and people. From Rouen he went to the border town of Gisors with its great castle for a meeting with Philip Augustus to settle various points at issue between them. Once again, the French king claimed both Gisors itself and that part of Normandy known as the Norman Vexin in which it stood, but dropped his claim in return for Richard's promise at last to marry his sister Alice. Of course, no one thought for a moment of consulting the lady herself, and we shall never know what she thought about the whole thing. She had been engaged to Richard since her earliest infancy, and she was now over twenty, and yet she was still being treated like a piece of land or an heirloom to be haggled over and eventually handed to the highest bidder, despite the fact that her potential value in the marriage market had been somewhat reduced by rumours that Henry had made her his mistress while she was in his care. But a flurry of righteous twentieth-century indignation over the customs of the twelfth would no doubt have been as unintelligible to Alice herself as her acceptance of her role in the social climate of her own class and time is incomprehensible to us; and yet she probably did accept it more or less happily, for she had no alternative but to do so.

Before parting, Richard and the French king settled a number of other issues which divided them; Richard renewed his homage to Philip Augustus as his feudal overlord, and they also agreed to set out on Crusade together in Lent of the next year. For another three weeks, Richard stayed in Normandy, winning all hearts according to Gervase of Canterbury by 'his gracious and affable demeanour', and it was not until 12 August that he eventually sailed for England from Barfleur. He landed at Southampton, and moved on to Winchester, where he took possession of the royal treasure, and there he was welcomed by his mother, Eleanor, and a concourse of assorted nobles and empurpled bishops. He was greeted enthusiastically by the common people of the place, who were delighted by his first actions as heir to the vacant throne; for one of these had been to pardon everyone under arrest or in prison for offences against the hated forest laws. At their worst, these ordained blinding or castration or both for commoners caught poaching in the royal forests and, at their most lenient, lengthy incarceration for the same offence; and the royal forests were enormously extensive. Even a hundred years after Richard's time, when they had shrunk a good deal, the whole of Essex lay under forest law, as did a broad band of land stretching from Stamford in Lincolnshire southward to the Thames at Oxford; even just north of the city of London, where Hackney and St Pancras now stand, there was 'a great forest with woodland pastures which are the lairs of wild animals: stags, fallow deer, wild boars and bulls,' according to William Fitz Stephen in his biography of Thomas Becket; and it is not surprising that people were tempted to indulge in a little poaching in such conveniently accessible woodlands, when hunger or poverty drove them to do so. Now, those who had fallen for such temptation found themselves suddenly freed, as did others imprisoned 'by the will of the king or his justiciar', or detained on appeal for various other offences. But although this made Richard highly popular with the majority of the people, there were those who were less enthusiastic; William of Newburgh complained that 'at that time, the gaols were crowded with criminals awaiting trial or punishment, but through Richard's clemency these pests came forth from prison, perhaps to become bolder thieves in the future.'

From Winchester Richard moved in easy stages to London, and although news of a Welsh raid reached him while he was on the way, on his mother's advice he ignored it, not wishing to become involved in war at this particular time. He entered London on 1 September from the Strand through Ludgate, and went in procession to St Paul's, while crowds of cheering people lined his route, waving and shouting as he passed. Two days later, he was crowned in Westminster Abbey, having first moved in an even more solemn and splendid procession from the palace of Westminster through even larger and more enthusiastic crowds. He was escorted by the archbishops of Canterbury, Rouen, Dublin, and Trèves and a large number of other bishops and clergy, and accompanied by the earls of Gloucester, Salisbury, Pembroke and Essex; on his right hand walked Hugh de Puiset, the bishop of Durham, and on his left, Reginald Fitz Jocelin, the bishop of Bath, while a silken canopy was held over his head on lances by four barons of the Cinque Ports, and the citizens of London roared themselves hoarse as he passed. Once inside the abbey, the pattern of the liturgy, which was destined to be followed at all subsequent coronations of the kings and queens of England down to our own time, was set. Richard took his seat on a chair at the centre of the crossing, and an antiphon was sung by the choir as he deposited an offering of a pound of gold on the altar; he knelt while the Litany was intoned, and stood to take the coronation oath, swearing on the Gospels to rule justly and in peace with the help of God. He was anointed with oil and balsam by the archbishop of Canterbury and invested with spurs, sword, stole and mantle by two earls before being conducted to the high altar to be crowned. The archbishop adjured him in the name of God not to assume the kingly office unless he was determined to keep his vow, and Richard answered that by the grace of God he would do so. Then he took the crown from the altar and handed it to the archbishop, who set it on his head, as the choir burst into singing the *Te Deum Laudamus* and the newly anointed king was led by the bishops and barons to his throne. Mass was then sung, and Richard made his communion with God before returning in solemn procession through cheering crowds to his rooms in Westminster palace, bearing the body and blood of Christ in himself and the weight of the kingdom on his shoulders.

The court festivities which followed the coronation lasted for three days, and were in marked contrast to the rough informality of the court in Henry's time. Richard sat at a high table with senior clergy of the land, while the nobility dined at other tables, and all were served with 'such an abundance of meats,' as one man remarked in near-lyrical enthusiasm, 'that none might keep account or tally of.' Unfortunately, the festivities were marred by a hideous outbreak of mob violence. In accordance with usual and long established custom, Richard had decreed that no woman and no Jew should be admitted to the palace during the feasting. The Jews as non-Christians would obviously have been out of place at a feast in celebration of a great Christian ceremony, but why women were barred is harder to understand; perhaps their exclusion had its roots in the traditional customs of a warrior society, evolved in the Dark Ages, when the only things worth celebrating had been bloody victories won by the men of the tribe. However the custom may have orginated, on this occasion protocol was ignored by some Jewish merchants, who presented themselves at the palace on the evening of the coronation with gifts for the king. As non-Christians and descendants of those who had killed Christ, the Jews had never been popular in England, but the hatred in which they were universally held in Richard's day was at least partly their own fault. After settling in a number of English cities at the time of the Norman Conquest, for nearly a century they had been tolerated and left to live peacefully enough in ghettos under the king's protection; but over the years they had become extremely rich, eventually owning a third of the movable wealth of the country, and they had never hesitated to flaunt their riches in the faces of their poorer Christian neighbours, many of whom were their debtors. Usurers are never popular, and dislike of the Jews grew steadily; but dislike turned to hatred as a result of their unconcealed contempt for the practices of Christianity. In the second half of the twelfth century matters were made worse by lurid stories of the ritual murder of Christian boys by Jews: stories which were widely believed despite their implausibility. One such told how a boy of twelve, William of Norwich, a tanner's apprentice, was enticed from his home by a Jew on Monday in Holy Week 1144; five days later, on Holy Saturday, his body was found with marks of violence in a neighbouring wood, and a monk of Norwich, Thomas of Monmouth, swore that he had evidence that the boy had been crucified by Jews during their celebration of the Passover. A converted Jew, Theobald by name, testified that according to Jewish religious practice a Christian child had to be sacrificed annually to obtain the deliverance of the Jewish people. The dead boy was canonized, and when his body was translated from the monastery in which he had originally been buried to Norwich Cathedral in 1151, it was said that many miracles took place at his tomb.

Hatred of the Jews as a result of such stories as this, reinforced by Crusaders returning from the Holy Land filled with distrust for all infidels, burst forth when the little bunch of Jews appeared at the palace gates. The crowds assembled there were incensed by the temerity of these alien usurers and hated sons of Belial attempting to gain entry where even decent Christians like themselves could not pass without a special invitation, and they were attacked, robbed, beaten up and driven away by the mob; some were mortally injured in the process, and some were killed on the spot, but by the time the tumult reached Richard's ears, things had already got so badly out of control that the justiciars arrived too late to restore order.

A great wave of anti-Jewish xenophobia and irrational hatred then swept through the city; before morning most Jewish houses had been sacked, some had been burnt with whole families of Jews inside them, while anyone who had tried to escape the flames had either been murdered on the spot or chased through the streets and lynched. As day broke, synagogues were desecrated, and Jewish shops looted and destroyed. The appalling ferocity of the anti-Jewish feeling, present at all times just below the surface and now openly discharged upon the unfortunate Jews of London, was demonstrated by a comment made by Richard of Devizes, an otherwise reasonable man, as the riots spread throughout the length and breadth of England. 'The other cities and towns of the kingdom emulated the faith of the Londoners,' he wrote, 'and with like devotion dispatched their bloodsuckers with blood to hell . . . Winchester alone spared the vermin.' The citizens of Lincoln, Norwich, Lynn, Stamford and many other cities may have 'emulated the faith of the Londoners' to the satisfaction of Richard of Devizes but only the citizens of York managed actually to exceed it; there, Jewish men, women, and children were hunted down and killed with as little compunction as might have been wasted on a plague of rats, and so fierce was the hunt that only about one hundred and fifty managed to escape and take refuge in the castle. The mob was not to be cheated of its prey, however, and urged on by a fanatical hermit, it besieged the place. When it became obvious to the Jews that they would not be able to hold out indefinitely, most of them committed suicide, having first killed their wives and children; a few, relying on promises that they would be spared if they allowed themselves to be baptised as Christians, surrendered, and were immediately slaughtered. It was the end of a shameful chapter in English history.

Richard was furious. He was a child of his own time and he held no special brief for the Jews, but he found them useful as a source of revenue and he disapproved of rioting and lawlessness against whomsoever it might be directed; but there was very little he could do about it. The strength of popular feeling was running so strongly against the Jews that any attempt to punish the rioters with a severity even remotely appropriate to their crimes would have been virtually impossible, and he was forced to content himself with punishing a few individuals who had robbed or killed Christians by mistake. Three of these were sent to the gallows, while for the rest, in the words of Roger of Howden, he had 'to condone what he could not avenge'. But he tried to prevent further anti-Jewish disturbances by sending letters into every shire commanding that the Jews be left in peace and that no one should molest them; and as long as he remained in the country, these orders were obeyed.

After his coronation, Richard set about the main task ahead of him: namely, preparing for the Crusade and for the continued government of the country in his absence. It was an enormous double task. Many of his latter-day critics, while admitting his brilliance as a soldier, have tended to dismiss him as no more than that: an efficient killing machine. But when one comes to think of what must have been involved in preparing a large expeditionary force for shipping to a theatre of war two and a half thousand miles away as the crow flies and farther than that by land and sea, equipping it properly before it embarked and set sail, maintaining it while it was abroad perhaps for years, and ensuring that it had the best possible medical and spiritual care that could be provided while it was overseas, the idea that the man at the head of it all was a mere military oaf and no administrator is absurd. It has been said that the secret of good administration is delegation, and Richard delegated as much as he could to others. He sent a number of officials touring round the coastal towns of England and France commandeering ships for the voyage on a massive scale; vessels were requisitioned in most of the ports and coastal towns of Normandy, Brittany and Aquitaine, but it was in England, a seafaring island, that the royal officials assembled the largest fleet. Over thirty ships were supplied by the Cinque Ports alone. As their name implies, originally there were five of them:

Hastings, New Romney, Hythe, Dover and Sandwich, though by
Richard's day Rye and Winchelsea had been added to their
number, while as time went by such places as Lydd, Deal,
Ramsgate, Reculver and others were loosely incorporated with
them. Because they were strategically important to the defence of
the realm against cross-Channel invasion before the existence of
a regular navy, certain tasks were required of them, and in return
they were granted certain privileges; up to the reign of Henry VII
they had to furnish the crown with most of the ships and men
needed by the state for its self-defence, and for many years after
that they were expected to give assistance to the permanent fleet.
However, in order to show that the crown was not ungrateful for
these services, the Cinque Ports were given certain profitable
exemptions and rights; they were exempt from tax and tallage,
the latter being a form of taxation abolished two hundred years
later in the fourteenth century; at the same time, they were
granted sac and soc, or the right to full legal cognizance of all
criminal and civil cases committed within their liberties; tol and
team, or the right to receive toll and the right to compel any
person in whose hands stolen property was found to name the
person from whom it was received; blodwit and fledwit, or the
right to punish shedders of blood and those seized in an attempt to
escape justice; mundbryce, or the right to break into another
man's *mund* or property in order to erect banks or dig dykes as a
defence against the sea; infangentheof and outfangentheof, or
the right to imprison and execute felons; and indeed a number of
other useful rights and powers defined by, and disguised under,
the kind of spectacularly incomprehensible names beloved of the
English legal profession. The ports also had the right to assemble
their own parliament at Shepway not far from Hythe and to
convene their own courts, while the highest office in connection
with them was that of Lord Warden, who also acted *ex officio* as
governor of Dover Castle, although officially he lived in Walmer
Castle.

Meanwhile, William of Ely, the new justiciar, was requisition-
ing horses; he 'took for the king's use from every city of England
two palfreys and two additional sumpter horses, and from every
manor of the king's own one palfrey and one sumpter horse.'
With others collected throughout the Angevin lands in France,

eventually over 10,000 animals were gathered up and made ready for shipping. Horses need to be shod from time to time, and while the justiciar's men were collecting the animals themselves, another party was charged with the task of purchasing 50,000 horseshoes from the iron works of the Forest of Dean; and so the work of preparation went on. But although these and a thousand other tasks were delegated to servants of the crown, Richard would have had to keep an overall eye on the progress of events in order to make sure that nothing was forgotten, and this was both a vast administrative task in itself and an immense responsibility. If the same sort of mistakes had been made in Richard's day as were made during the First World War, when, during the Gallipoli campaign, guns were shipped in one vessel and their breech blocks in another, Saladin could have slept more easily in his bed, and Richard would have had little or no success on arrival in the Holy Land.

However, there was one task which he delegated to no one. Having settled his father's debt of twenty thousand marks to the French king and having paid for his own coronation, the royal treasury was virtually empty. The preparations for the Crusade had to be paid for, and the sums involved were enormous; so Richard set out to raise as much money as he possibly could by almost all means short of the criminal. The most obvious device open to him was to levy a massive tax on his subjects, but he rejected the idea for various reasons. A so-called 'Saladin Tax' had been imposed by Henry not long before he died, and understandably it had proved to be highly unpopular. If Richard had levied yet another tax at this juncture, it would not only have antagonized his subjects, but it would also have taken months to collect, bringing in comparatively little at the end of the day. So he resorted to easier and quicker ways of solving his problem. When the news of the disastrous defeat of the Christians in the Holy Land in the battle of Hattin, followed by the fall of Jerusalem, had first reached England, very large numbers of people had responded to the pope's call for a new Crusade by taking the Cross in a moment of emotional enthusiasm; but by now the ardour of some had grown noticeably cooler, and Richard sought the pope's permission to allow those who wished to do so to purchase release from their crusading vows. The pope agreed, leaving it to

Richard to negotiate with each of his subjects an appropriate price for his freedom, and this Richard proceeded to do with enthusiasm and considerable financial acumen; those who could afford it had to pay through the nose, but on the whole they were happy enough to do so in view of what they were purchasing; freedom from absence from home with all that this entailed, from the perils of a long sea voyage, from the even worse perils posed by the numerous lethal middle eastern diseases to be encountered on arrival, and from the possibility of a premature and painful death in battle. Almost any sum of money which purchased so many desirable freedoms was considered to be a bargain by some people, especially by the rich who had more to lose than the poor, and Richard's coffers began to fill up in a most satisfactory manner.

But he had no intention of allowing those who had not joined the Crusade to avoid all responsibility for its financial support, and those eager to serve their monarch at home rather than overseas were now called upon to pay for the privilege. Neither the sale of public offices nor the even more general practice of requiring payment for royal grants of land, public offices, privileges, and benefits of various kinds was condemned by the current criteria of political morality in Richard's day, and he considered that men who wanted any of these things and had the wherewithal to pay for them should be made to contribute as handsomely as possible to the furtherance of the Crusade; so he set himself to exploit these sources of revenue. 'He induced many persons to vie with each other in spending money to purchase dignities or public offices, or even royal manors,' reported William of Newburgh, while Richard of Devizes remarked that 'all who were overburdened with money the king promptly relieved of it, giving them powers and possessions at their choice.' 'All things were for sale with him – powers, lordships, earldoms, sheriffdoms, castles, towns and manors,' said Roger of Howden, summing it all up; 'the king put up for sale everything he had.' When he was taxed with selling too much of his own royal demesne, he replied simply, 'I would sell London, if I could find a buyer for it.' The only unusual aspect of Richard's great auction of honours and offices was the speed and the thoroughness with which it was conducted: a speed and thoroughness dictated by the imminence of the Crusade. Similar auctions had been held often enough in the past by newly crowned monarchs but at a more leisurely pace over a number of years and perhaps not on such an all-inclusive scale with almost every official position up for grabs; but Richard needed the money, and he needed it urgently. Emergencies do not tolerate half-measures or procrastination, and Richard's whirlwind tactics were well timed. He got his money.

His other major task before setting out for the Holy Land was to ensure that the kingdom would be in safe hands during his absence abroad, and this meant dismissing those whom he did not trust and replacing them with people upon whom he could rely. With his brother John, he had already dealt as best he could, but his half-brother, Geoffrey, Henry's illegitimate son by Rosamund de Clifford, also posed a problem though a lesser one. Henry had tried to have him made bishop of Lincoln some years earlier, but he had been too young at the time, and as he grew older he had adamantly refused to be consecrated; he did not want to be a bishop. 'I much prefer horses and dogs to books and priests,' he announced firmly; but this may not have been his only reason for refusing to take holy orders. Once ordained, no man could ever become king, and it is just possible that Geoffrey had his eye on the throne; after all, there was nothing to stop a bastard becoming king; William the Conqueror had been an illegitimate child. Moreover, rumour had it that during a dinner party Geoffrey had once held the lid of a golden bowl over his head, and asked his friends whether they thought that a crown would suit him. Of course, he may have been slightly drunk or it may have been a joke, but Richard was determined that, joke or no joke, Geoffrey should never have the chance to discover whether a crown suited him or not, and he ordered the dean and chapter of York to elect him as archbishop and thus obey the dying wish of Henry, who had promised his bastard son the archbishopric as a reward for his faithfulness. Some of the canons objected that Geoffrey was a man of blood, conceived in adultery, and the son of a whore, but since none of these attributes were necessarily incompatible with episcopacy, the fastidious canons were overruled. His election being confirmed by a papal legate, he was ordained deacon, then priest, and consecrated bishop, and that was that. His other half-brother, William Longsword, posed no problem; he was not an ambitious man, eventually marrying the heiress to the earl of Salisbury, and making no further demands on good fortune in this mortal life.

Richard then turned to the task of filling the main offices of the crown with men he could trust, and this meant that some holding high office had to go. Amongst them, Ranulf Granville, who had been Henry's chief minister for many years as justiciar, was dismissed. The title 'justiciar' had been used ever since the Norman conquest to describe any officer of the king's court from the chief justice down to anyone qualified to act as *judices* in the shire-courts; it was only in the reign of Henry II that the title *justiciarus totius Angliae* or *summus justiciarus* was applied exclusively to the king's chief minister. The origin of this office was described by Stubbs in his *Constitutional History of England*, where he explained that the sheriff 'was the king's representative in all matters judicial, military and financial in the shire. From him, or from the courts of which he was the presiding officer, appeal lay to the king alone; but the king was often absent from England and did not understand the language of his subjects. In his absence the administration was entrusted to a justiciar, a regent or lieutenant of the kingdom; and the convenience being once ascertained of having a minister who could in the whole kingdom represent the king, as the sheriff did in the shire, the justiciar became a permanent functionary.' The fact that the king was often absent from England and that the justiciarship was usually held by great nobles or churchmen made the office of such importance that at times it threatened to rival or even overshadow that of the crown. The last of the great justiciars, Hubert de Burgh, who entered the royal service as a very young man during Richard's reign, went from strength to strength, making four dynastically and financially extremely advantageous marriages and eventually becoming earl of Kent and vastly wealthy before falling out of favour and being dismissed in 1231 after a number of violent disagreements with the then king, Henry III, a volatile, emotional and injudicious man, who found it hard to brook opposition of any kind, especially opposition to his madcap schemes to invade France and retrieve the Angevin dominions lost during the reign of his predecessor on the throne, King John.

The west front of the twelfth-century church in the village of Matha not far from Angoulême in Plantagenet country. In spite of the belligerence of the times, it was an age of more church building than at almost any other time before or since.

The tympanum of the south door of the Church of St Peter at Aulnay, a few miles north of Matha, provides another example of magnificent church building in Angevin territory in spite of the wars of the time. It is a little later than the church at Matha.

The island of Rhodes was a stronghold of the Crusaders for many years until eventually conquered by Suleiman the Magnificent in December 1522. As a gesture of courtesy to the Knights of St John – the Hospitallers – and as a tribute to their bravery in defence of the place, Suleiman gave orders that the escutcheons of the Knights carved on the walls of the city in various places should be left as a memorial of their courage and endurance. This is one of many still to be seen there.

The old Crusader walls of Acre fell into neglect after the victory of the Mamelukes and the expulsion of the Crusaders in 1291. They were repaired by a Turkish High Commissioner in 1775, and these sea walls are the result of his restoration of the original fortifications.

The sea walls of Acre. To the left is the Sea Gate into the town, while to the right the small lighthouse in its round tower and the jetty beyond were built in Crusader times, probably just after the capture of the town by Richard.

Known as the Crypt of St John and lying below the Turkish citadel at Acre, this splendid thirteenth-century hall with its great Gothic vaults probably was the refectory of the Hospitallers' palace there. Although built a few years later than Richard's day, it is typical of buildings which he would have known well.

A group of Crusaders receiving a delegation of Arabs treating for peace, while others to the right of the picture leave no doubt as to what will happen if a truce is not arranged. From a fourteenth-century French manuscript.

This is thought to be a portrait of Saladin by an Egyptian artist of the Fatimid school, perhaps because the man portrayed appears to be blind in one eye, as was Saladin. The picture dates from about 1180.

The most magnificent of all Crusader castles, Krak des Chevaliers in Syria, was described by T. E. Lawrence as 'perhaps the best preserved and most wholly admirable castle in the world'. It was built by the Knights of St John in mid-twelfth century, and though stronger than any other castle, it was typical of many. It was never taken by storm, only surrendering to the Mamelukes in 1271, when the last Crusaders were expelled from the land.

Plan of Jerusalem drawn in about 1150, probably by a monk of Voormezeele in Flanders. The draughtsman may have made a pilgrimage to the city, or he may have based his drawing on the accounts of others; but his drawing shows real knowledge of the place. The Church of the Holy Sepulchre can be seen at the bottom to the left.

The Dome of the Rock in Jerusalem. Built in the Temple area of the city, it covers a great outcrop of rock upon which traditionally Abraham prepared to sacrifice Isaac. On the same site once stood both Solomon's temple and later that of Herod. The present building was built as a Mosque by Abd al-Malik, the Arab conqueror of Jerusalem from the Byzantines, in AD 691, but the Crusaders believed it to be the old biblical Temple in which Jesus had walked and talked.

The east end of the Abbey at Fontev- raud, where Richard is buried next to his father, Henry II. His mother Eleanor, who survived them both, was also buried here by their side, when eventually she died on 1 April 1204.

The effigy of Richard on his tomb at Fontevraud. It was made some years after his death, and may not be much of a likeness of him; it has the air of being an idealized portrait with its youthful face and straighter than straight nose.

After de Burgh's dismissal, the office of justiciar was never revived, and it may be that Richard dismissed Ranulf Granville because he feared his power, though some have suggested that he did so in order to confiscate his considerable fortune. Whatever the truth may be, Granville had virtually ruled the country for years, making a huge fortune in the process, and too many tears need not be shed over his downfall. In his place, Richard appointed two very different men, one as justiciar in the north of England, the other in the south. In the north, he appointed Hugh de Puiset, who was almost the perfect type-piece of aristocratic Norman barons; he was tall, assured, and greatly experienced in the business of government, having been bishop of Durham for many years: a cultured man with a notable library and a taste for the arts, he had been on friendly terms of mutual respect with such influential and powerful people as the Percy family for years, and this made him an obvious choice for the job. But both he and the Percys were suspected of having had a hand in inciting the murderous anti-Jewish riots which had culminated in York, and this did not appeal to the man Richard appointed as justiciar in the south of the country. William Longchamp, bishop of Ely, has been described by the historian Philip Henderson as 'the son of a Norman labourer and a member of the master race, who made no secret of his contempt for the English . . . a lame stammering dwarf . . . with a particular aversion to women,' thus appearing to imply that he had some highly unepiscopal sexual tastes without actually saying so. However, there is not a scrap of evidence that William of Ely had homosexual tastes, nor much more that he was 'a lame stammering dwarf'. Everyone agrees that he was of humble origin, small in stature and plain featured, but according to another historian, John Gillingham, these physical shortcomings were more than outweighed by the fact that he was a man 'of considerable culture and learning . . . the king's most trusted servant and author of a treatise on civil law': a number of facts studiously ignored by Henderson. The truth seems to be that he was a celibate priest of proletarian origins, great natural endowments, and equally great ambition, who rose to eminence by taking advantage of the chances which came his way; he may well have had a very large chip on his shoulder against aristocrats such as Hugh de Puiset, with their entrenched positions in society, their snobberies and anti-semitisms, and their unquestioned and unquestioning arrogance.

Having made the necessary arrangements in England for the government of the country in his absence, Richard sailed for France, where he made similar plans for his continental dominions; this involved another meeting with Philip Augustus, this time at Nonancourt, where each agreed to bind his subjects by oath to respect the other's lands in their absence, and final arrangements for their departure were agreed between them. Richard then travelled south to make sure that Aquitaine would be adequately protected from the perennial hostility of Raymond of Toulouse during his absence on Crusade, and to this end he had various meetings with King Alfonso of Aragon and Sancho VI of Navarre. Alfonso had been his ally for many years, and no doubt Sancho's goodwill was secured by a remarkable new agreement between them; remarkable, that is to say, in that it represented a political *volte face* on Richard's part, which was bound to cause a diplomatic explosion once news of it became known, though for the time being both sides agreed to keep it secret. In fact, Richard agreed to marry Sancho's daughter, Berengaria of Navarre, in spite of his long engagement to the French king's sister, the unfortunate Alice. If Philip Augustus had heard of this extraordinary change of plan on Richard's part while they were both still in France, he would hardly have sat back and done nothing; but doubtless Richard felt that, if he waited to break the news until they were both well launched on crusade together, there was little that the French king could do but bluster and fume with anger and hurt pride; and in the event he was proved right.

With preparations for departure now virtually complete Richard held a final council at Chinon to ensure that nothing had been forgotten, and to make last-minute arrangements. These included the issuing of regulations for the maintenance of discipline on the long voyage to the Holy Land: regulations which have been cited by some people as yet more evidence of Richard's brutality and ruthlessness. They were simple enough. 'Any man, who kills another, shall be bound to the dead man and, if at sea, be thrown overboard, if on land, buried with him. If it be proved by lawful witnesses that any man has drawn his knife on another, or has struck him and drawn blood, his hand shall be cut off. If any man strikes another without drawing blood, he shall be ducked in the sea three times. Swearing at another man shall be punished by a fine. A man convicted of theft shall be shaved like a champion, tarred and feathered, and set ashore at the first landfall.' If these can be interpreted as evidence of a brutal streak in Richard, they may also bear witness to the explosive volatility and tendency to violence which lay just below the surface of the ordinary twelfth-century man. Similar tendencies probably lie below that of twentieth-century man, too, even if he manages to hide them most of the time rather better than his great-great medieval grandfather, unless he happens to be a Nazi storm trooper, Islamic fundamentalist or English football fan. However that may be, Richard's regulations ended with a royal command to all who were going to Jerusalem by sea, as they valued their lives and their return home, to obey the justiciars of the fleet, who were bidden to set out on their voyage as soon as possible; and this they did a few days before the Easter of 1190.

But before he himself was ready to sail, Richard had one more thing to do, and that perhaps from his point of view the most important of them all. He paid a visit to his favourite country seat at the little village of Talmont at the mouth of the river Jard, where in those days it flowed into the Atlantic, though today the sea has receded, and Talmont is no longer a port. The castle there had belonged to the lords of Poitou longer than almost any of their other possessions, forming part of the dowry of successive countesses of Poitou, and thus being known as 'the Land of the countess'. By agreement with his mother, who also knew it well, 'on the sea shore in the wood of La Roche, not far from the mouth of the Jard', Richard now founded a house of Augustinian canons. It was dedicated to 'our Lord and the glorious Virgin Mary his mother', and he endowed it with the whole Land of the countess as an offering to God for his safe return and for the success of his pious enterprise. Now, at last, having thus made his peace with God, Richard was ready to go.

VII

They that go down to the sea in ships, and occupy their business in great waters; these men see the works of the Lord and his wonders in the deep. For at his word the stormy wind ariseth, which lifteth up the waves thereof.

Psalm 107: 23–25

In the third week of June 1190, Richard received his pilgrim's scrip and staff from the hands of the archbishop of Tours in the cathedral there, while his followers crowded the city, almost blocking its streets. The poet Ambroise, one of the crusaders who kept a written record of the progress of events, noted that 'there were many good knights and crossbowmen there; and dames and damsels were sorrowful and heavy-hearted for their friends who were going away, and all the people were in sadness because of their valiant lord's departure.' Then on 27 June they all set out for Vézelay, where the two crusading armies, the English and the French, were due to meet. Medieval towns were small, and Vézelay could not possibly accommodate both the king of France's army and Richard's even larger force; instead, a miniature city of tents was pitched outside the city walls, while the people of Vézelay looked on in astonishment and awe at the sheer size of the army of crusaders, as they gathered there. We do not know precisely how many there were, but by modern standards the army was not very big: twelfth-century logistics limited the number of men who could be fed and supplied in the field to seven or eight thousand at the most. But while we do not know how big the whole force was, we do know that Richard's army was much bigger than that of Philip Augustus; to say that

Richard commanded about five thousand men, give or take a hundred or two, and Philip about half that number may well be as good a guess as any; and by medieval standards that was still a large army: indeed, a huge one.

On 3 or 4 July, the combined host set out for Lyon, 'the kings riding in front and discoursing of their great journey,' according to Ambroise. At Lyon, they intended to cross the Rhône before marching along its left bank, but when they arrived after a march of eight days, they had a first taste of disaster: as the men crowded on to the one and only narrow wooden bridge across the river, one of the arches collapsed, and they were pitched into the water. The river was in flood, but by good fortune only two men were drowned, while the rest somehow struggled to shore through the turbulent water. While theirs was a lucky escape, it left the rest of the army with the problem of how to cross the river; eventually, a large number of small boats were collected, lashed together and formed into a pontoon bridge, over which the men began once again to make their way gingerly to the east bank. The whole operation took three days, and at this point the two armies split up, having arranged to join forces again in Sicily. If they had continued to travel together, their passage would have put an insupportable strain on the resources of the countryside through which they had to pass, so Philip went ahead with his men to Genoa by way of the foothills of the Maritime Alps and the Apennines, while Richard and his larger force set out to march to Marseille, where they had arranged to meet the English fleet.

The march to Marseille was far from easy to accomplish. It is about a hundred and eighty miles from Lyon to Marseille, and in July southern France is hot; medieval roads were rough and dusty, the countryside provided little shade, and although most of the knights would have been able to load their heavy steel armour and their weapons on to carts or pack animals, the rank and file would have had to carry everything they possessed, many of them probably wearing the thickly padded leather coats which were their only protection against injury in battle. Baked by the sun all day, sleeping rough at night, and probably soaked to the skin by thunderstorms every now and again, they managed to march about fifteen miles a day, arriving in Marseille after a fortnight, on the last day of July, St Ignatius's Day, only to find that the English fleet had not arrived.

The story of the fleet's progress has a very twelfth-century ring to it. Over a hundred ships had set out more or less at the same time from a number of different ports in England, Normandy, Brittany and Poitou, and had begun their southward journey in a loose, informal convoy, for the most part hugging the coast of France in case they should have to run for shelter when a storm arose. They had no time to shelter, however, when they were struck by a violent gale in the bay of Biscay at about three o'clock in the morning of Ascension Day, and widely dispersed in the pitch darkness. Fortunately, at the height of the storm, when most people were praying fervently for divine deliverance, the blessed saint and martyr, Thomas of Canterbury, appeared to three men on a ship from the port of London, and assured them that he and two other saints, Edmund, the martyr of East Anglia, and Nicholas, the confessor of Myra, had been charged by God with the safety of the fleet, and as long as they resolved to behave themselves, all would be well. Thomas then disappeared, but as one might expect of such a saint, he was as good as his word; the storm subsided and the fleet re-grouped off the coast of Portugal, battered but still afloat.

Some ships in need of minor repairs then called in to the port of Silves, an outpost of Christendom which had been captured from the Moors of southern Spain barely a year previously, and some reports say that the crusaders joined in the continuing war against the Moors near the town. However, others suggest that in an excess of Christian zeal they attacked the few remaining Moslems who had been allowed to continue living in the city, finding it unbelievable that the Portuguese should tolerate the evil presence of infidels in their midst. However this may have been, there is no doubt that when the fleet put in to Lisbon the city's Moslems and Jews were viciously attacked, their houses burned, their property looted and their women raped by gangs of drunken sailors. Several hundred sailors were thrown into prison by the Portuguese authorities until such time as they should sober up and become less murderously xenophobic, and there they languished until the fleet sailed in the last week of July to creep slowly on its way, hugging the coast of Spain and eventually arriving in Marseille three weeks late. Meanwhile, Richard had already departed.

He had waited a week before doing so, but then his patience had run out, and he had hired some local ships for the onward voyage. Some of his men under the command of Baldwin, the archbishop of Canterbury and Ranulf Granville were sent ahead with orders to sail directly to the Holy Land and succour the hard-pressed Christians there until the main body of crusaders could arrive. As soon as they had gone, Richard and the rest of his men sailed in a more leisurely manner along the coast of Provence towards Italy, stopping at Genoa, where the French king lay sick. Philip loathed the sea, and suffered badly from seasickness; but, since he had travelled to Genoa overland, he could not have been suffering from *mal de mer* on this occasion. Whatever his illness may have been, Richard visited him before moving on to Portofino, where he received a message from the French king the next day asking for five of the ships which Richard had managed to hire. Richard replied that he could have three of them, but this did not satisfy Philip, who somewhat petulantly refused. It was a small matter, but it was a straw in what was to prove to be an ominously prevailing wind. From Portofino Richard sailed down the Italian coast in something very like holiday mood, calling in at many of the little ports on the way, where he hired horses and went riding with one or two companions, exploring the country-side and seeing the sights as though he had all the time in the world and the Crusade could wait. It was an uneventful period except for two incidents. On 25 August he landed at Ostia, where he was welcomed in style by the bishop of the place and a bunch of ecclesiastical dignitaries who had been sent by Pope Clement III to invite him to Rome; but this was an invitation which Richard curtly declined. Only a few months previously, Clement had demanded a large sum of money from him before he would agree to the appointment of William Longchamp as his legate to the Church in England, and Richard had not forgotten this piece of papal rapacity. Having therefore dismissed the discomfited bishop with a royal flea in his prelatical ear, Richard resumed his leisurely progress down the Italian coast, spending a fortnight at Naples before riding overland on horseback to Salerno. It was during this part of his journey that the second event worth recording took place. In a village through which he was passing, he caught sight of a falcon on a perch; it was such a splendid bird that Richard decided at once that he must have it, and promptly took it. The outraged owner of the bird protested volubly in Italian, and when Richard took no notice of his unintelligible outburst, he drew a knife and attacked him; some other villagers rallied to their friend's support, and Richard had difficulty in beating them off with the flat of his sword and escaping with his life. It was a discreditable little incident, but presumably Richard was so accustomed to getting his own way without contradiction in his own land that he expected no opposition, and it never occurred to him that anyone would object. As it was, he reached Salerno unscathed, and there on 13 September he heard that the English fleet had at last reached Sicily. The news put an end to his holiday and he left at once for Messina.

King William of Sicily, whose kingdom included much of southern Italy as well as Sicily itself, had invited the kings of England and France to use the island as the final assembly point for their forces before they set out on the last stage of their journey to the Holy Land, and both Richard and Philip Augustus had welcomed the idea; but William had died some months before they had set sail. He had been married to Richard's sister Joan, but they had had no children, and at the time of his death his next of kin was his aunt, Constance. However, she was married to Henry of Hohenstaufen, the German emperor's eldest son and heir, and for some reason the Germans were extremely unpopular on the island; so no one had wanted to see Constance on the throne. Moreover, Pope Clement III had been equally averse to the idea, for he dreaded the threat of German domination of southern Italy, which might well have been the result of her accession. Luckily, however, Constance had been in Germany at the time of William's death, and after a short intrigue, backed by the pope, her place had been usurped by a cousin of the late king, Tancred of Lecce. Ugly, dwarfish and a bastard, he had seized the throne only to find himself in trouble straight away; for he had been greeted by a Moslem revolt on the island of Sicily itself while, on hearing of his seizure of the throne, the Germans had invaded his lands on the mainland of Italy in support of Constance; but with the help of some Sicilian forces hastily recalled from the Holy Land, Tancred had succeeded in defeating his various enemies, and although he himself was in Palermo as Philip and Richard prepared to visit the island, he gave orders that they should be welcomed with appropriate solemnity.

The islanders themselves were agog at the prospect of the arrival of two such splendid royal visitors, and they were deeply disappointed when Philip slipped ashore on 14 September so unobtrusively that hardly anyone saw him; he hated pomp at the best of times, and he may well have been feeling sick on this particular occasion after sailing from Genoa. But Richard's arrival on 23 September more than compensated for the fiasco of Philip's entry. He assembled his whole fleet, boarding the leading galley himself, and ordered the trumpeters to be ready to announce his arrival at the appropriate moment. The ships were decked with brightly coloured standards and pennons fluttering in the breeze, their sides hung with shields glittering in the sun, and there at the head was Richard magnificently dressed and standing on a specially raised platform as the fleet entered Messina harbour to the sound of the trumpets and their accompanying clarions, while the people of the city crowded round and watched goggle-eyed at the splendour of it all. Philip, who had been alerted to the arrival of the English fleet by the noise, had come down to the harbour to meet his ally, and as Richard leaped ashore, the two kings embraced each other, while the people of Messina 'marvelled at that which they saw and heard of the king of England and his power': or so wrote Roger of Howden, who, with Ambroise, was the other great chronicler of the Crusade, and a spectator with an eye to the kind of curious and interesting little details which can bring the dead stuff of history alive; and yet at the same time he was a manifestly reliable and trustworthy eye-witness.

But the euphoria and the celebrations following Richard's arrival did not last long; the sudden influx of several thousand people into the island stretched its normal resources of food and wine, and as demand for these things increased sharply, so did their prices. As prices rose, so did tempers; arguments broke out between the crusaders and the islanders; there was the usual trouble created by drunken gangs in the streets, women were molested, and fights became common. Things were made worse by the mistrust and misunderstandings which arise between people of different ethnic origin and religious belief, especially when they speak different languages. Sicily had been part of the Greek-speaking Byzantine empire for centuries until conquered by the Saracens of north Africa, who had then ruled the island until the Normans wrested control from them about a hundred years before the arrival of Richard and his men. There was still a large population of Saracens all of whom were staunch Moslems, living side by side with an equally large number of Greeks who were members of the Orthodox Church, and they were ruled by a small oligarchy of Normans, who were Catholic. It was a potentially explosive scenario, but the three communities had learned over the years to live together, if not affectionately, at least with mutual forbearance; but to Richard's men from the north, none of whom could speak either Greek or Arabic, the Greeks were 'a parcel of thieving Griffons', while the Saracens, as Moslems, were enemies of Christ, for whom no treatment could be too bad. However, the crusaders had no monopoly in the art of insulting language and verbal abuse, and they themselves were soon dubbed 'the long-tailed English'. It is not entirely clear whether this was meant to imply that they were like devils, or to be rather more insulting than that, referring to the fact that after months at sea the English soldiers were often offensively unrestrained in their approaches to the women of Messina. Whichever meaning it carried, it infuriated the crusaders.

Meanwhile, matters were made worse by the fact that it soon became common knowledge that Richard was being cheated, and his sister ill treated, by the Sicilian king. The facts were simple enough: Tancred was not only refusing to hand over a large legacy left to Richard by the will of the late King William II, but also keeping his sister, Queen Joan, William's widow, a virtual prisoner and refusing to allow her access to her dower. Richard was fond of his sister and almost equally fond of money, and the legacy owing to him was a large one of gold plate, golden furniture, a huge silken pavilion large enough to stage a banquet for two hundred people and a number of ships and provisions for the Crusade. Before arriving on the island, he had sent a peremptory message to Tancred from Salerno demanding the release of his sister and her dower and the immediate delivery of his legacy. In an irenic gesture, Tancred responded by sending Joan with a royal escort to Richard in Sicily, while opening negotiations for a money settlement in place of the legacy and the dower; but Richard was not in an irenic mood. Instead he sent a small force across the straits with orders to attack and capture the fortified town of Bagnara, where he installed his sister in the castle dominating the town. Then he himself attacked a small island just off Messina, on which there was a Greek Orthodox monastery; to most Catholics, members of the Orthodox Church were almost as godforsaken as Moslems, and Richard had no hesitation in throwing the monks out to make place for his own troops – an action which horrified the Greeks of Sicily and convinced them that the English king was no better than his brutal troops.

On 3 October, less than a fortnight after Richard had landed on the island, an argument over the price of a loaf of bread between an English crusader and a woman baker selling her wares in one of the streets of Messina led to a fight, which rapidly turned into a full-scale riot. Blood was shed, and rumours began to spread that Richard was bent on conquering the whole island; the mob shut the gates of the city against his men, trapping some inside, whom they attacked. When the fleet made an attempt to force its way into the harbour, it was driven back. Philip Augustus, deeply alarmed by this violent turn of events, summoned the archbishop of Messina and a number of other pillars of Sicilian society to accompany him to see Richard in his camp outside the city walls in an attempt to make peace, and at first things seemed to go well. But then, three times during the conference, messengers arrived with news of the fighting: first that the English were everywhere under attack, next that they were being beaten, and finally that they were being killed 'both within and without the city'. The Sicilian members of the conference hurried away, ostensibly to stop the fighting. 'But they lied,' said Ambroise. Richard then went to see what was going on, and as he approached the city, a mob shouted abuse at him, 'the long-tailed English king', and he flew into a towering rage; wheeling his horse, he galloped back to the camp. Like his father he could be very volatile and on this occasion even people who had known him for years were surprised at the violence of his fury; he was choking with anger.

Donning his armour and accompanied by about twenty knights, he galloped back to the gate of the city, scattering the terrified crowd, and ordered a general assault on the place. The citizens were no match for their assailants despite the near equality of their numbers; they were caught off guard, and the city fell 'quicker than any priest could chant Mattins', or so it was said after the event: an exaggeration, but even so all resistance was overcome in a matter of four or five hours. Once the fighting was over, the long-tailed English soldiers vented their pent-up dislike of the Griffons by looting their houses and assaulting their women, while the Sicilian fleet at anchor in the harbour was burnt. Richard then gave the order to hoist his standard on the battlements of the city to signify its conquest.

Neither Philip nor any of his men had taken part in the fighting, but when the French king saw Richard's banners waving in the breeze over Messina, he was furious. As Richard's feudal superior, he demanded that they should be taken down and replaced by the fleurs-de-lis of France. At first, Richard refused, but two days later he agreed that the lilies of France should be set up beside the golden lions of England; the two kings had agreed at Vézelay that all conquests should be shared equally between them, and Philip was merely staking his claim to equal rights with Richard over the conquered city until such time as some sort of agreement could be reached with Tancred. Meanwhile, that little monarch was playing a devious game; he might be small, ugly and the untimely fruit of an adulterous union, but he was no fool diplomatically, and while Richard strengthened his position by building a great wooden castle outside the walls of Messina, naming it derisively 'Mategriffon' or 'Death to the Greeks', and announcing that unless those same Greeks behaved themselves he would conquer the whole island, Tancred began secret negotiations with the French king for an alliance between them against Richard. It should be cemented, he suggested, by the marriage of one of his daughters either to Philip himself or to his infant son Louis; but Philip was cautious, not wanting to antagonize the Germans by allying himself with someone who had just usurped a throne which by rights should have been occupied by Constance, the wife of Henry of Hohenstaufen, who was presently king of the Germans and emperor elect. He went as far as promising to support Tancred if he should attack Richard, but he would commit himself no further. While Philip hesitated, Tancred quietly made similar overtures of alliance to Richard, offering to give Joan twenty thousand ounces of gold in lieu of her dower and a similar amount to Richard in place of King William's legacy, while at the same time engaging one of his daughters to Richard's nephew, Arthur of Brittany. It was a good offer, and Richard was astute enough to realize that, if he rejected it, not only would he virtually throw Tancred into the arms of the French king, but it would make his continued stay on the island very difficult indeed; and yet, now that winter with its storms had made a voyage to the Holy Land almost impossible until the spring, he had little choice but to remain in Sicily with all his men until the weather improved. So Richard accepted the offer of an alliance, and promised in return to give aid to Tancred against anyone who should attack him or invade any of his lands, whether in Calabria on the mainland of Italy or on the island itself.

The treaty was duly drawn up and signed, and Tancred breathed a sigh of relief; he had secured a powerful ally against any possible invasion by the German emperor, and at the same time he had delivered his island from the threat posed by Richard. Richard, too, was pleased. He had made peace, solved his immediate problems, and made a useful ally, while denying a similar satisfaction to Philip. The fact that he had also made an enemy of the German emperor was not to have its full and disastrous consequences until much later, and Richard can hardly be blamed for not foreseeing them. The only person whose diplomatic nose had been put out of joint was Philip Augustus, and Richard realized that it was up to him to do something to repair their damaged relationship. He offered Philip part of the gold paid to him by Tancred and several of the ships which had recently arrived from England, while at the same time promising to renew his vows of friendship and alliance: offers which were gratefully accepted by the French king. To pacify the islanders, Richard insisted that his men should return the plunder they had taken after the capture of Messina, and when his own troops grumbled at this order, he pacified them too with gifts. Finally, the three kings, Richard, Philip and Tancred, sat down together and fixed the price of bread, thus removing the greatest cause of friction between the crusaders and their unwilling Sicilian hosts. Another cause of tension had been fights between the crusaders themselves, many of which had begun as a result of two things: alcohol and gambling; so all gambling was banned except in the presence of officers, and a measure of peace returned to the island and to the crusader camp, as everyone prepared to spend the winter in Sicily.

There is a sense in which Richard's many-sided nature with its almost paradoxical mixture of conflicting characteristics was as clearly revealed by the various parts he played in the events of his sojourn in Sicily as it was ever destined to show itself again. His deliberate sense of theatre, which he could turn on at a moment's notice, was magnificently displayed by his dramatic arrival on the island, as skilfully and splendidly stage-managed as a scene from an old-fashioned epic Hollywood film; he could scarcely have 'up-staged' the French king more effectively; but to write him off as a mere twelfth-century *prima donna*, as some people have tried to do, is to forget the diplomatic skill he showed in his bargaining with King Tancred, from whom in the end he got just what he wanted by applying a judicious mixture of the carrot and the stick, while outwitting Philip Augustus in the process. The fact that Philip outlived Richard and eventually ouwitted the whole house of Anjou – or, anyway, Richard's younger brother and successor, John – has tended to obscure the fact that Richard could be a diplomat of subtlety, distinction and determination when he chose. Yet, cool, calm, and calculating as he could be, like his father, every now and again sheer emotion transformed him into a different man altogether, as his anger before the capture of Messina demonstrated clearly enough. In a sense, this emotional inconstancy was typical, not just of Richard, but of the age in which he lived. Most men in the twelfth century lived lives of such radical insecurity that they were far more liable to sudden violent outbursts of anger, jealousy, religious fervour, xenophobia or some other emotion than is the average modern Western European in the twentieth; but even so Richard and his father seem to have excelled most of their contemporaries in this respect as in so much else.

Indeed, another respect in which Richard was very typical of his time also made one of its periodical appearances while he was in Sicily. The medieval church has often been accused of encouraging an exaggerated sense of guilt in its members, and this may or may not be true; what is beyond doubt is that the average man in those days was far more conscious of his moral responsibility to choose between good and evil and his consequent responsibility under God than those people today who bask in the belief that guilt is an irrational frame of mind to be dispelled by analysis rather than something to be acknowledged, confessed and forgiven. We suffer from guilt complexes which need explaining; our medieval ancestors were guilty of many things which seemed to them to cry out for God's forgiveness, and Richard was no exception. As a result, just before Christmas 1190, his sense of his own failure to live up to God's demands on him drove Richard to make a dramatic act of penitence which was superbly typical of his time and very similar to his father's contrition in Canterbury cathedral sixteen years earlier. He called together the various bishops who were accompanying the Crusade to a chapel in a house occupied by one of his knights, Reginald de Muhec, and there, falling naked at their feet, he made his confession to them. We have no idea what he confessed. Some twentieth-century biographers have assumed that, since in their view he was homosexually inclined, he must almost certainly have regaled the assembled bishops with accounts of his amorous adventures with sailors or other long-tailed Englishmen. It is a scenario which fits better our own rather limited view of sin than the twelfth-century's wider and more catholic view of the subject; but whatever sins Richard may or may not have confessed – lust, pride, anger or what-have-you – the bishops forgave him in the name of God, adjuring him to avoid them in the future, and Richard departed, determined to mend his ways and to enjoy Christmas to the full.

And so he did. He entertained King Philip and many of the French and English nobles to a magnificent banquet in Mategriffon together with some high-ranking Sicilians, and apart from a brawl down by the harbour between some Genoese sailors and some men from Richard's galleys, the island was momentarily wrapped in peace and goodwill. But the spirit of Christmas did not last into the new year, and as the month of

January went its somewhat dreary way, the combination of short, grey days, cold nights and boredom had its effect; tempers grew shorter, and fights became common. On 2 February, Candlemas and the Feast of the Purification of the Blessed Virgin Mary, Richard and a number of English and French knights went riding together, and on their way back they passed a peasant with a cart loaded with bamboo rods or some such straight canes. Laughing, Richard challenged one of the French knights, William des Barres, to a friendly tilting match with canes for weapons. William agreed, but as the match proceeded, Richard suddenly lost his temper, flying into one of his rare but terrifying rages; his mock lance broke, and he was unseated from his horse, but he remounted and charged his opponent in a fury, and even when the earl of Leicester and others managed to calm him down and stop the fight, he was still shaking with anger, warning his unfortunate opponent never to cross his path again. This tendency occasionally to lose control and fly into a violent rage was a characteristic shared by many of the Angevin family, and some of their contemporaries regarded it as a direct manifestation of the powers of darkness; Henry II had been even more prone to attacks of this sort than Richard. Whether the dark powers at work in mankind can be blamed for Richard's behaviour on this occasion – and both mythology and psychology in their rather similar ways tend to agree that they may indeed be blamed – it was another discreditable little incident which did little for Richard's reputation and even less for his relations with the French.

But those relations were soon to be put under a far greater strain than that arising from a petty quarrel. Queen Eleanor was due to reach the island with Berengaria, Richard's future bride, and their arrival would inevitably entail telling the French king that Richard was not going to marry Alice after all. But the two ladies broke their journey at Brindisi, and while they were there a document came into Richard's possession which greatly strengthened his hand. It was a letter from Philip to Tancred, and it had been written at the time when Richard and Philip had been intriguing against each other for an alliance with the Sicilian king. In it Philip had warned Tancred that Richard was a traitor, wholly untrustworthy and faithless, and had gone on to promise that, if

Tancred felt like attacking him, he, Philip, and all his men would help him destroy Richard and his army.

When Tancred had first shown him this letter, Richard had been genuinely shocked, and for a time he had refused to speak to the French king. Philip, who had heard rumours of Berengaria's forthcoming arrival and the purpose of her visit, attributed Richard's silence to an understandable reluctance on his part to admit that he had changed his mind about marrying Alice. Eventually, he tackled Richard and asked him why he was being shunned as though he were a leper. In reply, Richard produced the letter to Tancred, and handed it silently to Philip. According to Roger of Howden, at first 'the king of France was struck speechless by his evil conscience,' before recovering and swearing that the letter was a forgery, and that Richard had invented the whole thing as an excuse for not marrying his sister. Richard replied icily that he had no intention of marrying someone who had been his father's whore for years; having succeeded Rosamund de Clifford in one royal bed, Alice could not expect to occupy another. For a moment it looked as if the two kings would come to blows, and the count of Flanders stepped between them to prevent them from fighting; with an obvious effort, both men calmed down, and although Philip was still trembling with anger, he was the first to recover. In a remarkable *volte face*, he offered to release Richard from his obligation to marry his sister if Richard in his turn would promise to compensate her generously and send her back to her own people. It was more than Richard could have expected so soon after the two of them had been trading insults, and he agreed at once. Then, as sometimes happens after the emotional discharge of a violent quarrel followed by the relief of its ending, Philip went even further, suggesting that he and Richard should draw up a new treaty of friendship in which they would publicly avow once again their firm alliance, and in which Philip would grant to his 'friend and faithful liege, the illustrious king of England . . . freedom to marry whomsoever he will, notwithstanding the covenant made between ourselves and him regarding our sister Alice.'

At peace again and with the advent of spring weather, there was nothing to prevent the two kings from setting out at last on the final stage of their journey to the Holy Land, and having formally signed the new treaty with Richard, Philip set sail on 30 March. Richard kept him company for a few miles outside the harbour, and then turned and made for Reggio, having just heard that his mother and Berengaria had arrived there. Taking them on board his own ship, he delivered Berengaria into the care of his sister Joan in Bagnara Castle, and then sailed on to Messina with Eleanor, who stayed there with him for four days before saying goodbye and leaving for England. Women are often tougher and more durable than men, and Eleanor was no exception; she was almost seventy, and yet apparently she thought little of making the long, uncomfortable and hazardous journey from England to Sicily and back again to Normandy. Despite these exertions at her age, the indomitable old lady was destined to outlive all her sons except John, just as she had already outlived both her royal husbands. She was magnificent, and Richard must have been desolate to see her go. Once she had sailed for home, however, he, too, was ready to leave. The fleet was made ready, the men, the horses, and the provisions were embarked, and on 10 April 1191, Wednesday in Holy Week, Richard and the English host put to sea.

VIII

'The beautiful island of Cyprus . . . was the realm of the goddess Venus; and many there have been, who, impelled by her loveliness, have had their ships broken upon the rocks that lie among the seething waves.'

Leonardo da Vinci, quoted in *Journey into Cyprus*, Colin Thubron

The fleet which sailed from Messina was huge by any standards, let alone those of the twelfth century. It consisted of more than two hundred ships of various kinds of which about fifty were galleys – slender warships with long keels and armed prows, built along the same lines as the ships of Richard's Norse ancestors, and propelled by two banks of oars in the same way as the old Roman warships had once been driven into battle – while the rest were transport vessels. The fleet was led to sea by its three biggest ships, in one of which Richard's sister Joan together with Berengaria were travelling with their retinue of ladies; then came the transport vessels, and last of all the warships, but as soon as all were clear of land, Richard and the warships sailed ahead and took up position as the advanced guard of the whole fleet. Contact was kept between the various vessels by sailing close enough for men to shout to one another, while at night a great lantern was hung from the masthead of Richard's galley as a guiding light in the darkness.

Accustomed as we are to great liners with stabilizers, air-conditioned cabins, refrigerated food and constant radio contact with the rest of the world, it is difficult to imagine what conditions must have been like on board one of Richard's ships. The typical lading of each of them consisted of forty war-horses, forty knights with all their arms and accoutrements, forty foot soldiers and fifteen sailors, with food enough for both men and horses for a year as well as spare rudders, anchors, sails, oars and ropes of every kind; in even the calmest of calm seas, conditions must have been appalling, space acutely limited, comfort non-existent, and sanitary arrangements so primitive as to beggar description, while one can only dread to think what they must have been like in a storm with men being sick everywhere, and everything getting soaked with rain, spray and sea water. Yet even under such abysmal conditions, Roger of Howden, epitomizing the indomitable spirit of adventure and excitement which drove these twelfth-century men on their faithful, brutal, perilous way, had the time to describe with obvious delight 'some very strange fish . . . They can leap in the air and fly about a furlong before diving back into the water.' In order to assure his readers that he was not beguiling them with a mere traveller's tale, he told them how 'a man happened to be sitting at table on board ship, when one of these flying fish landed on the table in front of him, so he can vouch for the fact that these odd creatures really do exist.' To men, many of whom had probably never travelled further than ten miles or so from their native hamlet in the Yorkshire Dales or on the Marlborough Downs before setting out on Crusade, the sight of flying fish and of dolphins leaping from the water, the experience of finding themselves out of sight of land in the vastness of the open sea, and the terrible sight of the sky darkening for a storm must have been almost unimaginably vivid and overwhelming; and in fact it was not long before the sky did indeed darken.

The fleet had done well enough for the first two days at sea, but on Good Friday a gale blew up, and Richard had difficulty in keeping the ships together, even though, whenever he saw a vessel in difficulties or falling behind, he would go to the rescue or wait behind to encourage the laggard to keep up. But as the gale got worse, it became impossible to keep an eye on the whole fleet; the wind and the spray reduced visibility to a hundred yards or less by day, and at night there was no way in v. hich anyone could prevent some ships from being blown off course and becoming separated from the fleet. For the next few days, the gale became worse, blowing the ships along in the right direction, but making life hideous in the process; everyone was soaked to the skin, cold, dog-tired and extremely frightened, and many were seasick. The bishops and priests on board tried to say Mass on Easter Day, as the sun struggled up over the horizon, breaking through the clouds for a moment and turning the crests of the great grey waves gold against the stormy sky, but most of them were defeated by the pitching of the decks and the strength of the wind; so everyone prayed instead to the risen Lord, who had walked on the water and stilled the storm, and to his blessed Mother for protection in their dire extremity, and three days later, on the Wednesday in Easter Week, 17 April, their prayers were answered; the wind dropped, they sighted land, and a few hours later they dropped anchor off the coast of Crete. But twenty-five ships were missing, including the vessel carrying Joan and Berengaria and those with the greater part of Richard's treasure aboard. It was a disaster, and he was furious.

Since the gale had dropped a little, there was no reason to stay long off Crete, and the fleet sailed on to Rhodes in a high wind, but speedily and safely enough to convince all on board that God was pleased with them and the course they were setting. At Rhodes, they stayed ten days, while Richard's galleys scoured the seas for the missing ships, and at last they found most of them at anchor off Cyprus near the town and harbour of Limassol. Joan and Berengaria were safe; their ship had nearly been wrecked on the south coast of the island, but had managed to survive. Two other ships had been less fortunate; they had been driven on to the rocks near Limassol, and some of their crews, including the king's vice-chancellor and seal-bearer, had been drowned, while the rest had been seized and thrown into prison on the orders of the governor of the island, the self-styled emperor of Cyprus, Isaac Ducas Comnenus. Isaac was an aggressive, devious and rapacious man, who had seized the island by trickery five years previously, arriving with forged papers to say that he had been appointed governor by the Byzantine emperor in Constantinople and, once established, pronouncing himself to be emperor of the island in his own right. He had maintained himself in power by making alliances with such people as the Sicilians, the Armenians of Cilicia, and finally with Saladin and the Arabs, and not surprisingly the news that some ships full of armed men had been wrecked on the island had greatly alarmed him. He had hurried to Limassol, but by the time that he had reached the town, the shipwrecked knights had fought their way out of prison and, with the help of a landing party from the ships off shore, had been rescued and taken back to the fleet. On hearing that Queen Joan and Princess Berengaria were aboard one of the ships, Isaac had invited them to come ashore as his guests, but Joan was well aware of her own value as a hostage, and she had politely refused, asking permission instead to send some of the crew ashore to buy food and wine. Permission, however, had been curtly and rudely refused.

Two days later, on Sunday, 6 May, Richard's fleet appeared over the horizon. Nearly two hundred ships with their sails set against the sky, looking like a great flock of countless gulls, was an impressive sight, seeming to cover the sea from horizon to horizon, and Isaac flew into something very like a panic. He summoned some troops, ordered the citizens of Limassol to barricade the beach with anything and everything they could lay their hands on, and hurried down to the shore to await events. After all the alarms and excursions of his voyage, the loss of Joan and Berengaria, and the delay caused by the storm, Richard was not in the best of tempers, but nevertheless he sent a courteous message to Isaac Comnenus, requesting him politely to release the few prisoners he still held and to restore the loot he had taken from the ships which had been wrecked. Isaac greeted his messengers by cutting them short with an obscene oath in Greek, the meaning of which was hidden from them though the intention was crystal clear. Ambroise recorded Richard's response, which was equally brief. 'To arms!'

Between the fleet and the shore five armed Greek galleys lay in the harbour, while by this time Isaac's troops were drawn up on the beach behind a massive barricade of old barrels, casks, doors, window frames, shutters, wrecked ships, boats, planks, benches and every other kind of debris, while behind them again was the fortified town of Limassol crowned by a castle built on the summit of a rocky hill. Richard's men could land against this opposition only by crowding into a small armada of little cockleshell boats, weighed down by their armour and cumbrous weapons; but, as one of them said after the event, 'We knew most about war.' The attack was opened by crossbowmen, who brought such a devastating fire to bear on the galleys in the harbour that the Greek sailors leaped into the water and abandoned their ships. Meanwhile, knights and foot soldiers were rowing for the shore under a hail of arrows; they were led by Richard himself and watched by Ambroise, who described how the king 'leaped from his boat into the sea, making for the Greeks, and assailed them.' As his men followed him, they drove the defenders back, some into the town and others into the country, and Isaac mounted his horse and fled. For a moment, the scene was set for a little incident as typical in its way of one aspect of Richard's character as it was also of the spirit of the century in which he lived. Seeing an unattached horse 'with a sack attached to its saddle and stirrups of cords', Richard sprang on its back and, chasing Isaac, he shouted, 'Emperor, come and joust!' But jousting with Richard was the last thing that Isaac wanted, and being better mounted than the English king, he made his escape.

The town of Limassol now submitted, and Richard brought his sister and Berengaria ashore. That same night the horses were landed and exercised, and early next morning the king and about fifty knights rode out in search of the enemy. They found a small party of men in an olive grove, who ran away in terror, and were chased until the main body of Isaac's men was sighted. Isaac, half a mile away, hearing the noise of a sudden commotion and the shouts of his men, hurried to the scene, and was astonished to find his army confronting a little band of mounted knights, for he had no idea that Richard possessed horses. Although the Greeks greatly outnumbered their opponents, they seemed to be at a loss as to what to do, and in the event they did little but rattle their shields and shout insults at the little group of armoured knights, motionless on their horses a few hundred yards away. A certain Hugh de la Mare turned to Richard and said, 'Come away, Sire, their numbers are too great;' but Richard's brief reply was to leave matters of war to him, and moments later he gave the order to charge. The suddenness and the sheer weight of the massed onslaught of fifty knights in full armour, each armed with a lance half the length of a telegraph pole and sitting on a galloping horse weighing a ton or more, was enough to strike the fear of God into the hearts of the Greeks, and they broke and ran for their lives. Isaac fled to the mountains; his standard bearer was struck down, and the standard taken by Richard himself, and with the victory complete he called off his men from the pursuit, and returned to Limassol. Isaac's standard was sent back to England as a gift to the abbey church at Bury St Edmunds.

Before reaching Cyprus, Richard had sent a messenger to the Holy Land, where the king of France had by now arrived, to let the embattled crusaders know of his whereabouts and to explain the delays he had suffered. On 11 May, three galleys were sighted approaching Limassol, and on arrival they proved to be carrying some of the leading crusaders from Outremer including King Guy of Jerusalem, who, as Guy of Lusignan, was one of Richard's principal vassals in France; with him were his brother, Geoffrey of Lusignan, Humphrey of Toron, Bohemond, prince of Antioch, Raymond, count of Tripoli, Leon the brother of the prince of Armenia and a number of other high-ranking nobles. They had come to enlist Richard's aid against the French king, who was trying to replace Guy as king of Jerusalem by his own protégé, Conrad of Montferrat, the lord of Tyre, a ruthless, vigorous and brave man who had been involved in a murder in Constantinople before coming to the Holy Land, where he had been largely responsible for preventing Saladin from totally ejecting the crusaders from the land after their crushing defeat on the Horns of Hattin. Richard welcomed them warmly, and invited them to his wedding to Berengaria the next day and afterwards to a feast to mark the occasion.

To the historian, Berengaria is a shadowy creature floating elusively in and out of the pages of history, featureless and voiceless like some disembodied spirit, without ever becoming distinguishable or recognizable as a person. Ambroise described her as 'a prudent maid, a gentle lady, virtuous and fair, neither false nor double tongued', which sounds like a brave attempt to present an unpromising subject in the best possible light. Somehow, she managed to pass through the events of her time without leaving even the ghost of a trace behind her, and the only hints we get as to what sort of a person she may have been point to her as having been rather dull, plain and worthy. Nevertheless, all the records agree that Richard was in high spirits and euphoric mood when, on 12 May, he married her in the chapel of the castle of Limassol. Two remarks made at the time shed light on the vexed subject of Richard's sexual tastes. Richard of Devizes remarked rather cattily at the time of the wedding that 'presumably the bride was still a virgin', plainly implying that in his opinion Richard had probably already jumped the marital gun and gone to bed with her; while Walter of Hemmingburgh believed that Richard married her 'as a salubrious remedy against the great perils of fornication', to which, in the opinion of many people at the time, he was addicted. Indeed, rumours of his illicit affairs with women abounded during his lifetime, and after his death some stories became legendary. He was credited – or perhaps debited would be a more appropriate word – with lusting after all sorts of women, including a king's daughter, while he was a prisoner in Germany after the Crusade, and also after a nun in the abbey at Fontevraud, whom he wanted so badly that he threatened to burn the place down if he could not have her. Some credence is lent to these stories of his heterosexual tastes by the fact that he acknowledged an illegitimate son, Philip, whom he made lord of Cognac. Moreover, if the reason why his marriage to Berengaria proved to be childless was not that he was homosexual, but that his wife was barren, he may well have continued to seek solace and excitement in promiscuity, in which case it was probably his heterosexual adventures which brought down on his head the celebrated hermit's warning a few years after his marriage.

The story is well known. In 1195 or thereabouts, a saintly hermit confronted Richard and warned him to 'remember the destruction of Sodom, and abstain from illicit acts, for if you do not, God will punish you in fitting manner.' Since one of the few things that most people today know about the Old Testament is that the people of Sodom went in for sodomy, and brought down fire and brimstone on their heads as a result, it is understandable that they should conclude that Richard was being warned against that vice; and maybe he was. But, as those who know their Bible a little better will appreciate, it is just as likely that he was being reminded that all sin, not just the sin of sodomy, was liable to bring down the punishment of God on the head of the sinner unless he repented and changed his ways. The story of the destruction of the cities of the plain, Sodom and Gomorrah, was used by Old Testament prophets, by Jesus himself, by St Paul, and by many subsequent Christian preachers, mystics, hermits and self-appointed moral mentors of the societies of their day to warn people, not against sodomy in particular, but against sin in general: against the terrifying possibility of bringing the fire and brimstone of God's terrible wrath down upon their guilty heads as a punishment for whatever sins – idolatry, faithlessness, pride, greed, fornication or what-have-you – they happened to be practising at the time; and this is almost certainly what Richard's hermit was doing. Having heard the widespread rumours of his adultery and fornication and his open acknowledgement of an illegitimate child, and in all probability with a sideways look at the sins of pride, avarice and brutality, into which most medieval kings were liable to fall as an occupational hazard, the saintly, scandalized and ferocious old hermit was warning the king against the dire consequences of these abominable sins.

The feasting after the royal wedding lasted for two or three days, and when it was over Richard held a conference with King Guy of Jerusalem and other leaders of the Crusade. It was decided that Cyprus should be conquered; possession of the island would be of incalculable value to the Christians in the Holy Land, for in the short term its conquest would yield immensely rich pickings, while in the long run it was in a strategic position of such importance to anyone fighting a war in Syria, a mere sixty miles away across the sea to the east, that its possession could almost be regarded as essential. Richard's decision to delay his departure for Outremer in order to conquer the island was strengthened by the arrival of some of his ships which, by this time, had been written off as lost at sea with all hands during the recent gale; somehow, however, they had survived, and the reinforcements they brought were more than welcome at this particular juncture. But before he could resume his pursuit of Isaac Comnenus, the self-appointed emperor forestalled him by proposing that they should meet and discuss peace terms. According to a picturesque account by Ambroise, they met 'in a garden of fig trees between the shore and the Limassol road', while another contemporary source records that Richard went to the meeting dressed in a rose coloured silk tunic and cape embroidered with silver thread, wearing a scarlet cap and a gold-hilted sword; he was mounted on a Spanish horse of great beauty, the saddle was red, studded with little golden stars, and it had on its hinder part two golden lion-cubs rampant. It reads like a scene straight from a contemporary illuminated manuscript, and no doubt Richard's appearance was intended to overawe Isaac Comnenus. Whether it did so or not will never be known, for all that history records is that on arrival, the Greek promised to come on Crusade with the English king accompanied by five hundred knights and to hand over the castles of Cyprus as a pledge of his sincerity together with 3,500 marks. The two men then exchanged the kiss of peace, returned to Limassol together like brothers, dined together, and retired to bed; whereupon Isaac stole quietly from his room, mounted his horse – an animal named Fauvel, celebrated for its speed – and rode like the wind for Famagusta, for he had not the smallest intention of keeping any of his promises.

His flight was soon discovered, and the next morning Richard put to sea at the head of his galleys to sail round the coast to Famagusta, while at his request Guy of Lusignan led his land forces along the coast road to meet him there; but on arrival they found the town deserted. Isaac had fled. Before pursuing him farther, Richard sent some of his ships to blockade the other island ports in order to prevent his escape, and while he was in Famagusta, he received a delegation from the king of France pressing him to come and join him as soon as possible – almost ordering him to do so, in fact – and Richard fell into a rage at the bare-faced impudence of the French king. He dismissed Philip's envoys with a curt message that 'not for half the wealth of Russia' would he leave Cyprus until he had conquered it and made sure that both its harbours and its corn and wine were available for the Crusade. Having dismissed the French, he marched on Nicosia, where Isaac was said to have retired. With his usual military flair, he suspected that Isaac would attack him from behind, and took command of the rearguard; and so it turned out. Isaac laid an ambush near the village of Tremithius, waiting until the majority of Richard's men had passed by before attacking them, but in spite of the fact that he is said to have used poisoned arrows in his attack on the Crusaders, he was quickly repulsed. He himself escaped to Kantara on the matchless Fauvel, leaving his men to their fate, and although some got away, most were killed or captured. After the battle, Richard and his men went on to occupy Nicosia, where he was greeted by the inhabitants of the place as a liberator from the rule of the much hated Isaac.

Richard might have completed the conquest of the island in a matter of days, had he not fallen ill at Nicosia. As it was, Isaac, greatly heartened by the news of his enemy's incapacity, put his four great northern castles at Kantara, Buffavento, Saint Hilarion and Kyrenia on to a state of full alert, and determined to hold out until the English king should tire of the war and sail on to the Holy Land. But while Richard lay sick, King Guy marched on Kyrenia, and captured it together with Isaac's wife and little daughter, whom he had placed there for safety. Isaac was one of the least attractive members of the great Byzantine royal family, the Comneni; he was cruel, deceitful, unscrupulous, tyrannical and about as trustworthy as a pathological liar trained in ethics by an admirer of Judas Iscariot, but he had one amiable weakness: he loved his daughter, and when he heard of her capture, the fight went out of him. He surrendered to Richard unconditionally, begging only that he should not be cast into irons. Richard raised him to his feet, and relieved his anxiety about his daughter by bringing her to him, and promising that she would be treated with as much love and care as if she were his own offspring; and he was as good as his word, handing her over to his sister Joan, who brought her up as her own child. As for Isaac himself, his plea not to be placed in irons was also granted, but only in a way which appealed to a rather unattractive medieval sense of humour; he was cast into silver chains, wrought especially to spare him incarceration in irons, and despatched to Syria, where he was imprisoned in the great fortress at Marqab on the coast north of Tripoli. There, in all probability, he died, though history does not bother to say so; but then history is an incorrigible snob, meticulously recording the boring deaths of genuine emperors and kings, but dismissing the deaths of most other people as too trivial to be worth recording.

Thus, in less than a month Richard conquered Cyprus. The Cypriots shed no tears for Isaac Comnenus, for he had taxed them unmercifully, and the treasure he had amassed was enormous.

This now fell into Richard's acquiescent hands, which were never allergic to the touch of gold, and which might have been satisfied, one would have thought, with such a golden harvest; but Richard was not one to miss an opportunity of reaping an even richer harvest than that already gathered safely in, and in return for a promise to the islanders to restore the laws and institutes which they had enjoyed under the emperors of Constantinople, he imposed a fifty per cent capital levy on each of them. They were in no position to protest, and since it was to be levied once and once only, they paid up; but their initial relief at being liberated from Isaac's harsh and extortionate rule lost some of its pristine rapture as the Cypriots resigned themselves to settling down once again under a new set of tax-hungry alien rulers. Meanwhile there was nothing to detain Richard on the island, and on 5 June, Wednesday in Whitsun week, he set sail again with the fleet for the Holy Land.

IX

The voyage to the Syrian coast was uneventful, the fleet making landfall off Marqab in the first week of June. Turning south, the crusaders sailed down the coast past Tortosa, Tripoli and Beirut, until Richard in the leading galley suddenly sighted a ship of such enormous size that, in the words of Ambroise, 'We read of no larger one ever existing save the ark of Noah.' One of his men hailed it, enquiring where it was bound. 'We are Genoese bound for Tyre,' came the reply; but another of Richard's sailors called out to him in excitement, 'Hang me, Sire, if that ship be not Turkish!' Richard immediately ordered one of his galleys to approach the suspect vessel, which soon put her identity beyond doubt by opening fire on Richard's men as they closed the gap between them. There followed a sharp and bloody little fight, as attempt after attempt to board the enemy vessel was driven back, until at last Richard ordered his men to make a breach in the side and sink her, which they did. Most of the crew were either killed or drowned, but a few were taken prisoner, and from them it was learned that they had been trying to reinforce the besieged garrison of Acre with men and much needed supplies. The ship's loss was a serious blow to the city's defenders and a cause of much rejoicing to Richard and his men. Their jubilation was short-lived, however, for when they landed that evening near Tyre, intending to spend the night there, they were refused entry into the city on the orders of Conrad of Montferrat and the king of France. Richard was furious, but there was nothing he could do about it, and the following day he re-embarked his men and sailed on to Acre, arriving there without further incident on 8 June. He was welcomed rapturously by the besieging army; the celebrations went on into the small hours of the morning by the light of bonfires and torches, and the noise of the Christians singing and dancing 'to the sound of trumpets, clarions, and flutes', as one chronicler recorded the event, deeply depressed the half-starved garrison in the city and their Moslem compatriots encamped on the hills inland. But the general situation which greeted Richard on his arrival in the country was not such as to give him or any Christian much cause for rejoicing.

It was almost a hundred years since pope Urban II had called the first Crusade into existence, and the imagination of Christian Europe had been lit up by the idea of recovering the holy places of their faith from the shame of infidel rule. Against astonishing odds and at the cost of endless endurance, suffering and self-sacrifice, the men and women of France, Germany, England and almost every country in western Europe had succeeded in establishing a number of Christian principalities there and opening the land where Christ had lived and died and risen from the dead once again to pilgrims from all over Christendom. It had been an extraordinary achievement, but the position of the Christian rulers of these new kingdoms in Syria and the Holy Land had always been precarious and insecure; they had been vastly outnumbered at all times by their Moslem subjects, with whom relations had never been happy, although occasionally after a few years of peace they had begun to tolerate each other rather better than usual; but such periods had been brief, invariably ending abruptly as new recruits from Europe had arrived filled with Christian determination to go out and kill a few Turks for the love of God. The success of the first Crusade had been partly due to the disunity of the Moslems and the unity of their Christian enemies, but as the years had gone by, the rulers of the Christian kingdoms had become progressively quarrelsome, while the Moslems had learned the bitter lessons of their defeat and had joined together more and more in their determination to expel the Christian invaders from their lands. The appearance of Saladin on the stage of middle eastern politics had marked the climax of this dual process of growing Moslem unity and Christian disarray, and the result had been inevitable: the Christian forces had been almost obliterated in battle on the Horns of Hattin on Saturday, 4 July 1187, almost four years before Richard's arrival. Jerusalem had fallen into Saladin's hands, and only in Tyre had a handful of Christians under the leadership of Conrad of Montferrat succeeded by a near miracle in holding out against him. On 1 January 1188, Saladin had raised his siege of the city, and Conrad had become everyman's hero, his name a legend throughout Christendom.

By birth, Saladin was a native of Kurdistan. His father had risen to become a general in the army of Nur ed-Din, the emir of Aleppo; later he had been governor of Baalbek, and later still he had joined his master's court at Damascus, where his children had been brought up. Saladin had been educated there in the most illustrious centre of Islamic learning outside Cairo, and he had grown up to be a devout Moslem, so although he nearly always treated his Christian foes with courtesy and even respect, he knew perfectly well that they were all doomed to hell. Physically, he was unimpressive, short, rather stout, red faced and blind in one eye; no one could have guessed from his appearance at the greatness of the man, and as a young officer in Nur ed-Din's army he had shown little talent other than some skill at polo. He could be ruthless; his rise to power was not impeded by many scruples, and he never shrank from bloodshed when he deemed it to be necessary. Indeed, after the battle of Hattin, he killed one of his most obnoxious captives, Reynald of Châtillon, with his own hand, and he ordered the cold-blooded execution of all the Knights Hospitaller and the Templars without turning a hair. But with all that, he was modest, courteous, highly intelligent, well read, and a brilliant soldier with simple tastes and a dislike of ostentation, and he was greatly respected by both friend and foe alike.

But despite their defeat by him on the Horns of Hattin, the Christians had not learned the lessons of their disunity. King Guy had been captured at Hattin, but when Saladin had released him on condition that he would take no further part in the war,

Conrad of Montferrat had refused to recognize him or even allow him inside the city of Tyre, and once again the Christian camp had been rent by bitter feuds between its leaders. Conrad had been in far the stronger position; even if Guy was the rightful king, he was a king without a kingdom or much of a reputation after his catastrophic defeat at Hattin, and the majority of the other leading Christians had favoured Conrad. But then to everyone's surprise, in August of the following year Guy had stolen a march on his rival by moving south with a small army of his supporters and besieging Acre, blithely breaking his promise to Saladin in the process; but as every good Christian knew, a promise made to an infidel – a man cursed by God – was not binding, and Guy had soon found a priest to release him from his vow and allow him to resume the war. On the face of it, however, his attempt on Acre had seemed to nearly everyone at the time to be an insane enterprise; his little army had no chance of taking the place, and it had been only a matter of days before Saladin had swooped down with his much larger host, and pinned down the little group of Christians between the walls of Acre and his army on the hills inland, thus besieging the besiegers. Even so Guy and his men had succeeded in keeping Saladin at bay while at the same time preventing him from relieving his fellow Moslems in the city, and as a result he had regained much of the respect and esteem which he had lost at Hattin; indeed, his political stock had risen higher than ever before, so that even Conrad had been forced to recognize that for the time being the tide had turned in Guy's favour. As a result, in the spring of 1190 he had recognized him as king, and he and most of his supporters had joined him below the walls of Acre. Other crusaders from France and England, exasperated by the slow progress of the two kings in Sicily, had also made their way there to reinforce Guy's hard-pressed little army, and the siege of Acre had gone on.

Political tides are both less predictable and less reliable than those which rule the motion of the seas, and before the arrival of either King Philip or a little later King Richard the tide had turned once again against Guy and in favour of Conrad of Montferrat; for Guy's wife, Queen Sibylla, together with two of his little daughters, had been taken ill and had died, and since he had become king of Jerusalem only by virtue of his marriage to her as the rightful queen, her death had made many people question his right to remain king. Guy himself had argued that, since he had been anointed, nothing could remove his divine right to the throne; but there seems to have been some doubt about the strict legality of his anointing and subsequent coronation, and by no means everyone had been convinced. Instead, many had declared that Sibylla's younger sister, Princess Isabella, was the rightful heir and should marry Conrad of Montferrat, who would make a much better king than Guy. Unfortunately there were difficulties to be overcome before this plan could be adopted: difficulties which, to a simple man, might have seemed serious. Not only was Isabella already married to a youth named Humphrey of Toron but Conrad almost certainly had one wife in Constantinople and probably another somewhere in Italy. However, minor details of this sort never daunted ecclesiastical lawyers or medieval theologians when power politics were involved, and Isabella had been firmly told that her marriage to Humphrey, a charming but rather effeminate young man, was null and void – or soon would be, when a convenient archbishop could be persuaded to say so – and that she should marry Conrad. The lady had pointed out with understandable warmth that the last thing she wanted to do was to exchange the young husband she knew for a middle-aged bigamist and murderer whom she had hardly met, but her objections had been brushed aside as too trivial to be worthy of note, and Archbishop Baldwin of Canterbury had been asked to annul her marriage to Humphrey. To many people's surprise, he had refused to do so, declaring that since Conrad already had a wife, any marriage between him and Isabella, who had a husband, would be doubly bigamist; but their surprise at this odd ruling had soon given way to understanding when it was quietly explained to them that his real reason for refusing to sanction the marriage had not been a misguided fidelity to the finicky ecclesiastical rules governing matrimony, but rather his loyalty to King Richard, whom he knew to favour Guy against Conrad. The archbishop of Pisa had then been approached as papal legate with a request to overrule Baldwin's judgement, and after a few carefully phrased hints had been dropped that under certain circumstances Pisa might be offered some highly advantageous trade concessions, the archiepiscopal eyes had suddenly been opened to the truth, which had been staring everyone else in the face for a long time: namely, that Isabella's marriage had obviously been null and void from the beginning, and that since both Conrad's wives were a long way off, they would be extremely unlikely to cause any trouble if he were to marry again. Isabella's marriage to Humphrey of Toron had then been duly annulled, and on 24 November 1190, the bishop of Beauvais, by a lucky chance a cousin of the king of France, had married Princess Isabella to Conrad of Montferrat, thus greatly strengthening his claim to the throne of Jerusalem.

Into this extremely complicated military and political situation Richard and his men sailed on Saturday, 8 June 1191. According to Ambroise as they approached the coast from the sea, they were greeted by the sight of 'Acre with its towers and the flower of the world's people seated round about it, and beyond them the hill peaks and the mountains and the valleys and the plains, covered with the tents of Saladin and his brother Safadin and their troops, pressing hard on our Christian host.' Presumably, at first, all that Richard saw was the immediate military situation of the besieging army below the city walls; but after the celebrations to mark his arrival were over, it would not have been long before the realities of the political situation would also have begun to press in on him, and they would have made him no fonder of the king of France. But he was pre-eminently a soldier, and it was the tactical problem which fascinated him. Acre was built on a promontory of land jutting out into the gulf of Haifa; to the south and west it was protected by sea walls and by the sea itself, while the harbour was protected by a mole running out south-eastwards to a large rock, on which a fort named the Tower of the Flies had been built to guard the harbour entrance, which was made even more secure by a great chain across its mouth. Meanwhile, the landward side of the city was protected by two formidable walls running from sea to sea across the promontory, and joined by another fort called the Accursed Tower, and these walls were themselves protected by a deep fosse at their base. The city was capable of resisting a long siege, but although King Philip had been acknowledged as supreme commander of the crusaders since his arrival in April, he had done nothing much to prosecute the siege after his first assault on the place had been defeated by a counter-attack by Saladin's troops on his rear. Instead, he had busied himself with setting up some large siege engines, which he had brought with him from France, and supervising the business of filling the fosse with stones and rocks from the surrounding countryside.

But after his tumultuous welcome, Richard was not content with such inactivity, and having exchanged polite greetings with Philip, he set about the business of making sure that he, not Philip, should be in command in future. Having discovered that the French king was paying his followers three gold bezants a month, he issued a proclamation offering four to any knight of any nationality who would take service under his banner. Numbers of men from Pisa and elsewhere immediately joined him, including a few Germans, who had reached the country after the collapse of the German Crusade, when the Emperor Frederick Barbarossa had been drowned in a river on his way through Asia Minor, and who were dissatisfied with the meagre pay they were receiving from their leader, Duke Leopold of Austria. Another remarkable recruit was Henry, the count of Champagne and nephew of the king of France, who pledged himself to fight under Richard's banner rather than that of his uncle, largely because of Richard's generosity when compared with the niggardly manner in which the French king had so far treated him. Needless to say, neither Duke Leopold nor King Philip were pleased, but there was little that either of them could do but nurse a sense of grievance in private, though in Leopold's case the incident was the first in a chain which was to have disastrous consequences for Richard at a later date.

Talk of the city of Acre with its towers and walls and harbour can easily mislead one into imagining that it was a much bigger place than it actually was. In fact, by today's standards it was little larger than a big village covering an area of no more than half a square mile, and conditions inside it for its six thousand defenders, crammed into a warren of small insanitary houses in a maze of dusty narrow streets, must have been appalling; they were short of water, half starved, and under constant bombardment by the crusaders' siege machines, but at least they were accustomed to the heat. Their enemies, on the other hand, were not; and they, too, were packed together far too tightly for either health or comfort. The walls of the little city were only half a mile long from sea to sea, and between them and Saladin's army less than a mile inland on the hills was the entire Christian host; men and a few women from France, England, Germany and Italy were crowded together with their animals, their engines of war, their baggage trains, their supplies and their tents in a temperature which seldom fell below eighty degrees Fahrenheit, and often rose much higher. As soldiers, they were almost as varied in experience as they were in nationality. Some had fought the Moslems before, having been living in Outremer for many years before the battle of Hattin; indeed, a few had actually been born there. Others had arrived from Europe since the disaster on the Horns of Hattin, volunteers who had not been content to wait until their leaders should stop quarrelling among themselves before going to the assistance of their fellow Christians in the Holy Land in their moment of desperate need. They had made their way in groups large and small, some travelling overland by way of Constantinople, others by sea, and on arrival they had joined either King Guy and his army or Conrad of Montferrat and his rival force, and their advent had been invaluable to the remnant of Christians, still alive and eager to prevent Saladin from achieving total victory. All were welcome, but some were little more than armed yokels, who had responded to the pope's plea for help, but who knew little of warfare before arriving in Outremer, while at the other end of the spectrum were the Hospitallers and the Templars – or, to give them their full titles, the Knights of the Order of the Hospital of St John the Baptist in Jerusalem, on the one hand, and the Poor Knights of Christ and the Temple of Solomon, on the other.

The Hospitallers had been founded by a monk named Gerard, who had been in Jerusalem when the first crusaders had besieged it; he had been in charge of a small Christian hospital, and it was said of him at the time that during the siege he had helped his fellow Christians outside the city by throwing loaves of bread to them from the walls, when they were at their most hungry, while telling the defenders of the place that he was bombarding them with stones. It was an improbable story, and he had been arrested and dragged before the Moslem governor of the city charged with treachery, but when the incriminating loaves had been produced in evidence, they had been miraculously turned to stone, and Gerard had been acquitted. The story had won him immense popularity after the capture of the city, and he had taken the opportunity to enlarge his hospital and to recruit more monks to serve in a reconstituted Order. It had not been long before kings, grandees and princes of the Church throughout western Christendom had begun showering Gerard with properties in Provence, Spain, England, Italy, Portugal and Germany to endow his new Order; recruits had also flowed in, for the new Order had been constituted as semi-monastic and semi-military, fulfilling a need for many men who longed to dedicate themselves to the religious life, but who were better fitted by nature to an active rather than a contemplative existence. The Knights Templar had been founded at about the same time by a Burgundian knight, Hugh of Payens, with the object of protecting pilgrims from attack by Moslems or robbers on their way to Jerusalem and the other holy places, and they too had grown in numbers with prodigious speed. Both these Orders, the Templars and the Hospitallers, had the same structure, being divided into three classes: the Knights, from whose number was chosen a Grand Master, who ruled with autocratic powers, and who had to be of noble birth; the Sergeants, who sprang from less aristocratic families; and finally the Clergy, who acted as chaplains and performed other non-military duties. Vowed to poverty, chastity and obedience, as time had gone by the members of each Order had become a corps of utterly dedicated professional soldiers, who had no rivals in the world of their day; they were an élite body, and they knew it. Their courage became a by-word amongst friends and enemies alike, for they were willing to go anywhere at any time at a moment's notice, and they were invariably found fighting in the most dangerous places. Needless to say, they were invaluable to the Christian rulers of the crusader kingdoms in the Holy Land, who used them rather as Commando troops are used today, and Richard was to prove no exception.

As if the heat and overcrowding were not enough to plague the Christians below the walls of Acre, occasional dust storms, brought by hot winds from the deserts to the south, made life hideous now and again, the fine grit getting into the men's ears, between their teeth, under their eyelids, up their nostrils, and into their food; meanwhile, the swarms of middle eastern flies, which are bad enough under normal conditions, were made even worse by the abundant nourishment to be had from rotting bodies and bits of bodies lying in positions too dangerous for them to be retrieved for burial, and from piles of human and animal faeces. There may have been latrines of a sort, but Ambroise recalls one vivid little incident, which proves that they were not always used, even if they existed at all. 'It happened,' he wrote, 'that a knight was down in a ditch just outside the camp on an affair of his own that no one can do without. As he placed himself so, a Turk in one of the enemy outposts, to which he was paying no attention, separated from his companions and raced his horse forward. It was villainous and discourteous to seek to surprise the knight while so occupied. The Turk was already far from his own people and was approaching the knight with lance to slay him, when our men shouted, "Run, Sir, run!" He had barely time to get up. The Turk came at full gallop, believing that he would be able to turn his horse and wheel back, if he needed to do so, but by God's grace he did not succeed. The knight cast himself to one side, and took up two stones in his hands; but listen to how God takes vengeance! As the Turk checked his horse to turn back on him, the knight saw him clearly, and as he drew near, struck him with one of the stones on the temple. The Turk fell dead, and the knight took his horse, and led it away by the rein.' It is a magnificently graphic little story, bringing the past alive as almost nothing else could, but it is also evidence that sanitary conditions in the crusader camp below the walls of Acre must have been almost unendurable, the stench appalling, and the prevalence of disease inevitable.

Richard had brought with him the materials out of which his wooden fortress, Mategriffon, had been built in Sicily, and by 10 June it had been reassembled close to the walls of Acre, so that from its top English archers could look down into the city and harass its defenders, while all along the line the great siege engines – The Cat, God's Own Sling, The Evil Neighbour, as some of them were called – hurled great rocks at the enemy. The coming of the English king had lifted everyone's spirits; his vigour and enthusiasm were in such marked contrast to the dejection and apathy of the French king, who obviously disliked the whole business of war and did little but sit gloomily in his tent, that the morale of the crusaders rose higher every day. Richard of Devizes records how Richard 'went about among the troops, instructing some, criticizing others, encouraging everyone; he seemed to be everywhere at once and at every man's side.' Within a day or two, however, he was struck down by a strange disease, which the French called *arnaldia*, a fever which resulted in the loss of a man's hair and nails; but although at first he was so ill that there were fears for his life, he continued to direct the war from his bed as best he could. He was furious when the king of France, refusing to take his advice, ordered an attack on the walls on 14 June and again a few days later, and it was not much satisfaction to have his opinion vindicated by the bloody failure of both attacks. During his sickness, he sent a message to Saladin suggesting that they might meet, and sending him the gift of a negro slave; but Saladin replied politely that the time for a meeting was when peace was in prospect, not during the middle of a war. He wished Richard a speedy recovery, and sent him a present of fresh fruit.

Philip succumbed to the same disease, but he was much less seriously ill than Richard, who was confined to his bed for nearly a fortnight; but eventually he recovered, and as he brought his own siege engines into action – long-range catapults, which hurled huge rocks at the defenders of the city from a safe distance – and set his sappers to work on undermining the walls, the fighting took on something of the ferocity of despair on the Arab side. The harbour was closed, and the defenders of the place were receiving no more supplies of either food or ammunition; Richard's sappers were undermining the walls so inexorably that hardly a day passed without a section collapsing into rubble with a great roar in a cloud of choking dust, whereupon men rushed into the breach to fight like devils as the crusaders tried to hack their way into the city over the rubble; drums were immediately beaten by the defenders as a signal to Saladin to launch an attack on the Christian rear, which he invariably did; but there is a limit to human endurance, and the city's defenders had very nearly reached it. The fighting at this time was described from the Arab point of view by the Moslem counterpart of Ambroise, a man named Beha ed-Din ibn Shedad, who had this to say of one of Saladin's counter-attacks. 'The Frankish fanatics, standing in their trenches, presented the appearance of a solid wall. Several of our men penetrated into the camp, only to be met by an unbreakable resistance. An enormous Frank, standing on the parapet, drove our men back single-handed, hurling stones with which his comrades kept him supplied. He had more than fifty wounds from arrows and stones, but nothing stopped him. He held up our men until he was burnt alive by a bottle of naphtha thrown over him by one of our officers.' Apparently, the feat of this indomitable giant of a man was rivalled by that of a formidable woman, who did not stop shooting at the enemy, until she was trampled to death. 'We killed her,' says Beha ed-Din, 'and took her bow to the Sultan.' The picture conjured up of the sheer horror of this kind of hand-to-hand fighting, the cries of the dying and the agony of the wounded, the blood, the flies, and the stench of sweat and death in the heat of the middle eastern sun, is terrifying; and yet in accounts of it from both sides there runs a thread of mutual admiration for the courage of the other. Why else did her killers take that dead woman's bow to Saladin? It was a tribute and a salute to her invincible courage; and much the same respect for the bravery and endurance of the Moslem defenders of Acre was shown by their besiegers. 'What can we say of this race of infidels,' wrote one of their Christian foes, 'who thus defend their city? Never were there braver soldiers than these, the honour of their nation. If only they had been of the true faith, it would not have been possible, anywhere in the world, to find men to surpass them.' But as the siege with its attacks and counter-attacks went from horror to horror, even if nothing could quite destroy this deep seated mutual admiration, a kind of bitter desperation set in on both sides, and each fought the other without giving or expecting mercy. Some newcomers, who had arrived with Robert, earl of Leicester, burnt a Moslem prisoner alive within sight of the wall, and the garrison immediately took their revenge by burning a captive crusader at the stake.

By 12 July, the defenders had reached breaking point. They had been warning Saladin for over a week that, unless he did something to relieve the city, they would surrender with or without his consent, and now they offered to do so 'at the will of the Christian kings'. After conferring together with the leading crusaders, Richard and Philip replied that they would accept the surrender of the city on certain conditions: Acre was to be handed over at once; fifteen hundred of the sultan's Christian prisoners were to be released immediately; a payment of two hundred thousand gold bezants was to be made to the two kings; and the True Cross was to be restored to Christian keeping. In return, the lives of the garrison would be spared, and they would be kept as hostages for the fulfilment of these conditions of surrender. The commanders of the garrison had little choice but to accept these terms of surrender, and they duly did so, sending a swimmer with a message to Saladin to tell him what they had done. When he heard of the conditions, he was appalled, but it was too late to forbid their acceptance; as he looked over towards the stricken city, he could see French and English standards already waving in the breeze over the battered walls of the city. Acre had fallen, and being a man of remarkable integrity and honour, he determined to abide by these conditions made in his name.

The rejoicing of the Christians at their victory was marred by two events, one apparently quite a minor little affair, the other a much more serious matter, though as things turned out the comparatively trivial incident eventually proved to have greater consequences than could have been foreseen at the time. For when Duke Leopold of Austria had his banner planted on the walls of the city alongside those of the king of England and the king of France, some of Richard's men tore it down, and threw it into the ditch. Understandably, Leopold was furious, and his own countrymen probably sympathized with his anger; but no one else did so. There were very few Austrians amongst the crusaders, and Leopold himself, a single German nobleman with a handful of men salvaged from the wreckage of the German Crusade after the death of Frederick Barbarossa, did not count for much in the *realpolitik* of the Christian camp. It was a pity that he had taken offence, but he should not have planted his flag beside those of the two kings in the first place, for by so doing he was in effect claiming an equal share with them in the loot from the conquered city. Neither Richard nor Philip had any intention of allowing him to do that, and so his flag was cast down by Richard's men and probably on the orders of Richard himself in one of his more tactless and high-handed moods, although Philip would certainly have agreed with the order to remove it; but since it was Richard who had given the order, he was blamed for the incident by Leopold, who promptly went home to Austria feeling humiliated and full of hatred for Richard; and this was to have results which were far from trivial a couple of years later.

At the time, however, the event which totally overshadowed the offence to Leopold's *amour propre* was the announcement by the French king that he, too, was going home. Richard begged him to stay, entreating him to sign a declaration of intent to stay for three years or until Saladin had been driven out of the Kingdom of Jerusalem; and the French nobles, some with tears in their eyes at the prospect of seeing their king sail away from his Christian duty and from the dangers and hardships of the war like a common coward, did their appalled best to make him change his mind; but they had no success. Philip was not a coward, but unlike Richard, he had neither the talent nor a liking for war. He much preferred getting his own way by subtler means; diplomacy, patience, and intrigue were his weapons, and sowing dissension in the ranks of his enemies by fair means or foul suited him better than fighting them. If the Latin tag, *divide et impera*, had never been invented, Philip would have had to invent it. He had also been ill, and an insanitary medieval army camp infested with man-eating middle eastern flies in the heat of a Levantine summer was not the best place to ensure a quick return to health. Moreover, he had urgent business awaiting him in France where the count of Flanders had died leaving a large share in his inheritance to be claimed by the king. So in spite of all protests and deaf to all entreaties, on 3 August Philip sailed for France. The best that Richard could do was to extract an oath from him before he left that, when he got back to France, he would not attack any of Richard's lands in his absence. Knowing full well the value of Philip's solemn promises and oaths, Richard sent some of his own men to warn his people at home to be on their guard against the perfidious French king.

But if the relationship between the two kings was one of mutual suspicion, distrust and dislike, before Philip departed, he and Richard together with the other leading crusaders did at least manage to solve the dispute between Guy of Lusignan and Conrad of Montferrat over the kingship of Jerusalem. A compromise was reached: Guy was to remain king during his lifetime, and on his death Conrad was to inherit the crown by virtue of his marriage to Princess Isabella. Both men agreed to abide by this decision, allowing bygones to be bygones and bringing a new measure of unity to the Christian camp, though below the specious surface that unity was far from complete. The only thing now to be done before continuing the war was to wait for Saladin to do what the garrison of Acre had promised in his name, when they had surrendered, and Richard was getting a little tired of waiting. But Saladin had his difficulties; the sum of two hundred thousand gold bezants could not be raised by the flick of his fingers, and he asked for time. Richard agreed to payment by instalments, the first and much the largest to be paid on 20 August, by which time he, Richard, who also had his difficulties, hoped to have persuaded Conrad of Montferrat to return some of the Acre captives, whom he had in effect hijacked and taken off to Tyre as part of his personal booty, but who had been promised to Saladin in return for payment of the agreed indemnity. At the same time there were as always those who made life no easier by arguing that any fool could see that Saladin was dragging his feet in order to gain time; the longer Richard and the crusading army could be pinned down in Acre, the better prepared their enemies would be, when eventually they moved on again, and obviously Saladin had no intention of honouring his promises; or so they argued, and there was some truth in what they said. As the deadline approached, however, these prophets of woe went further, spreading the rumour that Saladin had massacred his Christian prisoners, and that instead of making payment on 20 August, he would launch an attack on the unsuspecting Christians. It is doubtful whether Richard believed this, but when the deadline arrived, and there was still no sign of any message or communication from Saladin, he decided to wait no longer. The Moslem prisoners were marched out of Acre in batches, and methodically butchered – men, women and children – in full view of Saladin's camp.

That this was a brutal and abhorrent action is undeniable, and it would be both absurd and useless to argue otherwise, for no one would be persuaded; as a result, Richard has been roundly condemned as a barbarian for ordering the massacre. However, merely to throw one's hands up in the air in righteous horror and condemnation without first asking a few questions is a little too easy. When Saladin failed to keep his promise to begin to pay Richard what he had agreed to pay on that particular August day, Richard found himself in a military dilemma. He could not wait indefinitely for Saladin to make a move in his direction in case he was indeed preparing to attack, as even the Arab historian Beha ed-Din admits that he was doing. On the other hand, Richard could not march away from Acre leaving several thousand prisoners behind him, for he had neither the men to guard them nor the food to feed them. So what was he to do? Appalling as it may sound, he had them killed as a matter of inescapable, if unfortunate, military necessity: a fact which his own age seems to have understood, for even his enemies did not condemn him for it. But his enemies would have remembered that after the battle of Hattin Saladin had ordered the massacre of all captive Templars and Hospitallers on the rather less inescapable grounds that they were simply too dangerous to be allowed to live. Just as no one had condemned Saladin for this, now no one condemned Richard for doing likewise. Richard's contemporaries were more understanding of the true situation than some recent historians have been.

Two days later, on 22 August, Richard led the crusaders out of Acre. They had been there for just over six weeks, and many were reluctant to leave. It is difficult to imagine why: to envisage what sort of pleasures or delights a little dusty Levantine town, battered by warfare and not much bigger than a modern village, could possibly have offered its conquerors; but apparently, as soon as it had fallen to the besieging Christian host, a miraculous army of prostitutes had descended on the place from nowhere, like phoney manna falling down unannounced from some black market heaven, intent on doing a roaring trade with the crusaders by offering them a welcome escape from their long bondage to involuntary celibacy. With touching simplicity, Ambroise says that 'Acre was full of delights, good wines and girls, who were often very beautiful,' adding with a touch of hastily remembered propriety that 'the men abandoned themselves to wine and women and all manner of follies as a result.' In less simple vein, the contemporary Arab historian, Imad ed-Din, was more explicit. 'Tinted and painted, desirable and appetising, bold and ardent, with nasal voices and fleshy thighs . . . these girls offered their wares for enjoyment, brought their silver anklets up to touch their golden ear-rings, making themselves targets for men's darts, offering themselves to the lance's blows, making javelins rise towards shields . . . They interwove leg with leg, caught lizard after lizard in their holes, guided pens to inkwells, torrents to the valley bottom, swords to scabbards . . . and they maintained that this was an act of piety without equal, especially to those who were far from home and wives.' But Richard was having no purveyors of such pleasures and distractions from duty with the army on its march south, though a few women were allowed out of Acre with the assembled troops as they prepared to leave, most of whom were probably cooks, washerwomen or maids-of-all-work.

It is difficult, however, to be sure of the roles played by the various women who accompanied the Crusade; a few are known to have fought the enemy as ferociously as the men, as did the woman killed below the walls of Acre; but who she was, how old, whether French or English, and why she was there are mysteries. She may have been a local Christian, born and bred in the Holy Land, who had joined Richard's men on their arrival, or she may have joined the Crusade in England or France, perhaps as the wife of one of the men who had taken the Cross, though most men left their wives behind. One of the knights, Conon de Béthune, recorded his sorrow at parting from his lady: 'Alas, my love! What a cruel leave I must take from the best lady who was ever loved and served! May the good God restore me to her, as surely as I leave her with sorrow. What have I said? If the body goes forth to serve the Lord, the heart remains entirely in her power. On to Syria, sighing for her.' But this chivalrous and romantic attitude to women – this *courtoisie* as it was known at the time: a word with a richer and deeper meaning than mere courtesy – was both a comparatively new phenomenon in Richard's day and a rare one. Most women were treated as inferior to men and created by God to be subservient to their husbands, many of whom did not hesitate to beat their wives when they felt like doing so. Since most medieval girls were looked upon as being adult in their mid-teens, marrying at fourteen or fifteen, while the daughters of the aristocracy might be legally wed in infancy, it is not surprising that many women soon became bored with their lot as wives; most of their husbands took it for granted that they might stray from the marriage bed from time to time, and many women saw no reason why they should not do so, though they were more circumspect than their husbands. Not surprisingly, wives left behind by crusaders, sometimes for years, alleviated their loneliness by allowing others into their beds from time to time, and this may be why the first chastity belts were imported into Europe by crusaders returning from Moslem countries where infibulation – or the physical padlocking of the female genitalia – was practised. It may also be why some young husbands decided to take their teenage wives with them on Crusade, rather than leaving them at home.

Many women, especially educated women, became extremely bitter at their subservience to men, though few had the opportunity to record their resentment. Heloise, Abelard's lover, was an exception, not attempting to hide her anger at society's treatment of her as a woman. As medieval society changed and the idea of chivalry spread, women began to take their revenge on men for centuries of dominance; but the chivalrous enthronement by men of women as near-goddesses was more often a matter of romantic theory than mundane practice, and it was at all times offset by a very different attitude to women as portrayed in bawdy stories. There, both their pretensions to romantic perfection and their actual licentiousness were often lampooned. One such story, current in the later Middle Ages, told of a game being played at a certain court, in which the players had to answer questions put to them truthfully or not at all. A knight is asked by the Queen whether he has ever fathered any children, and admits that he has not done so. This surprises no one, 'for he did not have the look of a man who could please his mistress when he held her naked in his arms; his beard was little more than the kind of fuzz that ladies have in certain parts.' The Queen remarks that she does not doubt his word, 'for it is easy to judge from the state of the hay whether the pitchfork is any good.' Not to be outdone, however, the knight then puts a question. 'Lady,' he demands of the Queen, 'is there hair between your legs?' When she replies, 'No, none at all,' he remarks, 'I believe you, for grass does not grow on a well-beaten path.' This ambivalence of medieval society's attitude to women, enthroning them in theory as little short of divine while treating them in practice as lecherous, shameless – and according to Vincent de Beauvais just after Richard's time – 'the confusion of men, insatiable beasts, and houses of ruin' may well have been rooted in the church's ambiguity to sex; for while it proclaimed that the procreation of children was a godly task, it also denounced copulation for the sake of pleasure as sinful.

Once on the march again with the sensual delights of Acre behind them, it is doubtful whether the men of Richard's army were much bothered by the presence of the few women, whatever their various functions may have been, who were allowed to accompany them. The eventual goal of the Crusade was Jerusalem, and from Acre two roads led there. The most direct route was inland through the hill country of Samaria and Judea, but it was a long way, and an army travelling along it would have been wide open to attack from both sides and to ambush in the hills. The other route was by way of the coast road to Jaffa and thence inland, and this was by far the safest. The army would be protected by the sea on its right, and since most of the country through which it would pass would be flat coastal land, the chances of an ambush were small, though it was ideal country for Saladin's light cavalry, his most formidable arm. So Richard chose the coast road, and on Sunday, 25 August, he led the vanguard out of camp with the duke of Burgundy in command of the rear, and the long march south began. If the delights of Acre were difficult to envisage before learning of the miraculous windfall of women with fleshy thighs, it is almost equally difficult to imagine the desperate discomforts and arduous conditions endured by Richard and his men on the march south. The temperature in late August thereabouts is seldom less than 80 degrees Fahrenheit (27 Celsius), and quite often rises to 100 or even 105 (38 to 40 degrees Celsius), and while choking dust storms brought by the *khamsin* wind blowing from the deserts of north Africa are more common earlier in the year, they are not unknown in late summer, when violent thunderstorms and torrential rain also occur from time to time. As protection from the arrows of Saladin's light cavalry, the rank and file of Richard's army wore thick leather jackets, often studded with metal plates, in which they had to march with packs weighing anything from 50 to 80 pounds (23 to 36 kilograms) or more on their backs, and in which presumably they must have been virtually roasted alive except when they were soaked to the skin by a storm; while many of the knights wore armour. Enduring all this, everyone had to be ready at a moment's notice to turn and fight off an attack by the enemy. In fact, they had not moved more than a mile or two from Acre before they were attacked by Saladin's cavalry, who swooped down on the baggage train and tried to drive it into the sea. A certain John Fitzluke galloped forward to tell Richard what was happening, and according to one account 'the king with his meinie [his retinue] galloped back at a great pace; he fell upon the Turks like a thunderbolt – I know not how many he slew – and they fled before him like the Philistines of old from the face of the Maccabees.' Cheered by this initial success, they pushed on to camp near the mouth of the brook Kishon, by whose banks years ago Elijah in godly vein had supervised the slaughter of the prophets of Baal. The next day they moved on to Haifa, where they rested for a couple of days, having travelled ten miles from their starting point at Acre. It was not much, but considering the conditions which they had had to endure in order to reach it, it was triumph enough for the time being. At least, they had made a start.

They resumed their march on Tuesday, 27 August, this time with the Templars and the Hospitallers taking turns to man the rearguard. The main body of marching troops was divided into three closely knit columns; in the centre marched the mounted knights and their horses, protected on the landward side by a screen of marching infantry, archers and pikemen, who kept the enemy's light cavalry at a safe distance with their arrows and the bolts from their crossbows; this was both the most arduous and the most dangerous position, and after a spell of duty there, the men were relieved by other infantrymen who had been marching in comparative safety between the knights and the sea, where the army was protected by the fleet. It was a tightly disciplined formation calling for great steadiness in everyone, and it was made no easier by the heat, which was appalling. Every now and again someone would cry out in prayer, 'Sanctum Sepulchrum *adjuva!'* – 'Help us Holy Sepulchre!' – and every now and again, too, someone would die of a heat stroke and be hastily buried where he had dropped; but invariably someone else took his place, so that Beha ed-Din could not stifle his admiration for his Christian foes. 'One cannot help admiring the wonderful patience displayed by these people,' he wrote. 'I saw some Frankish foot soldiers with from one to ten arrows sticking into them, and still advancing at their usual pace without leaving the ranks.' The arrows would have been sticking in the soldiers' thick leather coats, under which many of them – though not all – wore singlets of chain mail, in which the arrow points became embedded without seriously wounding the men inside; but, even so, many of them must have been suffering from scratches and bruises and minor wounds, which would have been enough to cause them acute discomfort, while every day a few were seriously wounded and others killed by arrows which penetrated their owners' defensive clothing. Yet doggedly, day after day, this great clumsy column of hot, dusty, suffering, grumbling but determined men crawled down the ruins of the old Roman road leading from Syria to Egypt like some huge, ponderous, thick-skinned brontosaurus or other prehistoric reptile left over from the past, with arrows bouncing off its armoured hide, as Saladin's horsemen buzzed round it like a cloud of gnats or mosquitoes without managing to provoke it into rash retaliation. The march south by Richard and his army was proof, if proof were needed, that medieval warfare was not all a matter of gallant knights making romantic charges, but a highly professional business of sound tactics, discipline, endurance and courage; and if he had not known it before, Saladin certainly discovered at this point that Richard was a master of such warfare. He had already defeated him below the walls of Acre, and now he had shown him that the traditional Moslem tactics of using the fast-moving Turkish cavalry to provoke the Christian enemy into an unwise response would not work either, and Saladin called off their attacks. Instead, he drew his whole army up across Richard's line of march ahead of him at Arsuf, and waited there to give him battle.

On Saturday, 1 September, the Christians emerged from the forest of Arsuf on to the open plain to find themselves threatened by an apparently vast army drawn up in battle array on their left flank, challenging their line of advance. The host menacing their path was estimated to outnumber Richard's men by three to one; it was obvious that Saladin, like the good general that he was, had decided to make his challenge on ground of his own choosing and at a time of his own choosing too, having first gathered the maximum number of his own forces together, so that he should be at his strongest when the decisive moment should come. Under a threat such as this, Richard was at his best; he had no intention of allowing Saladin to divert him from his chosen path or purpose, and in such moments of stress, where other men might have shown some evidence of nerves, Richard became, if anything, cooler, calmer and more relaxed than at any other time. He divided the army into five divisions; the vanguard consisted of the Templars; next came the Bretons and the men of Anjou, then the Poitevins under the command of King Guy, followed by the Normans and the English with the Standard; and last of all in the rear, the position of greatest danger, were the Hospitallers. Each of these divisions was divided into two battalions, horse and foot, which marched parallel to each other as on previous days, while Richard and the duke of Burgundy and a few other picked French and English knights rode up and down the line, watching the enemy for any movement and keeping their own men in tight formation. As usual, the task of the infantry was to resist all enemy attacks, while the knights were under strict orders not to break ranks and charge until two trumpets in the rear, two in the centre, and two in the van should simultaneously sound the moment to do so.

Saladin waited until the whole of Richard's army was well clear of the forest, his own men 'as thick as drops of rain' on the hills inland, motionless, as they watched the Christian host move steadily forward in a great cloud of whitish dust, the armour of the knights glinting in the sun and only the occasional neighing of a horse breaking the silence of the morning. But the silence was not destined to last very long. At about nine o'clock, Saladin made his move, sending wave upon wave of Turkish cavalry down from the hills to the terrifying din of drums and tabors and trumpets and cries of 'Allah akhbar!' and the thunder of horses' hoofs; they were closely followed by swarms of dark-skinned Arab pikemen and black-faced Nubian archers yelling and screaming and looking so like demons from hell as painted on the walls of many of the crusaders' churches at home that they had no doubt that they were being attacked by the shock troops of Satan himself and the powers of darkness; but the Christian line held, and their march went on. The attack was hottest in the rear, where the Hospitallers were 'packed together so closely that you could not have thrown an apple at them without hitting either man or horse,' but although they were strained nearly to breaking point, their line held, and attack after attack was beaten off. As casualties mounted on both sides, the fighting took on a desperation which was made no less desperate as the sun reached its zenith at midday, and the knights in their armour sweltered in the heat; again and again they sent messages to Richard, begging him to sound the charge, but even when the Grand Master of the Hospitallers rode forward in person to entreat him to allow them to launch their long-delayed attack, he replied, 'Be patient, good Master.' He was determined not to risk a charge until he judged the moment to be right, and despite the terrible strain of waiting and waiting under constant provocation and attack, while men and horses were being killed and wounded, the march went on, ranks were not broken, and discipline was maintained. It was a remarkable achievement due as much to Richard's extraordinary talent as a soldier, his *sangfroid* and military judgement, as to the discipline and powers of endurance of the ordinary rank and file crusader, who is so often written off as a mere latter-day barbarian, and who could sometimes behave like one. But endurance can endure just so long and no longer, and there came a moment in the early afternoon, when a Norman knight of the Hospital named Baldwin le Caron reached breaking point, and crying 'Saint George!' he wheeled his horse, and drove it furiously at the enemy. As though a shot had been fired, all along the Christian line the knights broke ranks with a great shout, and charged the enemy. It could have been a disaster, but Richard reacted with such speed, ordering the trumpets to sound the charge and spurring his own horse 'quicker than a quarrel from a cross bow' that the Turks never seem to have realized that the onslaught upon them was not deliberately planned for that moment.

The brunt of the Christian attack fell on the men who had been harrying the rear of the crusaders' column, and as Richard and the knights of Anjou, Brittany and Poitou thundered down to join the Hospitallers, the combined weight of virtually the whole chivalry of France completely shattered Saladin's light cavalry, who were routed and cut to pieces as they were driven down on to the shore. Saladin counter-attacked, sending in his reserves against the centre of the Christian line, but Richard had foreseen just such a move; he had already called off the pursuit in the rear, and now at the head of his English and Norman knights he led a charge against the enemy centre and left wing, and once again the sheer weight of his attack carried everything before it. The enemy's rout was so complete that Beha ed-Din, escaping from the total confusion at the centre, tried to rejoin first the left wing and then the right, but found each division in a greater panic than the one he had quitted; and when he reached Saladin's reserve, he found only seventeen men remaining to guard the Standard, all the rest having been sent by the sultan to support their comrades, and having shared their fate. But Richard was not tempted to jeopardize his victory by allowing his men to chase the enemy too far, and when they reached the hills, he called off the pursuit. His triumph was complete, but it was not final or decisive; Saladin had lost a large number of men and suffered a tremendous blow to his prestige, but he had not been rendered incapable of re-forming and attacking his enemies once again. 'We were all wounded,' wrote Beha ed-Din without trying to minimize the seriousness of their defeat, 'either in our bodies or in our hearts.' But they resumed their harrying tactics the next day, as the Christians marched on down the coast.

Three days later, Richard reached Jaffa. Saladin had destroyed the city walls and done so much damage to the place that the crusaders pitched their tents in an olive grove outside the town, but this did not disturb them very much; the surrounding countryside consisting of cornfields, orchards, palm groves and vineyards could not have been a pleasanter place in which to rest for a few days after the dangers and exertions of their march from Acre, and the army settled down to refresh itself. Jaffa, too, is the nearest port to Jerusalem and therefore the obvious starting point for a drive on that city, but Richard hesitated. His instinct was to carry on marching south to Ascalon, for whoever held Ascalon controlled the all-important military road to Egypt, and Richard felt that the safety of his base on the coast and his sea-borne supply route depended on capturing that city before moving on Jerusalem. Although he had no way of knowing it, in fact Saladin agreed with him so whole-heartedly that he had given orders that Ascalon should be demolished, stone by stone and brick by brick, as speedily and as secretly as possible in order to deny the place to his enemies. The wretched inhabitants, seeing their city demolished and their homes reduced to heaps of rubble, had no alternative but to seek somewhere else to live, and after a few days one or two desolate little families wandered into Jaffa in search of new homes. When Richard and the other crusaders heard their tale, at first they could not believe that Saladin would destroy one of his strategically most important fortresses and ports. King Guy's brother, Geoffrey of Lusignan, was sent by sea to discover what was happening, and in due course he returned and confirmed the unwelcome fact that Ascalon was a heap of ruins. An army council was held to decide on the crusaders' next move, and although Richard still wanted to press on and refortify Ascalon, the majority were in favour of resting for a while at Jaffa, making the city their main base and eventually launching a drive on Jerusalem from there. Bowing reluctantly to the majority, Richard agreed.

X

___

The discipline of the crusaders on their march south under the heat of the August sun, while being constantly harassed by their enemies, had been remarkable, but after the capture of Jaffa they settled down to enjoy themselves. During September and October they began in a desultory way to rebuild the town and repair its fortifications, but they did not allow this work to deprive them of the delights of the surrounding countryside; at first, these were mainly pastoral, but as at Acre it was not long before a small army of prostitutes descended on the town as if from nowhere, and did a roaring trade. Indeed, after their clients had drunk enough of the local wine, the description of their trade as 'roaring' was no exaggeration, and discipline became a thing of the past. Some men even returned to Acre in order to enjoy its greater variety of lascivious pleasures, and Richard had to send King Guy to recall them to their military duties: a task which he signally failed to accomplish, for none of the men took the smallest notice of him. It took a visit from Richard himself to persuade them to return to Jaffa.

Meanwhile, from time to time the king and some of the leading French and English nobles also enjoyed themselves, combining business with pleasure by spying out the countryside for enemy activity while at the same time flying their falcons at hares and rock partridges. It was on such an occasion in mid-October, when Richard was out hunting with a small escort of friends, that he barely escaped capture. They had stopped for a rest at midday and had fallen asleep when they were surprised by a small party of Turkish horsemen. Awaking just in time, Richard leapt on his horse, shouting to his companions to wake up, and between them they drove the Turks off; but as they chased them, they were led into an ambush, and Richard was saved from capture only by the devotion and quick-wittedness of one of his knights, William des Préaux, who knew a little Arabic, and shouted out that he was the king, whereupon he was surrounded and captured as Richard and most of the others galloped away. Happily, about a year later William des Préaux was released by Saladin in return for ten Moslem prisoners as part of the final settlement with Richard. In the meanwhile, however, four of Richard's party were killed in their brief encounter, which could so easily have resulted in his own capture, and when the story of his escape became known, people were horrified that he should take such risks; but however much they begged him to take greater care of himself, Richard just laughed in an amiable way. 'In every conflict,' wrote Ambroise, 'he delighted in being the first to attack and the last to return.'

Below the surface, however, he was worried; for although he had inflicted two major defeats on Saladin, greatly damaging his military reputation while raising his own almost to the point of legend, since his victory at Arsuf what semblance of unity there may have once been in the crusaders' ranks had largely disappeared. The French under the duke of Burgundy were profoundly jealous of him, asking themselves why they should risk their lives to the greater glory of the king of England while little or none of that glory reflected on France; the tension between the Pisans and the Genoese, traditional enemies as they were, had nearly reached breaking point; and Conrad of Montferrat had retreated to Tyre, where he refused to take any further part in the Crusade. Indeed, he had opened secret negotiations with Saladin, offering to make peace with him at the expense of the other crusaders, although Richard did not yet know this. His overall objective remained the recapture of the city of Jerusalem, but despite his victories it seemed no nearer, and the difficulties in the way of attaining it were made no less by the onset of winter.

It was in this frame of mind that Richard decided to try to achieve his objective by treaty, if that proved to be at all possible, rather than by continuing the war. He wrote to Saladin, pointing out that 'the Moslems and the Franks are reduced to the last extremity, their towns destroyed, and the resources on both sides in men and goods reduced to nothing. Surely,' he wrote, 'it is time to stop fighting each other. The three things dividing us are Jerusalem, the True Cross, and the land which comprises the kingdom of Jerusalem. Jerusalem for us is a holy city, which we could not give up even if there was only one of us alive. We must also have our old kingdom of Jerusalem back. Meanwhile, the Cross, which to you is a mere bit of wood of no value, is sacred to us. If you will return it to us, we shall have peace, and both of us can rest again.' Saladin replied that Jerusalem was just as important to Moslems as the place from which the Prophet had ascended into heaven, and indeed more important to them than to Christians, for it was also the gathering place of the faithful on the last day. As to what Richard called the kingdom of Jerusalem, the land had belonged to the Moslem people long before the first crusaders had stolen it from them, and it could not be returned. Finally, as regarding the Cross, its possession was valuable as a bargaining counter, and he would not realease it without a *quid pro quo* in return.

That might have been the end of the matter, but Richard was not disheartened, and when he asked for an interview with Saladin to talk things over, arrangements were made for him to meet the sultan's brother, al-Adil Saif ed-Din, whom the crusaders called Safadin, an experienced, subtle and accomplished diplomat, destined to become sultan after his brother's death. To a modern eye, the negotiations which followed were conducted with absurdly exaggerated courtesy in a manner more suited to comic opera than to what the Germans call *realpolitik*. Richard prepared for his meeting with al-Adil by sending him a superb horse as an opening gambit in the diplomatic game, and when the two men met, they got on extremely well. Richard liked and admired al-Adil, and it seems that this feeling of admiration was mutual. After the preliminary courtesies had been exchanged, Richard put forward some highly original and startling proposals. If Saladin would make his brother Safadin lord of Palestine, he, Richard, would give his sister Joan to al-Adil as his bride, endowing her with the coastal towns which he had recently conquered as her dowry; after their honeymoon, the lucky couple could settle in Jerusalem, and under their joint rule Christians could be given free and safe access to the city and its holy places. When al-Adil told Saladin what Richard had proposed, the sultan burst out laughing; plainly the whole thing was a joke, and he sent his brother back with instructions to call Richard's bluff by accepting his offer unconditionally. When he did so, Richard told him apologetically that his sister had been enraged by the whole idea; she would never agree to marriage with an infidel, and so perhaps the best thing would be for al-Adil to become a Christian. Confirmed in his view that the whole thing had been a huge diplomatic jest, al-Adil politely refused the honour, but invited Richard to a banquet at Lydda on 8 November, where the two men exchanged a number of splendid gifts and enjoyed a sumptuous dinner together.

The question as to whether Richard was joking or in earnest when he offered his sister's hand to al-Adil may never be answered for certain; some historians have concluded that he was entirely serious in doing so, but it is difficult to understand how they have come to this conclusion. Whatever else he may have been, Richard was not politically naïve; he had been raised from childhood at the centre of twelfth-century power politics, and he knew their brutal realities better than anyone. There would have been an immediate outcry from all his subjects, nobles and commoners alike and above all by churchmen, at the idea of a Christian princess becoming one flesh with that most loathsome thing, an infidel son of perdition, and he must have known that to be so. Moreover, he was devoted to his sister Joan, and even if, in a moment of political aberration, he had forgotten to take into account the predictable fury of his subjects at the idea of her marriage to al-Adil, he could not possibly have failed to foresee her own reaction. It therefore seems much more likely that, when he made his wholly impracticable proposal, Saladin was right: he was not doing so with serious intent. But why should he have made the suggestion at all if he was not serious about it? The answer could be that he was playing for time, and was taken aback when Saladin accepted the idea. This involved him in the absurdity of coming back to the negotiating table and suggesting that al-Adil should embrace the Christian faith, against which he had been fighting all his life. It was patently ridiculous, but it gained more time, and meanwhile it gave him the chance to get to know his principal enemies a little better. A rumour had been circulating in the Christian camp that Saladin and his brother al-Adil were at odds with each other in some respects, and Richard may have been trying to widen the split between them by offering to help al-Adil become king of Jerusalem; but this seems a little improbable. It is more likely that Saladin was also playing for time in the hope of deepening the divisions in the Christian ranks as he continued his secret talks with Conrad of Montferrat. Whatever the truth may be, it was a bizarre situation.

By the end of October, however, Richard could delay no longer. He and his much reduced army set out on their march to Jerusalem. Progress was desperately slow, for before he dared penetrate too deeply inland, the various castles along his route, destroyed by Saladin precisely in order to deny them to the crusaders, had to be taken and repaired; and this took time. Saladin did little more than send out troops of light cavalry to attack any foraging parties which they could surprise, leaving the main body of crusaders alone. On one such occasion, a party out in search of grass for the horses and fodder for the mules with only a small escort of Templars was suddenly surrounded by a much larger body of Turkish horsemen than anyone had seen for a long time; the situation of the crusaders looked so perilous that the Templars dismounted, and prepared to sell their lives as dearly as possible. Somehow, however, a messenger succeeded in summoning help, and Richard accompanied by the earl of Leicester, the count of St Pol and a number of others hurried to the scene, but on arrival it was obvious that they were so far outnumbered by the Turks that his companions warned Richard not to endanger his life in a futile attempt to rescue the beleaguered Templars and foragers; it was better that they should die than that the whole Crusade should be put at risk by the death of the king. It is easy enough in the comfort of an armchair to raise a cynical eyebrow when reading slightly embarrassing tales of other men's heroics; indeed, it was this kind of healthy scepticism that made many people during the last world war describe some bloody military disaster in which they had been involved as 'a bit of a tea party', while categorizing a thoroughly boring social occasion as 'a bloody disaster'; but it would be a pity if this admirable tendency to dismiss bravado for what it is were to allow people to confuse moments of genuine heroism with those of empty vainglory. Richard was neither boasting nor indulging in bogus heroics when he replied to those who advised him to save himself for the greater good of the Christian cause, 'I sent those men here. If they die without me, I do not wish to be called king any longer.' Whereupon he spurred his horse and led an attack on the Turks, falling on them 'like a thunderbolt', to use Ambroise's often repeated simile, and after a short but bloody little encounter routing them and emerging once again unscathed. It was an incident demonstrating once again the quality in Richard which won him the total devotion of his own men and the awestruck admiration of his enemies, in whom the mere mention of his name struck such terror that after his death for many years distraught Arab and Turkish mothers, driven mad by the antics of their naughty children, would warn them that, if they did not behave themselves, *Malek Rik* would come and get them (*malek* being the Arabic for 'king').

The progress of the army was tediously slow. By the last week of November they had gone no farther than Ramleh, less than half way to Jerusalem, and there they stayed for six weeks, while the rain poured down almost without ceasing. The tents in which the men lived became sodden, the camp sites seas of mud, and no one could remember what it had once been like to feel warm and dry; their clothes were permanently wet, their leather jackets covered in mildew, their armour red with rust. Water seeped into their sacks of flour, bacon rotted in the barrel, and the country-side fell so far short of its reputation as a 'land flowing with milk and honey' that foraging parties had to travel farther and farther afield to find fodder for the animals, let alone food for the men. But morale remained astonishingly high, for everyone was convinced that Jerusalem would be theirs in a matter of weeks, if not days, and the Holy Sepulchre would once again be in Christian hands: everyone, that is to say, with the exception of some of the more senior and experienced officers, who took a less sanguine view of the situation as the army moved up to Beit Nuba less than twelve miles from the city. These men argued that, although the army was now within striking distance of its objective, and although Saladin was known to have sent many of his men home for the winter, the walls of Jerusalem were still manned, and it would not easily be captured. Even if it were to fall after a short siege, Richard's chances of holding it against a counter-attack by Saladin were minimal; more than half the crusaders, their pilgrimage to the holy places now achieved, would go home, and the army's strength would be so disastrously depleted that it would be impossible to defend the place, let alone maintain contact with their bases on the coast, whence alone they could hope for supplies and reinforcements. The Hospitallers and the Templars would stay, and on them the task of defending any territorial gains made during the Crusade would fall, and they were insistent that the only possible course open to Richard now was to retreat to the coast. Once there, he should fortify Ascalon as strongly as possible, thus turning the tables on Saladin by breaking his lines of communication with Egypt, whence came the bulk of his own reinforcements and supplies. Later, when more recruits from Europe had arrived, it should be possible to take Jerusalem and hold it.

Richard was too good a soldier to be in any doubt that they were right. The duke of Burgundy agreed, and on 10 January 1192, the orders were given to retire. The men were shattered. From a peak of wild enthusiasm with Jerusalem almost in view and by anticipation already theirs, they were cast down into the very depths of depression and defeat. They had suffered hardship, deprivation, danger and the death of some of their comrades only now to be told that it had all been in vain. The weather was even colder and wetter than before Christmas, and as they slithered back to the coast on roads turned into seas of mud by the rain and the passage of many feet, many of the men blamed Richard for their misery: Richard who had led them from victory to victory, but who was now branded as the man who had cheated them of the one victory that mattered, the conquest of Jerusalem, for which they had taken their vows, left their families, and risked their lives. Richard himself was said at the time to be 'worn out with grief and toil such as no tongue nor pen can describe'. On arrival at Ascalon, the fact that it was in almost total ruins did nothing to raise the men's spirits. Many of the French deserted to Jaffa and Acre, while others joined Conrad of Montferrat in Tyre; even the duke of Burgundy left the entire task of refortifying Ascalon to Richard. But if his own men were as dispirited as the rest, at least they remained loyal to him, and during the next four months they transformed Ascalon from a heap of ruins into the strongest fortress on the coast of the Holy Land. It cut the road to Egypt, and it was not long before some very profitable raids were made on caravans, as they tried to by-pass the city with supplies for Saladin.

Disappointment and bitterness over the retreat from Jerusalem widened the divisions in the Christian ranks to such a dangerous extent that the Genoese and the French began fighting the Pisans in Acre for control of the city; Conrad of Montferrat, a ruthless and enthusiastic fisherman in troubled waters, soon joined his fellow countrymen, but the men of Pisa refused to be intimidated, fighting back with ferocity and success, while sending an urgent plea for help to the king. Richard hurried to the scene, and news of his coming was enough to persuade the duke of Burgundy and Conrad to retreat in a hurry to Tyre. On arrival, Richard was able to pacify the Pisans and the Genoese, even if only on a temporary basis, before going in search of Conrad. The two men met at Casal Imbert half way between Tyre and Acre, but once again Conrad flatly refused to take any part in the Crusade, and when Richard berated him for his recent part in the fighting in Acre, he offered no apology, and they parted in anger. These internecine quarrels were so obviously fatal to any hope of Christian success in the fight against Saladin that despite his anger Richard realized that something would have to be done to reconcile the two rival factions at the root of all the trouble, headed respectively by Guy of Lusignan and Conrad of Montferrat. Hitherto, he had supported Guy, but Conrad had refused to give up his claim to the throne, and he was supported by the French. An end to this ruinous feud was made even more urgently necessary by some bad news from home, brought by the prior of Hereford with a message from William Longchamp, bishop of Ely and chancellor of England, who warned Richard that his brother John was creating a good deal of trouble in England, and the king of France, blithely ignoring his oath to Richard, was preparing to invade Normandy. If Richard was forced by these events to go home without first bringing some sort of peace to the warring Christian factions in Outremer, all the military gains of the last few months would be put in jeopardy, and the faith and dedication of the crusaders would turn out to have been, in Shakespeare's words, no more than 'an expense of spirit in a waste of shame'. With all this in mind, he summoned the leading crusaders to a conference at Ascalon on 16 April, and called on them to decide who should be king of Jerusalem, Guy or Conrad.

Without a dissentient voice, they voted for Conrad, and their reasons for doing so are not difficult to understand; Guy was a nice enough man, but when compared with the marquis of Montferrat he was unimpressive and ineffective. He was still remembered as the man who had lost the battle of Hattin, and thus as the man who had allowed both the kingdom and the city of Jerusalem to fall into the hands of infidels. The picture in everyone's mind of Conrad, however, was that of the man who had arrived in the nick of time to cheat the victor of Hattin of the full fruits of his victory by rallying the few remaining able-bodied Christians to the defence of Tyre, and against all odds doing so successfully. Moreover, though Guy might call himself king, since Richard's arrival he had exercised no real authority, and when Richard eventually left, it seemed unlikely that anyone would take much notice of him. Plainly, Richard must have known all this, and equally plainly he must have been prepared to see Conrad become king in Guy's place, or he would never have called a conference to discuss the matter of a possible change; but however obvious this may be, some historians have asserted that Richard was appalled by the unanimous decision of the conference, bowing to it only with the greatest dismay. This cannot possibly be true; on the contrary, Richard had almost certainly foreseen the outcome of the vote, and in the event he accepted it without argument, though no doubt he did so with a few tactful words of thanks to Guy for all that he had done in the past and of sympathy for him in his present disappointment. Fortunately, he was able to offer him handsome compensation for the loss of Jerusalem. He had sold Cyprus to the Templars for a hundred thousand bezants, of which he had received no more than forty thousand, and the knights were having difficulty in raising the rest of the money; as a result, they were happy enough to cut their losses by selling the island to Guy for forty thousand, and Richard did not press him for the remaining sixty thousand, which in fact was never paid. Thus Guy handed the throne of Jerusalem over to Conrad and became king of Cyprus instead; and although he could not have known it, his descendants were to rule the island for three hundred years until the year 1489, whereas Conrad was to have no such good fortune. For Guy the bargain could scarcely have been a better one, while from Richard's point of view, although he did not like Conrad, it must have been almost equally welcome politically, putting an end at last to the feud which had bedevilled the Christian cause ever since he had landed in Outremer.

On 20 April 1192, Henry of Champagne was despatched to tell Conrad that he had been elected king in Guy's place. When he heard the news, he fell on his knees asking God not to grant him the kingship if he were unworthy of it. Henry raised him to his feet, and discussed arrangements for the coronation within the next few days; there should be no delay, now that the matter was at last settled. But a week later, on Tuesday, 28 April, Conrad was kept waiting for his dinner by his wife, the Princess Isabella, who was lying longer than usual in her bath. She had been born and brought up in Outremer, where those living in the crusader kingdoms had long ago adopted many of the habits of their Arab and Turkish neighbours. Ever since Roman days, there had been public baths in most cities. They were similar to the Turkish baths of today, and at first the crusaders had shunned them, for in Europe washing was despised as effeminate and unmanly. But as the years had passed, the climate of the Middle East had had its effect, and bathing had become increasingly popular. On entering one of the public baths, the bather was expected to undress and don a towel, but according to a certain Prince Usamah, a member of an independent dynasty of Munqidhite Arabs, who travelled widely through Outremer and made many Frankish friends in the process, some of them did not bother to do so, greatly shocking the Arabs by bathing naked. (In passing, it is interesting to discover that history does indeed repeat itself; for recently, when a small party of English and American tourists were in the city of

Kayseri in Asiatic Turkey – the ancient city of Caesarea Mazaca – two young Americans profoundly shocked the Turks by appearing naked in the local Turkish bath.) To return to Princess Isabella in her bath, however, in all probability Conrad, a recent arrival from Europe, thought little or nothing of his wife's indulgence in the alien and slightly depraved habit of bathing, but rather than waiting for her to emerge from her ablutions, he decided to go and dine with the bishop of Beauvais, an old friend and near neighbour; but the bishop had already dined, and although he pressed Conrad to stay while the servants prepared a meal for him, Conrad would not hear of it. He did not want to be a nuisance, and he was perfectly happy to walk home again, where, by this time, his wife would have finished bathing. On the way back, however, as he turned the corner, he was accosted by two men dressed as monks, and while one of them held his attention, the other stabbed him in the chest. He was carried home a dying man. One of his murderers was killed on the spot, and the other arrested. They were Assassins, members of a sect dedicated to murder as a political weapon, the name 'Assassin' being derived from the Arabic *hashish*, which their agents were believed to take before carrying out their frenzied crimes. The head of the sect was a certain Sheikh Rashid ed-Din Sinan, who was known as the Old Man of the Mountains, and whose name spread terror wherever and whenever it was mentioned. The surviving Assassin confessed that he had been ordered by Sinan to murder Conrad, who had offended him in the past by attacking a merchant ship loaded with a cargo destined for the Assassins and already paid for by them: a fact which had not deterred Conrad from stealing it. But despite this confession, it was not long before some people were claiming that Richard had secretly ordered the murder, while others attributed the crime to Saladin. Such malicious rumours were probably inevitable given the tensions and rivalries of the time, but as Runciman said in his *History of the Crusades*, 'Saladin's connivance is not to be credited; while Richard, much as he disliked Conrad, never made use of such a weapon.'

The men of the twelfth century were nothing if they were not practical, and their ability to act decisively in a crisis has seldom been surpassed. For obvious political reasons, it was imperative that Conrad's widow, the Princess Isabella, as heiress of the kingdom of Jerusalem should choose another husband as soon as possible. In spite of the fact that she had been married twice, she was still only twenty-one years of age, and by all accounts ravishingly beautiful, so that it was not difficult to find a suitable candidate for her hand in marriage; but the speed with which she was married to Henry of Troyes, the count of Champagne, nephew of both the king of England and the king of France, takes the breath away. In less than a week after the death of Conrad, she and Henry were man and wife. Although theirs was very obviously a marriage of political convenience, it turned out to be a very happy one; Henry fell passionately in love with his wife, and Isabella found him a most welcome change from Conrad, who had been both middle-aged and rather forbidding as a husband. As when she had married Conrad, however, there were those who had raised the question of the validity of her marriage before it was solemnized; but once again the exigencies of the situation were such that it had been decided that they should marry first and argue about the validity afterwards, and this they had done. Henry never took the title of king of Jerusalem, perhaps in part because of lingering doubts about the whole question of the validity of his union with Isabella, but after Richard's return home he became the effective ruler of the kingdom until five years later, when he stepped backwards out of an upper story window by mistake and fell to his death. Isabella, still under thirty years of age, then married one of Guy of Lusignan's brothers, Amalric, as her fourth husband, but he had little better luck than his predecessors, dying in 1205 after eating too much fish; they were white mullet. There cannot have been very many women, royal or otherwise, even in the twelfth century, who lost four husbands before they themselves had reached the age of thirty-five.

With the feud over the kingship of Jerusalem settled at last, a new spirit of unity and cooperation began to replace the bitterness of the past, just as the bitter weather of winter also began to give way to the warmth and miracle of a Judean spring. As the sun was reborn, the marble hills of Judea clothed themselves with wild anemones and the lilies of the field of biblical fame in such profusion as to put Solomon in all his glory to shame all over again, while on the coastal plain around the villages, where, as in the days of Christ, the peasants tilled the soil, their gardens and their orchards decked themselves with blossom as if specifically to celebrate the glory of Easter. Practical as always, Richard decided to take advantage of this welcome new spirit to attack the coastal fortress of Darum twenty miles south of Ascalon, and thus to endanger Saladin's lifeline to Egypt even more seriously than was already the case. Henry of Champagne and the duke Hugh of Burgundy agreed to play their part in the attack, promising to join Richard as soon as they had martialled their men; but while Richard was duly grateful, he decided not to wait until they were ready, and before they could reach him, he delivered a lightning attack on the place and captured it. It was not a great victory, but it was a small triumph, which helped to raise everyone's spirits even higher than they had already been raised by the coming of spring and the end of the old feuds: everyone's, that is to say, except Richard's. For a few days later, yet another messenger arrived from England with an even more urgent summons to him to come home; and it now appeared that his brother John and the French king were in full conspiracy together against him although no one could be sure of their plans. This news put Richard into a dilemma, for how could he desert the Crusade at this moment when it was about to decide whether to attack Jerusalem again? And yet how could he sit back and ignore the warnings coming from England? He summoned an army council, and while not mentioning that he suspected treachery on the part of the king of France, he described his problem in outline. The leading crusaders listened sympathetic- ally, but did not feel able to advise him what to do; however, they told him that whether he stayed or went home, they would go ahead and attack Jerusalem.

When their decision was published, the men went mad with delight, dancing round camp fires all night and singing them- selves hoarse, while Richard retired to his tent, depressed and still undecided as to what he should do. It is said that his problem was solved a few days later, when he noticed a priest, one of the chaplains to the army, in tears outside his tent. He asked him in, and enquired what was the matter, and the man replied that he, Richard, was the matter. How could he possibly think of deserting God's cause, the man asked him, after all that God had done for him in the past, giving him victory after victory, bringing him unscathed out of battle after battle, escapade after escapade, and now at last bringing him to the brink of the finest victory of them all: the recapture of the holy city of Jerusalem from the hands of unbelievers? Apparently, Richard listened in silence; the next day he announced that he would stay until the following Easter and lead the Crusade to Jerusalem. it was an immensely popular decision.

On 6 June, Richard led the army out of Ascalon in perfect weather, taking the same road as that over which they had marched in such misery a few months earlier. Apart from the occasional skirmish with foraging parties, there was no sign of the enemy; the only casualties were due to snakebite, from which two men died, and five days after leaving the coast the army reached Beit Nuba, the point from which they had turned back the previous winter. Once again, they halted to await Henry of Champagne with some reinforcements. To have advanced farther before their arrival, venturing into the barren hills around Jerusalem where water was known to be short, would have been foolish. The city was strongly garrisoned; Saladin was there in person; and the Christians needed to be at full strength before attempting to lay siege to it. Meanwhile, however, scouts were sent out to reconnoitre the country and gather information about any movements by the enemy, and it was not long before one of them returned with a report that the Turks were busy laying an ambush near a village a few miles from the city. Rising at dawn the next day, Richard and a strong party of knights rode out to attack them, and after a careful approach they took them completely by surprise. Some of them were killed, and the rest fled in the direction of Jerusalem, hotly pursued by Richard and his companions, who slew a few more of the fugitives before relinquishing the chase, their horses exhausted, as they reached the top of a great limestone ridge overlooking the holy city. It was the hill which had been named Montjoie by the men of the first Crusade, who had had their first glimpse of Jerusalem from its summit almost exactly a century previously; and there was the city shining in the sun across a waste of little marble hills dotted with olive trees and cypresses, and crowned by the great mosque known as the Dome of the Rock. It was to be Richard's first and last sight of the city which he had come so far to see: the city of David, of Solomon's Temple, of the death and resurrection of the Son of God: the citadel of Christian faith and hope, and Richard is said to have wept when he set eyes on it.

It was to be his only sight of the city because, when he and the army council sat down to assess the military situation, they came to the conclusion that nothing had changed since the winter except the weather. Jerusalem was extremely strong, even stronger than before; the wells around the city had been polluted or poisoned on Saladin's orders, and water was almost non-existent; their lines of communication with the coast were highly vulnerable, and the risks in making an attempt on the city were too great to be worth taking. What Richard and his lieutenants did not know was that Saladin's generals were feeling almost equally pessimistic about their chances of resisting a Christian assault. In Saladin's presence, the emirs tried to put a brave face on their weaknesses, but in reality they were ready to surrender the city and go home, so frightened were they of *Malek Rik* and his invincible army of Christian devils from hell, who had beaten them on every occasion that the two sides had met in battle since Richard's arrival. According to Beha ed-Din, Saladin, too, was depressed, unable to sleep, and perplexed as to what he should do. Should he risk the capture or even the annihilation of his army by defending Jerusalem to the last man? Or should he risk humiliation by abandoning it to the enemy with all the political consequences which would flow from such a course of action? He did not know the answer, and while Richard and his army stayed at Beit Nuba without attacking the city, Saladin continued to struggle with the problem without coming to any conclusion, while Richard, a few miles away, was in a similar state of painful indecision.

But fortunately for the crusaders the state of indecision in their camp was enlivened by a few enjoyable diversions, while Saladin's men within the walls of Jerusalem had nothing to distract them from worrying about the coming attack. An ancient, saintly and shaggy old man with a huge beard and long matted grey hair appeared in the camp one morning to say that he knew where a portion of the True Cross could be found. He was the abbot of a nearby monastery dedicated to Elijah, and he had buried it himself in order to keep it safe from pollution by the hands of unbelievers, but if Richard would like to have it, he would give it to him. Its arrival in the camp aroused great enthusiasm amongst the men, who were convinced that with such a holy thing in their possession nothing could now prevent them from taking the city when at last they were allowed by their commanders to attack it; but Richard and their leaders were less certain of the strictly military advantages conferred on them by the relic, however great its religious value might be; and they still held back.

It was at this point that a different diversion helped to relieve the men's frustration at yet another delay. On 20 June, some scouts reached the camp with news of the approach of an enormous caravan bringing supplies from Egypt to Saladin; it was winding its slow northward way through the difficult desert country south of Hebron, where the stony hills of Judea run down to the Dead Sea in a barren desolation of rock and dust. According to Beha ed-Din, who later heard the story from some survivors of the caravan, 'When this was reported by some Arabs to the king of England, he did not believe it, but mounted and set out with the Arabs and a small escort. When he came up to the caravan, he disguised himself as an Arab and went all round it. When he saw that quiet reigned in the camp and that everyone was fast asleep, he returned and ordered his men into the saddle.' Another authority relates that Richard was challenged by some of the Moslem sentries guarding the camp, but that one of his Bedouin companions, motioning him to be silent, answered the men in Arabic without checking his horse, and the little party was soon swallowed up in the darkness. Returning to Beit Nuba, Richard formed a strong raiding party of knights and archers and, marching by night 'beneath the splendour of the moon', they fell upon the luckless Egyptians while they still slept. Their escort of armed men was greatly outnumbered by the attackers, and those of them who were not killed were only too happy to save their lives by flight, though very few escaped. Large numbers of prisoners, both soldiers and merchants and their wares, Saladir. ɔ supplies of food and war material, over a thousand horses and as many camels, all fell into Richard's hands. It was a disaster for Saladin, and the sheer quantity of the loot did much to cheer the crusading men. But on returning to camp at Beit Nuba laden with booty, Richard and the army council finally decided to abandon the attack on Jerusalem and return to Jaffa, there to plan an invasion of Saladin's base, Egypt, and the bitterness and disappointment of the men knew no bounds. Moreover, things were made no easier by the fact that, although the majority of the council had voted against pressing an attack on Jerusalem, Hugh of Burgundy and most of the French had disagreed; and once again the ranks of the crusaders were split by bitterness and division. The French troops began singing an insulting song about Richard, composed – it was said – by the duke of Burgundy, and the English promptly retaliated by bawling an equally scurrilous ditty about the nasty habits of the French duke.

The retreat to the coast was a miserable time for everyone except Saladin and his Emirs, who could hardly believe their ears when one of their reconnaissance parties reported that the Christian host was marching away from Jerusalem instead of launching the long-dreaded attack. But the Christian retreat was soon confirmed beyond possibility of doubt. As soon as Richard reached Acre, negotiations for a truce were opened once again, and at first it looked as though agreement might not be too far away; Saladin agreed to allow pilgrims to travel safely to and from Jerusalem and to leave the coastal cities in Christian hands, as long as Richard first demolished Ascalon; he could not allow them to sit across the main road to his base in Egypt. But Richard refused to consider pulling down Ascalon so shortly after he had rebuilt it at such a cost in labour and in treasure, and once again stalemate seemed inevitable. While these negotiations dragged on, Richard began to plan an attack on Beirut to the north; if he could capture that city before reaching agreement with Saladin, not only would it strengthen his bargaining hand at the conference table, but possession of almost the last great fortified town on the coast of Outremer would be invaluable to the Christians remaining there after the war. But for once Richard was outpaced by Saladin. Before the attack on Beirut had got beyond the planning stage, on 27 July Saladin launched a lightning assault on Jaffa.

Although the garrison was outnumbered by the enemy, the Christians fought with such stubborn bravery as once again to elicit Beha ed-Din's admiration. 'The sultan conducted the attack on the besieged with the greatest energy,' he wrote, 'but what fine soldiers they were, how brave and courageous!' He went on to describe how a large section of the wall had fallen with a great crash during the course of the next day, having first been undermined by Saladin's engineers. 'Then a mighty shout was raised, the drums sounded, the trumpets blared . . . the sun lost its light, and none of the besiegers dared enter the breach. When the cloud of dust cleared away, we could see the ramparts of halberds and lances that now took the place of what had fallen, closing up the breach so well that not even the eyes could pierce it; it was a terrible sight to see the courage, the fearless aspect, and the cool precise movements of the enemy.' But despite their courage, after three days the defenders were forced to retire into the citadel, and Saladin's troops swarmed into the city and sacked it. When news of the attack reached Richard at Acre, he sent a large body of Templars and Hospitallers under Henry of Champagne to march by road to Jaffa as fast as they could, while he himself set out by sea with a similar body of men. He was held up by contrary winds off Mount Carmel, but eventually arrived during the night of 31 July. At dawn, he could see Saladin's soldiers on the beach and on the walls of the city, and concluded that it had already fallen. He had no way of knowing that the men of the garrison had not surrendered, but were still holding out in the citadel, until a priest jumped from the walls into the harbour and swam out to Richard's galley, easily recognizable from the other ships, for it was painted red and had a prow carved in the shape of a dragon's head. Climbing on board out of breath and dripping with water, he poured out his story to Richard: the garrison was intact; on seeing his ships arrive the men had launched an attack on the enemy, but they were greatly outnumbered, and they could not hold out for much longer. Richard gave immediate orders to the crew of his galley to row for the shore and beach the ship. Without even waiting to put on his full armour, he leapt into the water as soon as the ship grounded, and waded ashore followed by his men, scattering the startled Moslem soldiers on the beach as he went. He had only a handful of knights and a few hundred infantrymen with him, but he burst into the city at their head with such ferocity that Saladin's men were taken by complete surprise and routed before they had recovered sufficiently to ask what had hit them. They spilled out of the city in panic, fleeing for their lives, chased by packs of jubilant, whooping crusaders, and they did not stop until they were five miles inland.

Saladin had come within a hair's breadth of a resounding triumph, which would not only have restored his tattered reputation as a soldier, but would also have put a wedge between the northern and southern halves of the crusaders' recent conquests on the coast, thus dangerously undermining their whole position. As it was, Richard had arrived in the nick of time to turn the tables, and with his usual *élan* he had inflicted yet another humiliating defeat on his opponents: a defeat which it was essential for Saladin to avenge and reverse at almost any cost, if he was to shore up a few shreds of respect against the ruins of his prestige. He knew that Henry of Champagne was on his way, for his scouts had told him so, and he determined to attack before these reinforcements could reach Richard. Normally, the crusaders' greatest strength lay in their heavy cavalry, but Richard had only fifty-four knights with him with fifteen horses between them. The Moslems outnumbered their opponents by at least three to one, and the sultan was fully aware that he would probably never again have such a golden opportunity to take his revenge on *Malek Rik*, as he had outside the walls of Jaffa in that first week in August 1192. Moreover, Richard seemed almost to be inviting him to attack, for instead of remaining within the comparative safety of the battered walls of Jaffa, he and his little army had chosen to camp outside the city walls in the open countryside.

During the night of 4 August, Saladin moved his army up towards the crusaders' camp. His men were under strict orders to keep silence and to move as stealthily as possible, but if men can be persuaded not to make a sound, horses cannot be so tightly controlled. A Genoese sentry who had strolled a little way out of the camp just before sunrise heard horses whinnying and men moving nearby, and as the sky began to lighten in the east, he saw a glint of steel and heard the chinking of metal on metal a field's length away. Running back to the camp, he raised the alarm, and although some of the men were barely half dressed by the time that Saladin moved up to the attack, he found them waiting for him. Richard had drawn up his infantry in a tight half circle; the men in the front rank were kneeling behind a protective wall consisting of their shields with their lances planted in the ground, pointing outwards at the enemy like a great steel hedgehog, while behind them crossbowmen were stationed in pairs, one acting as loader for the other, so that the enemy could be subjected to an almost uninterrupted fire, when they launched their assault. It came soon enough. Saladin ordered his cavalry to attack, and a thousand horsemen charged to within a few yards of the solid, bristling mass of Christian pikes; but there they checked their horses before they were impaled, wheeling them round under a murderous fire from the crossbowmen, the horses rearing and bucking in a confusion of hoofs, limbs, fallen riders and corpses, while the air was rent by the screams of the wounded. Again and again they charged, and again and again they were stopped and forced to retreat, leaving both men and horses wounded or dead on the ground around the perimeter of the crusaders' defensive position, until by afternoon their losses were so heavy and the survivors so tired that Saladin called them off. Then a quite astonishing thing happened. Before the sultan could decide which of his forces to launch next against the still unbroken Christian hedgehog, in spite of his enormous inferiority in numbers, Richard and his little handful of knights charged at the head of his spearmen, falling on the exhausted enemy with such impetuosity and vigour that they broke in disorder and near disbelief, while Saladin watched in grudging admiration at the sheer indomitable resolution of his opponent. Indeed, so moved was he by Richard's dauntless spirit that, when the English king's horse was killed under him, he ordered one of his grooms to lead a pair of horses across the battlefield under a flag of truce as a present to Richard with his compliments. It was a gesture as immortal in its way as Richard's valour.

But devastating as their sudden attack had been, Richard knew that the enemy was too numerous for him to follow up his success by chasing them off the field, and leaving Saladin's dazed troops to count their dead, he called his men back and regrouped them in their original hedgehog position. A little later, Saladin sent some of his men round the Christian flank in an attack on the town as an alternative to yet another suicidal frontal attack on the embattled crusaders. Some Genoese sailors fled to the shelter of their ships, but before the Moslems could exploit their success, Richard galloped up with a party of knights and rallied the town's defenders. By evening, Saladin's men had had enough; they could do no more, and the sultan gave the order to retreat. Leaving their dead on the field, they marched wearily back to Jerusalem, more than ever convinced that the terrible golden-haired *Malek Rik* was invincible. Many of Richard's own men tended to agree with their enemies on this if on nothing else. 'The king was a giant in the battle,' wrote one of them. 'He was everywhere, now here, now there, wherever the attacks of the enemy were at their most fierce. On that day his sword shone like lightning . . . He mowed men down as harvesters mow corn with their scythes. Whoever felt one of his blows had no need of another. He was an Alexander, an Achilles, a Roland!' He was indeed, but his victory outside Jaffa was due at least as much to the professional way in which he had disposed his small army in defence before the battle had begun and to the precise timing of his counter-attack, as it was to his prodigious performance in the sickening cut and murderous thrust of the fighting itself.

It is easy to forget that battles are brutal and messy, but it is important not to do so; for the messy aftermath of a battle can be more lethal than the fighting itself, and in the days before modern surgery and antibiotics such as penicillin, it often was much more lethal than the clash of arms. At the risk of repetition, then, it is worth recollecting that after a battle such as that outside the walls of Jaffa, where men had been killing each other for over a week, the place would have been littered with corpses and black with flies. It was high summer, and in the heat of the middle eastern sun, the corpses would soon have swollen and turned purplish black with putrefaction. Black kites would have gorged on the dead, until they were driven away by scavenging dogs, growling and snarling as they ripped them to pieces, tearing off a hand here or a bit of leg there, or capturing a liver and bearing it away in their jaws to be eaten at leisure in the shade of some dusty bush or ancient fig tree. The stench of death would have been every-where, and so would that of ordure; for during the course of a battle men would not have been able to retire modestly to the decent privacy of latrines, when they had wanted to defecate;

they would have done what they had to do, where and when they could, and the resulting threat to the health of those who survived the battle would have been deadly; and so it was after the killing outside Jaffa. Richard was one of the first to fall ill, succumbing to a fever which soon reached epidemic proportions, making any thought of following up the victory over Saladin impossible.

For a time he was very ill indeed. 'The king lay sick on his couch,' wrote Richard of Devizes. 'The typhus continued, and the leeches were whispering about the greater semi-Tertian fever. They began to despair of his life, and wild despair spread through the camp.' But in spite of his illness, he kept in touch with Saladin, whose Emirs were pressing him to make peace at almost any cost. They argued that, once a truce had been signed, Richard and most of the crusaders would go home leaving their fellow Christians virtually defenceless, whereupon the Sultan could renew the war at a moment of his own choosing with the certain prospect of victory. By this time, Richard, too, was eager to make peace as soon as possible, so that he could sail for home and cope with the various troubles there. Once again, however, the stumbling block was Ascalon; Saladin was determined not to leave it in Christian hands, and Richard was determined not to hand it over to him after what it had cost him in terms of sweat and toil to recapture and refortify it. The turning point in the negotiations came at the beginning of September, when – or so it is uncharitably related – Richard was so cheered by news of the death of the duke of Burgundy at Acre that he immediately took a turn for the better, and decided to compromise with Saladin. He agreed to cede Ascalon to him but only after the demolition of its fortifications and on condition that it should remain an open city. The other coastal cities were to remain in Christian hands, and pilgrims should be allowed free access to Jerusalem and the various other places like Bethlehem regarded by them as sacred. Saladin agreed, and a truce to last for three years was signed by their representatives on 2 September to almost everyone's great relief. The war was officially over, and Richard was free to go home.

Before recounting the saga of that remarkable journey, however, a moment should be spent remembering that the war was over for Saladin, too; he also was free at last from the alarms and excursions of the last four years of war. He stayed in Jerusalem until Richard had sailed for home, then went on to Damascus, there to pick up the threads of government again after four years of absence with the army in the field. His greatest ambition was to make a pilgrimage to Mecca, but the pile of business awaiting him in Damascus made it impossible for him to contemplate any such thing for the time being. The winter was a harsh one, and although he was only fifty-four, the strains of the war had taken their toll; he was tired and ill, and those who knew him best were worried. He complained of lassitude and forgetfulness; everything was an effort, and it was obvious that his health was failing. On Friday, 19 February 1193, a bitterly cold day with a dry northerly wind whipping up the dust of Syria and piercing even the warmest clothing, he rode out to welcome the pilgrims returning from Mecca, though he could hardly make the effort to mount his horse; that evening he took to his bed with a fever. As the days passed, his condition grew worse, and Saladin realized that he had not much longer to live: a fact which he accepted calmly and without complaint. On 1 March he lapsed into unconsciousness, and many of his entourage who had been obsequious fellow travellers in the days of his power deserted him; even his son, al-Afdal, scurried off to try and win the Emirs to his own cause, leaving his father to die virtually alone. But he was not completely alone, for the Cadi of Damascus and a few faithful servants refused to leave his bedside. On Wednesday, 3 March, as the Cadi was reading the Koran over him, he came to the words, 'There is no God but God, in Him do I trust.' Hearing them, Saladin opened his eyes, smiled, and died.

XI

*Then the nations set against him on every side from the provinces, and
spread their net over him; he was taken in their pit, and they put him in a
cage.*

Ezekiel 19: 8

On 9 October 1192 Richard at last set sail for home from Acre.
That sounds a simple enough thing to have done, but in fact it was
fraught with dangers and difficulties of many kinds, and Richard
must have been worried: worried about the weather so late in the
year for a sea voyage, but worried above all about the safest route
to take. By twelfth-century standards, October was not a good
month in which to travel, for storms were commonplace even in
the Mediterranean, while any idea of going home by way of the
Straits of Gibraltar was unthinkable at that time of year because of
the near certainty of gales and mountainous seas in the Atlantic.
Moreover, both sides of the Straits were in the hands of Moslem
powers, who would have been only too delighted to capture the
dreaded *Malek Rik*, as he sailed past their front door, before he
even reached the terrible Atlantic. It might have been all right in
summer with a large fleet to support and protect him, but in early
winter it would have been suicide.

The alternatives were neither numerous nor attractive.
Normally, his best route would have been by way of Sicily to a
southern French port, and thence overland through his own
domains of Gascony and Aquitaine, and it is not entirely clear
why he did not choose to travel that way; but it seems probable
that he was loth to go anywhere near the county of Toulouse,

where his old enemy Raymond would have been even more delighted than the Moslems of Gibraltar and Tangier to prepare a prison cell for him. Once again, it would have been safe enough to sail along the coast of Toulouse with a large fleet in summer weather, but to do so alone and unprotected with the possibility of being shipwrecked by a winter gale on your oldest enemy's front doorstep was not to be considered. For the same reasons, the idea of sailing as far as northern Spain, where he would have been safe enough with his ally Sancho of Navarre, was equally unattractive, and he decided against it. Even in the best summer weather, medieval sailors always sailed as close to land as possible, hugging the coasts in case they had to run for shelter. The worst fate a seaman could experience was to be caught by a gale out of sight of land and be blown God knew where to be lost at sea in that terrifying desolation of waters, the open ocean, which was known to swallow men and ships as the great Leviathan had swallowed up Jonah in biblical days. Anything was better than that, but Richard was left with few alternatives.

In the end, he chose what he considered to be the lesser of the various evils open to him. He sailed up the Adriatic, intending to make his way home by way of Germany. Of course, he knew that Leopold of Austria had been offended when he had ordered his men to cast down his standard from the conquered walls of Acre, and he must have known too that he had offended the German emperor's wife, Constance, by supporting Tancred on the throne of Sicily in her stead; but he may well have reckoned that these were less dangerous enemies than Raymond of Toulouse or the winter weather in league with the great Leviathan. One historian has attributed his choice of route to a schoolboyish love of adventure, condemning the resulting journey as 'a ridiculous escapade'; but this is to treat Richard's intelligence with patronizing contempt, and whatever else he may have been, Richard was not a fool. He knew the dangers of the German route, and he knew its advantages, one of which may well have been – or so it may have seemed to him at the time – that it was probably the last on which anyone would have expected to find him, and therefore the one route on which no one would be actively looking out for him. Yet another advantage was that, once he reached the territory ruled by the Welf clan headed by his brother-in-law,

Henry the Lion, he would be amongst friends. Many of the east German princes were at loggerheads with the Emperor Henry VI and would both welcome him and help him on his way to a northern port from which he could sail to England. The disadvantages, on the other hand, were obvious, and far the greatest was the risk of being recognized and apprehended by his enemies before he reached friendly territory, and Richard realized this and took precautions against such an eventuality.

However, the first disaster to overtake him was due to the weather not to his enemies. He sailed as far as Corfu in a large ship named the *Franche-Nef*, making very good time from Acre, but there he and his small number of companions trans-shipped to a little fleet of three small galleys, which were less conspicuous than the larger vessel and thus less likely to attract attention. It is said that they were manned by local pirates, who knew the area well; but whether they were pirates or merely local Greek seamen, they agreed to carry Richard and his little party up the Dalmatian coast as inconspicuously as possible, and this they did. All went well until they had passed through the Gulf of Trieste, when a storm blew up, and they were wrecked. Luckily, no one was either drowned or hurt, and having said goodbye to the Greek sailors, Richard and his party disguised themselves as pilgrims returning from the Holy Land – a common enough sight – and set off to walk. They travelled north-eastwards, avoiding the Alpine passes, which would not only have been impassable at that time of year, but which would have led them into the heart of the Emperor Henry VI's domain. Inevitably, this meant that they had to pass through Leopold of Austria's duchy, but they hoped to be able to do so without being spotted. One or two of Richard's companions could speak German; indeed, one of them – his standard bearer in many of the battles in the past two years – may well have been a German by birth, for he was affectionately known as Henry the German, and thus detection on linguistic grounds was rendered unlikely. Even if they had been detected as foreigners, however, they should still have been safe enough, for people were used to giving safe passage to parties of foreign pilgrims passing through their lands; both pilgrims and crusaders were under the protection of the pope, and few people dared to incur excommunication by molesting them.

Thus all might have been well if there had not been aspects of Richard's little group which attracted people's attention. They spent money a great deal more lavishly than most pilgrims, and even though some spoke fluent German, once they had drawn attention to themselves, there were those who found it odd that English and Norman pilgrims should be travelling by such an easterly route. It did not take someone with a pathologically suspicious nature to ask himself whether this might not be the king of England, who was known to be on his way home. As a result, a local nobleman, Meinhard of Görz, who heard of this rather strange band of pilgrims passing his way, arrested some of Richard's party in the hope of making sure of their identity. The king and most of his companions escaped, but from this moment they became fugitives, whose chances of making their way safely through Leopold of Austria's domain had become extremely slim. In the event, it is said that Richard was eventually discovered dressed as a cook in menial clothes, stirring a pot in the kitchen of a farmhouse, but having overlooked one fatal flaw in his otherwise admirable disguise: the cook was wearing a huge ruby ring. The story is probably apocryphal, but it may well represent the truth that Richard and his companions gave themselves away by failing to hide their wealth; not many twelfth-century pilgrims returning after a long and impoverishing journey to the holy places of their faith were likely to be laden with this world's riches, but Richard and his companions were so accustomed to affluence that it would hardly have occurred to them that, to protect themselves from recognition, they should have lived as meagrely as the poorest of the poor, even begging their bread from time to time, as other pilgrims often had no option but to do.

The arrest took place just outside Vienna in the heart of Leopold of Austria's duchy; nothing could have pleased Leopold more than suddenly to find himself master of the man who had had his standard cast into the dust from the battlements of Acre, and as news of his capture spread through Europe, others who either hated or envied Richard were equally delighted. The Emperor Henry VI was one of the first to be told, and he sat down at once and wrote a gloating letter to Philip of France, telling him the news. 'Our dearly beloved cousin Leopold, duke of Austria, captured the king in a humble house in the vicinity of Vienna.

Inasmuch as he is now in our power, and has always done his utmost for your annoyance and disturbance, what we have above stated we have thought proper to notify to your Majesty, knowing that the same is well pleasing to your kindly affection for us, and will afford most abundant joy to your feelings. Given at Creutz, on the fifth day before the Calends of January.' The king of France did indeed find the news well pleasing, as did Richard's brother John, who for some time had been plotting the dismemberment of Richard's French possessions with Philip Augustus. Philip immediately wrote to Leopold imploring him not to release Richard without first consulting him, and John hurried across the Channel to do homage to the French king for the whole of his brother's lands. The only person to make a move on Richard's behalf was Pope Celestine III, who promptly excommunicated Leopold for molesting a crusader, a man under both divine protection and the protection of the church. He also promised Richard's mother, Eleanor, whom he met at Châteauroux in order to discuss the whole affair, that as soon as possible he would send a delegation to Austria to arrange her son's release. But as the days passed and nothing much happened, Eleanor became more and more furious, eventually writing a splendidly savage letter to the pope, rebuking him for his failure to keep his promise, and inscribing herself as 'Eleanor, by the wrath of God, queen of England'. 'The kings and princes of the world have conspired against my son, the anointed of the Lord,' she wrote. 'One holds him in chains, while another ravishes his lands; another holds him by the heels, while yet another skins him alive. And while all this goes on, the sword of St Peter remains in its scabbard. Three times you have promised to send legates, and they have not been sent . . . Is this the meaning of your promises to me at Châteauroux?' But the pope's dilemma was that, while it was easy enough to excommunicate Leopold of Austria, to threaten Philip of France with an interdict was a little more difficult, and to menace the Holy Roman Emperor, Henry VI, with a similar penalty was another matter altogether. For he had already shown himself to be no respecter of ecclesiastical persons, not hesitating to murder some unfortunate papal nuncios, when it had suited him to do so, and Celestine did not want to give him an excuse to do so again.

When the news of Richard's fate reached England, reactions differed. His mother, Eleanor, remained totally loyal, while his brother John did his best to stir up rebellion against him. He tried to enlist William the Lion, the Scottish king, in his perfidious schemes; but Richard had always been open, honest and generous to the Scottish king, and William refused to have anything to do with John's particular brand of fraternal treachery while the object of his spite was a prisoner in Austria and unable to defend himself. When John turned abroad for help from the count of Flanders, the successor to Count Philip who had been killed at Acre, initially he had better luck; but an invasion planned from Flanders never materialized, though a few luckless mercenaries landed in East Anglia, and were gleefully chased to their deaths or to imprisonment by some local levies raised by Queen Eleanor for the defence of her son's realm. Frustrated by the king of Scotland and defeated in East Anglia, John decided to announce that Richard was dead, and that he, John, was therefore king; very few people believed him, but at least it gave him the opportunity to organize yet another criminal enterprise ostensibly with royal authority. While the true government of the country was collecting money for Richard's ransom, John had a duplicate of the chancellor's seal forged, and used it to collect money for his own pocket. But this devious and unedifying stratagem did him little good, even though it was not discovered for some time; for the majority of Richard's subjects greatly preferred their legitimate king to his unsavoury brother. When the great council of the realm met at Oxford in late February 1193 to decide how best to obtain Richard's release, the first thing they did was to despatch two men – they were abbots – to Austria to gather more information and if possible to see Richard.

Meanwhile, as soon as Leopold had made sure that he had indeed captured the king of England, he sent him under escort to Durnstein castle, a formidable fortress perched on a rock over-looking the Danube, and here - legend would have it – the minstrel, Blondel, found him. It is a charming story of how the troubadour wandered disconsolately all over Bohemia in search of his lord, singing a song which they had composed together, until at last under the frowning walls of Durnstein he heard Richard's voice take up the refrain from inside his prison; but the story appeared for the first time over a hundred years after the event, and is unlikely to have much grounding in fact, though it may reflect the truth that Richard spent some of his time in captivity writing poems and setting them to music in order to while away his time. At least one such poem is known, the so-called Prison Song, and a most accomplished and graceful piece it is in the original Norman French, though inevitably much of the beauty of the language is lost in translation. In it he complained of his fate and of the dilatoriness of his friends in ransoming him:

> No prisoner can tell his honest thought,
>   Unless he speaks as one who suffers wrong;
>   But for his comfort he may make a song.
> My friends are many, but their gifts are naught.
> Shame will be theirs, if for my ransom here
>   I lie another year.

He complains, too, of the way in which the French king was ignoring his oath and doing his best to ravage Richard's French dominions:

> What marvel that my heart is sad and sore,
>   When my own lord torments my helpless lands!
>   Well do I know that, if he held his hands,
> Remembering the common oath we swore,
> I should not here imprisoned with my song
>   Remain a prisoner for long.

But despite these poetic complaints, Richard was by no means overcome with self-pity during his captivity; on the contrary, he won the respect and admiration of all who came in contact with him at this time by the dignity with which he bore the various indignities thrust upon him by his enemies and the uncomplaining fortitude with which he supported his ordeal by imprisonment, while his captors haggled over his body, the most valuable piece of human real estate to come on the ransom market for years.

The two main contestants for his possession were Leopold of Austria, who held him, and the Emperor Henry VI, who wanted him. Henry VI, the eldest son of a much greater man, Frederick Barbarossa, was a little man with a vast ambition, cruel, treacherous and tactless. There was nothing he would not do to attain his ends, and his genius for doing things in the most authoritarian and offensive way possible managed to alienate many of the subjects of his widespread empire most of the time. This was fortunate for Richard, for it meant that when at last, after almost a year's haggling over the price, Henry bought him from Leopold for seventy-five thousand marks, Richard found himself warmly supported by a large number of the emperor's most powerful subjects, who were so disgusted by Henry's dictatorial tactlessness that they were prepared to support almost anyone as long as their support irritated the emperor and helped whomsoever was presently opposing him. Richard was handed over to Henry at the time of the arrival of the two Cistercian abbots, who met him at Ochsenfurt on the river Main on 19 March 1193, while he was being escorted to Speyer, where he was to be handed over to the emperor. In his *Chronica*, Roger of Howden is another witness to Richard's unfailing courtesy and composure during this time of his captivity, and of how much it impressed everyone who had anything to do with him. It was fortunate for Richard that God had endowed him with the qualities of steadiness and resolution, which he showed during the whole of this period, if it is indeed the Almighty who breathes a few virtues into us at our births, to be developed or neglected, as the whole twelfth century believed. He had every possible need of them on arrival at the imperial court at Speyer, where in effect he was put on trial.

He was charged with a long list of crimes: of betraying the Holy Land by making a treaty with Saladin, of murdering Conrad of Montferrat, of the rape of Cyprus, the imprisonment of Isaac Comnenus and kidnapping his daughter, of supporting Tancred in his unlawful seizure of the throne of Sicily, and of grossly insulting Leopold of Austria at Acre. But if Henry VI had counted on bullying Richard into submission or overawing him by the splendour of his court, he had picked on the wrong man. Richard rose to his feet and defended himself with such dignity, cogency and force that he impressed even his enemies, 'When Richard replied,' wrote William the Breton, court poet to the king of France, 'he spoke so eloquently and regally, in so lion-hearted a manner, that it was as though he had forgotten where he was and the undignified circumstances in which he had been captured, and imagined himself to be seated on the throne of his ancestors at Lincoln or at Caen.' He began by reminding the court that he had been born in a rank which recognized no superior but God, to whom alone he was responsible for his actions, thus firmly denying that either Henry or his court had any right to try him, let alone to judge him; but he went on to say that, since he had done nothing of which he was ashamed, he was happy to give an account of himself, not only to the present assembly, but to the whole world; and he defied anyone to call his actions criminal. To suggest that he had betrayed the Holy Land by signing a treaty with Saladin was absurd; the record of his battles against the sultan – and indeed of his victories over him – was sufficient proof of that, and if anyone was to be accused of aiding and abetting the enemies of the Holy Land, the finger should be pointed at the king of France and Leopold of Austria, who had deserted the Christian cause after the fall of Acre, leaving him virtually single-handed to continue the war against the infidel; and the duke of Burgundy had not behaved much better. He had had no hand in the murder of Conrad of Montferrat, and he had no need to prove it, for the assassins themselves had admitted that they had been sent by the Old Man of the Mountains to kill him. Turning to the next charge against him, he could not understand how anyone could accuse him of doing anything wrong in Cyprus; he had avenged injuries done to his own men and the human race by punishing a tyrant and dethroning a usurper. As to his support for Tancred in Sicily and the treaties he had signed with him, he defied anyone to discover anything in either which infringed the law of nations. Finally, as to Leopold of Austria, if he considered that he had been insulted at Acre, why had he not behaved like a man of honour by avenging the insult on the spot or by forgetting it long ago, instead of running home like a whipped schoolboy and harbouring a grudge?

It was heady stuff. He had spoken so well and with such obvious sincerity that the whole assembly of bishops and barons burst into spontaneous applause as Richard sat down. Their verdict was so obviously not only one of acquittal but of rapturous support that the emperor, only too well aware of the sense of the meeting and of Richard's triumph, was constrained to run forward and give his prisoner the kiss of peace and, with tears running down his face, pledge himself to sign a treaty of friendship with Richard and to do his best to bring about a reconciliation between him and the king of France. The assembly, already deeply moved by Richard's self-defence, now emulated the emperor by bursting into tears of joy at the pacific outcome of the day's events, and Richard was invited to be the emperor's honoured guest for Easter, so that they might celebrate the mysteries of the resurrection of the Son of God together like brothers. It was all very touching, but after Easter Henry VI reverted to his more normal form, and sent Richard under close guard to the gloomy castle of Trifels in the fastness of the mountains to the west of Speyer, having first told him that, brother in Christ or no brother in Christ, he still wanted a hundred thousand marks with the service of fifty galleys and two hundred knights for a year to help him conquer Sicily, before he would release him.

This return to something like solitary confinement in order to keep him away from his many German sympathizers must have been a bitter disappointment to Richard after his pre-Easter triumph and the emperor's profession of brotherhood and good will, and he was only rescued from it eventually by someone who has not appeared in the story since Richard left England three years previously: William Longchamp, the chancellor, to whom much had happened in the interim. The tale is worth telling, not only because it is germane to the story of Richard's life at this time, but because it also gives a vivid little glimpse of what it was like to be alive in that remarkable time. After Richard left the country on Crusade, the chancellor's behaviour was described by Roger of Howden. 'William, bishop of Ely, legate of the Apostolic See, chancellor of our Lord the king and justiciar of England, oppressed the people entrusted to his charge with heavy exactions; for in the first place he despised all his fellows, whom the king had associated with him in the government of the kingdom, and disregarded their advice. Indeed, he considered no one of his associates in the kingdom his equal, not even John, the king's brother. Accordingly, he laid claim to the castles, estates, abbeys, churches, and all the rights of the king as his own. On the authority of his legateship, he came to take up his lodging at bishoprics and abbeys, priories, and other houses of religious orders with such a vast array of men, horses, hounds and hawks, that a house where he took up his abode for only a single night was hardly able within the three following years to recover its former state.' That is probably a biased account, but there is likely to be some truth in it, and certainly Longchamp became very unpopular. However, worse was to come when his unpopularity was turned overnight into hatred by something done by his servants, for which he was blamed. About a year after Richard's departure for the Holy Land, his half-brother, Geoffrey, who had been consecrated archbishop of York on condition that he should remain out of England for three years – a stratagem to keep him out of harm's way during Richard's absence, for he was an ambitious and troublesome young man – decided to return despite his oath, landing at Dover in mid-September 1191. Longchamp asked the constable of Dover Castle, who happened to be his brother-in-law, to arrest him on landing; but the archbishop was too quick for his would-be apprehenders, taking refuge in St Martin's priory, where he was promptly besieged. All might still have been well, if patience and common sense had prevailed, but after four days Longchamp's men broke into the church, and seizing the archbishop by his legs dragged him out of the place, his head bumping down the altar steps as they did so.

The news of this unedifying event shocked the nation. Thomas Becket had not been long in his grave, and for another consecrated archbishop in God's holy Catholic Church to be treated in much the same way as Henry II had treated that popular saint appalled everyone, especially the clergy, who turned against Longchamp to a man. The fact that he had ordered Geoffrey's arrest out of loyalty to King Richard counted for nothing, and Richard's enemies chortled with delight that at last they could vilify this tiresomely over-loyal man whom they liked to portray as an evil little deformed ape with a great fondness for small boys. One of the most scurrilous of his attackers was Hugh, bishop of Coventry, of whom it was rumoured that just before his death no one could be found to give him absolution, for his sins were too black, too great, and too numerous: a highly improbable story, but one reflecting the popular idea of the man. However this may have been, the bishop described how Longchamp, after taking refuge from the popular fury in Dover Castle, went down to the harbour to look for a boat to take him across the Channel until the rumpus over Geoffrey's arrest should die down. 'Pretending to be a woman,' the bishop of Coventry wrote, 'a sex which he had always hated, he changed his priest's robes into a harlot's dress. The shame of it! The man became a woman, the bishop a buffoon. Dressed in a green gown of enormous length he hurriedly limped – for the poor little fellow was lame – from the castle heights to the sea shore, and then sat down on a rock to rest. There he attracted the attention of a half naked fisherman, who was wet and cold from the sea, and who thought that the bishop was the sort of woman who might warm him up. He put his left arm round Longchamp's neck, while his right hand roamed lower down. Suddenly pulling up the gown, he plunged unblushingly in, only to be confronted with the irrefutable evidence that the woman was a man. The fisherman then called his mates over to have a look at this truly remarkable creature.' Eventually, Longchamp was rescued from the fishermen only to end up for a week in Dover gaol before being released and allowed to find his way to France.

This and many other accounts of Longchamp, coming from the pens of his enemies, are inevitably biased against him and it is certain that there was another side to the man. Even his enemies had to admit that he was unfailingly loyal to Richard, and there are other reports of him as a cultured and learned man who, unlike many of his fellow Normans, had a liking for the poor and under-privileged and for taking their side against their over-powerful feudal masters. One might have thought this to be a fitting quality in a bishop, but it may also have been one of the reasons that he was so unpopular amongst his peers. At all events, it was Longchamp who rescued Richard from his solitary confinement by persuading the emperor to allow him to return to the imperial court – moved by this time to Hagenau – though how he managed to change the emperor's mind no one knows. Richard, who had made him chancellor in the first place and had never doubted the wisdom of that appointment, now had proof of the invincibility of the little man's loyalty, and was duly grateful; he sent him home with letters to his mother Eleanor and the other leaders of the realm, commending him to them, and giving them news of his own welfare and the emperor's demand for seventy thousand marks as a down payment on his ransom.

Longchamp reached England in late April 1193, and as soon as Eleanor and the other officers of state had read Richard's letters, they began to collect the money needed to free him; a twenty-five per cent tax was levied on income and on the value of certain kinds of property; some of the monasteries were compelled to hand over the produce of their farm lands; and the churches were told to surrender some of their more easily realizable treasures such as silver plate, golden vessels of various kinds, and jewellery. Richard's brother John did everything he could to hinder all this, but he had very little success, and when he launched into something very like open rebellion, his forces were driven back into Windsor castle and the fortress at Tickhill in Yorkshire by forces loyal to the government under the energetic direction of Eleanor, who had little time for her youngest son. Fearing that Richard might soon be released, trouble also broke out in his French possessions, where Ademar of Angoulême attacked some of Richard's estates in Poitou; but here too, as in England, most people remained loyal to their absent crusading liege lord, and Ademar was decisively repulsed. Philip Augustus invaded Normandy, where his army had some early success. The defenders of such places as Gisors and a few others, which either surrendered or put up very little resistance to Philip, probably reckoned that there was not much point in risking their lives and those of their men out of loyalty to someone who might never return from captivity in Germany; but when, flushed with his early triumphs, Philip marched on Rouen, he was defied by the earl of Leicester, who jokingly invited him to enter the city; he would be warmly welcomed, said the earl. Furious, Philip laid siege to the place, but the stout resistance of its citizens and the continuing mockery coming from the noble lord of Leicester discouraged him to such an extent that after a fortnight he lifted the siege and moved on. It was fortunate for Richard that the place held out, for a number of other strongholds in the Vexin surrendered to Philip, and if the capital city of Normandy had also fallen to him, Richard's position when eventually he returned would have been even more difficult than in fact it was.

Back at the emperor's court, Richard was busy enlisting some of the German princes in his campaign to persuade the emperor to release him. He knew that his brother John and Philip Augustus were doing everything they could to ensure that he should not be released, and when he heard that Henry was proposing to meet Philip, he scented danger. Henry was interested above all in money, and Richard suspected that if Philip offered him a large enough sum, Henry would not hesitate to hand his prisoner over to the king of France, who would take the greatest pleasure in locking him up for life. The undercurrents of bargaining, treachery, greed and fear beneath the bland diplomatic surface of twelfth-century Europe at this time were so complex, devious and malodorous that even now it is difficult to be sure about what was really going on; but it seems certain that Richard's only hope of defeating the king of France's murky scheming was to ensure that his ransom money was raised in full, while at the same time outbidding Philip in another direction too; and that was where the German princes were a godsend to him. For some of them had been in revolt against the emperor ever since an occasion some time previously, when a certain Albert of Brabant had been murdered by some knights believed to have been acting on Henry's orders. The murdered man had been one of three candidates for the bishopric of Liège, which was vacant at the time, and since he was by no means the candidate favoured by the emperor, Henry was blamed for his death. Many of the murdered man's supporters came from the Rhineland and from Thuringia, and these were the princes in more or less open revolt as a result of the murder. England had valuable trading relations with many of them, while others were related to Richard by ties of blood or of marriage, and he suspected that if he could use his influence to effect a reconciliation between them and Henry, the emperor might well release him in return.

In June 1193, at Richard's request, the emperor opened a great court at Worms, to which his various subjects were summoned, and there he publicly swore on the Gospels that he had had no hand in the murder of Albert of Brabant. To his great relief, the rebellious princes from the Rhineland publicly accepted his word and renewed their pledges of loyalty to him, though what they thought in the privacy of their own hearts about his protestations of innocence we shall never know. It was the end of a long and difficult period for the emperor and a diplomatic triumph for Richard, and since most of the ransom money demanded by Henry was known to be on its way from England, a date was set for his release amongst much brotherly kissing and courtly tears. It looked at last as though nothing could now stop Richard from returning home. But this was to count without the determination and malevolence of the king of France, who was so appalled at the prospect of Richard's freedom that together with John he raised the stakes by offering the emperor a larger sum of money than the hundred thousand marks being raised in England for his ransom. Henry VI was as well endowed with moral scruples as a hyena is instinct with compassion for its prey, and he was tempted to accept Philip's money; but once again the German princes came to Richard's aid, insisting that the emperor should keep his word and honour the agreement he had made at Worms in June. The result was that after Henry had received the greater part of the ransom money from England and taken hostages for the remainder, Richard was at last set free. Even then, however, Henry extorted one further concession; before Richard was finally released, the emperor persuaded him to do him homage for the kingdom of England, thus technically acknowledging it to be a fief of the Holy Roman Empire. This further humiliation of the king of England was seen by everyone to be a farce, the only point of which was to pander to Henry's vanity, and it did little to raise him in his subjects' esteem: not that that worried Henry very much, for he had squeezed an enormous – for that time an almost unimaginably large – sum out of Richard: literally a king's ransom.

Richard's other enemies had done less well than the emperor. The king of France had taken some important Norman castles, but he had failed to capture Rouen, the capital of Richard's duchy, or to persuade the emperor to sell Richard to him. When the news of Richard's release reached him, understandably alarmed, he sent an urgent message to John in England, 'Look to yourself; the devil is unbound.' John had even more cause for alarm than Philip, and so did those who had supported him in his treachery. They had gained almost nothing, and now stood to lose every-thing, while John could only hope for leniency by throwing himself at his brother's feet with a plea for mercy. As to the prime mover in Richard's long captivity, Leopold of Austria had gained the least of all, for he saw only a small part of the ransom money, while the emperor kept the rest. He had been excommunicated by the pope for imprisoning a crusader, and now the pope ordered him to hand the ransom money back to Richard in part compensation for his crimes against him. He refused to do so, but he did not live long to enjoy his small gains. Less than a year after Richard's release, on the day after Christmas, the Feast of St Stephen, his horse fell, when he was out riding, badly crushing one of his feet. Taken home and put to bed, his foot turned gangrenous, and he was advised to have it off; but in spite of Leopold's pleading, no one could be found to perform the gruesome and agonizing operation. In the end, he himself held an axe in place on his leg, and ordered one of his servants to hit it with a huge mallet. After one or two violent blows, the man succeeded in severing the black and festering foot; but gangrene was not to be so easily defeated. Five days later Leopold died.

PART 4

Final Battles

XII

For God's sake, let us sit upon the ground
And tell sad stories of the death of kings:
How some have been depos'd, some slain in war,
Some haunted by the ghosts they have depos'd,
Some poison'd by their wives, some sleeping kill'd;
All murder'd: for within the hollow crown
That rounds the mortal temples of a king
Keeps Death his court.

Shakespeare, *King Richard II*

After his release, Richard did not hurry to return to England; instead, he travelled in a leisurely way down the Rhine with Eleanor, who had come out to Germany to meet him. They stayed at various places on their way as guests of the local dignitaries, cementing a number of useful relationships and alliances with the German princes: alliances which were to stand England in good stead for a number of years to come in her wars with Philip Augustus. At Cologne, Richard was lavishly entertained by the archbishop, who paid Eleanor an unexpected compliment when she and Richard attended Mass in the cathedral on Sunday; for the Introit as he approached the altar, he intoned the words, 'Now know that the Lord hath sent his angel to snatch me from the hand of Herod.' Richard was delighted, though whether the emperor was equally pleased to be likened to Herod – and he would undoubtedly have been told about the archbishop's choice of scriptural passage – is not known; it seems unlikely. Before Richard left Cologne, he made an alliance with the archbishop, and received his homage as his vassal. Similar alliances were concluded with the archbishop of Mainz, the bishop of Liège, the duke of Brabant, and most of the princes of the lower Rhineland, who had been helpful in insisting upon his release, and who, though now reconciled to the emperor through Richard's good offices, were far from enamoured of their imperial master. Indeed, as Richard and his mother made their unhurried way down the Rhine, their journey became something of a triumphal progress; people in the cities and the villages turned out in their thousands to give a hero's welcome to the crusader king about whose victories and deeds of prowess in the Holy Land they had all heard, and as reports of their enthusiasm reached Philip of France, he became so enraged that he wrote to the emperor rebuking him for releasing Richard at all and demanding that he should be re-arrested. According to William of Newburgh, the emperor, too, was incensed that the man whom he had so recently and so satisfactorily humiliated should now be being treated with far greater honour and greeted with far greater warmth by his own imperial subjects than he had ever received from them, and he despatched a small posse of men to re-arrest the English king; but if he really did so, his orders were not carried out, for Richard reached Louvain unmolested on 16 February 1194, having been fêted everywhere along his route. A day or two later, on 4 March, he sailed from Antwerp in an English vessel from the Cinque Port of Rye, which had been awaiting his coming. The ship was held up by gales and contrary winds in the mouth of the Scheldt, and it was not until a week later on 13 March that Richard landed at Sandwich, another of the ancient Cinque Ports, at about nine o'clock in the morning. It was a brilliant, sunny spring morning, and the radiance of the day was taken by many people to be a good omen for the king as he returned at last to his own country.

But there were those, including John's partisans, who found the news of his return anything but bright and sunny. The seneschal of St Michael's Mount in Cornwall died of fright when he heard of the king's landing, and there were others who, if they did not die, were equally terrified. Before dealing with these rebels, however, Richard went to the shrine of St Thomas of Canterbury to give thanks to God for his deliverance from captivity, and only then did he press on to London, which he reached three days later on 16 March. He was given a rapturous welcome by the citizens of the place, as he rode to St Paul's to attend a service of thanksgiving before setting out on yet another pilgrimage, this time to the shrine of St Edmund at Bury, that popular ninth-century saint who, as king of East Anglia, had chosen to become a target for the bows of some pagan Danish archers rather than share his throne with one of them. Having thus amply discharged his religious duty of thanksgiving to God, Richard turned to the more mundane business of dealing with his rebellious brother John and his supporters. Most of the castles under their control had already surrendered to forces sent against them by Hubert Walter, the archbishop of Canterbury, who had succeeded William Longchamp as chancellor and justiciar of England at the time of the latter's fall from grace while Richard was still the emperor's captive. Of the castles remaining in John's power, Marlborough and Lancaster had recently surrendered; Hugh de Puiset, bishop of Durham and justiciar in the north of England, was besieging Tickhill in Yorkshire, and Walter's men were laying siege to Nottingham, where Richard arrived on 25 March. The garrison of Nottingham had been one of the few groups of people to have believed John when, some time previously, he had announced that Richard was dead, and apparently they still believed it; as a result, they now refused to believe that Richard had joined their besiegers, suspecting it to be a trick to weaken their resolve. Angered by their stubborn resistance, Richard set up an enormous gallows just below the walls of the city with the obvious intention of intimidating them, and ordered an attack on the place. As usual, he himself took part in the fighting, risking his life as he had so often done in the Holy Land, and once again emerging unscathed, though some of his men were killed at his side. A few of the city's defenders were captured during the battle, and these were then hanged in full view of the walls as an example to the watching defenders. By any standards, this was a brutal thing to do, although in the end it probably saved lives; for it shocked the men of the garrison into making overtures of peace. As Richard sat down to dinner on 27 March, two envoys from the constables of the city came under a safe-conduct to see for themselves whether the king was dead or not. When they were ushered into his presence, he turned to them, and said, 'Well now, what do you think? Am I the king, or am I not?' 'You are,' they replied. 'Then go and tell your masters so,' he told them. When the constables heard their report, they and twelve other senior citizens of the place left the castle immediately, and surrendered to the king, and the rest of the garrison followed suit the next day. Richard spared them, but made them pay fairly heavy fines before setting them free. He needed the money to raise an army against Philip Augustus of France.

After a day's hunting in Sherwood forest, Richard called a great council of state at Nottingham on the last day of the month but one. His mother attended, as did his half-brother, Geoffrey, as archbishop of York, together with Hubert Walter, the archbishop of Canterbury and chancellor of the realm, Hugh de Puiset the bishop of Durham, William Longchamp who, though no longer chancellor, was still the bishop of Ely, the saintly Bishop Hugh of Lincoln, and the bishops of Exeter, Worcester and Hereford. King William of Scotland's brother, David, was invited to attend, and for four days the council wrestled with the problems confronting the nation. Finance took pride of place, and once again Richard put many of the most lucrative ecclesiastical and secular offices of state up for sale to the highest bidders. Geoffrey was forced to bid against William Longchamp in order to retain his archbishopric of York and eventually outbid him, whereupon Longchamp paid an almost equally princely sum to retain his position at Ely; and they were typical of many others. Immoral as it sounds to modern ears, it was one way of soaking the rich, though neither so efficient nor perhaps so unblushingly extortionate as some latter-day forms of taxation. In view of his treachery, the council wanted to confiscate and auction John's English possessions but Eleanor argued against such a course on the grounds that it would merely drive John into the willing arms of the king of France, and the council eventually agreed with her. Even so, John and his unsavoury *particeps criminis*, the bishop of Coventry, were summoned to appear before Richard's court before 10 May to explain themselves. If John failed to do so, he would be banished from the kingdom, while the bishop of Coventry would have to submit, both to the judgement of his fellow bishops and to that of the king's court or regard himself as both unfrocked and banished, and in either case his property and whatever wealth he might have accumulated would be confiscated. Other more general ways of raising money were also adopted: a land tax was imposed, and anyone liable to military service who wanted to opt out of his duty to serve in the coming war against Philip Augustus of France had to pay scutage for the privilege, while various ethnic minorities, like the Jews of York and certain other cities, were granted certain privileges and protection from harassment on due payment of an appropriate sum of money to the king. Finally, the conference decided to stage a great ceremony in Winchester cathedral during which Richard would appear in full regalia, wearing the crown, as a public demonstration that he had returned to his kingdom after his imprisonment by the emperor with his kingly authority unimpaired. The date was fixed for 17 April 1194.

Richard spent the next weekend hunting again in nearby Sherwood forest. A popular ballad tells how, at this time, he disguised himself as a monk in order to meet Robin Hood and his band of merry men and how well the two got on together. There is no doubt that throughout the Norman period there were outlaws, many of whom were driven into hiding in the country's forests and other wild places in a kind of unorganized Anglo-Saxon resistance movement against their conquerors from across the Channel, rather as many Frenchmen were driven to resist the Germans in a more organized way during the second world war from their hiding places in rural France. Robin Hood may well be a personification of these popular, patriotic resistance fighters, even if historically there was no single leader called Robin Hood. He may also be a latter-day version of an ancient, pagan woodland elf or sprite with deep animistic roots – a spirit of the trees – in whom country people had believed from time immemorial, and who had slowly been assimilated into medieval Christian mythology with Friar Tuck bringing the blessing of the church upon the little band of outlaws as the years went by; but none of this means that Richard's meeting with Robin Hood must be treated as mere nonsense – unhistorical romantic rubbish – or that such stories cannot be taken seriously. To assume any such thing would be to treat the twelfth century as at best childish and at worst nit-witted without bothering first to wonder why anyone should have bothered to compose a song that suggested that the non-existent outlaw of Sherwood forest and the Norman king of England should have met and liked each other, an event which must have seemed highly improbable to everyone alive at the time, including the singer of the song. So why did he sing his song? Shortly after Richard's hunting expedition in Sherwood forest, at the time of his crown-wearing ceremony in Winchester cathedral, one of the things he did was to order a relaxation of the draconian forest laws which decreed such penalties as blinding and castration for people under the rank of knight or clerk caught poaching in the royal hunting reserves; and it seems at least possible that the popular imagination, wondering what had induced a Norman king to do something so un-Norman as to make life a little less dangerous and uncomfortable for the Anglo-Saxon poachers in the greenwoods of England, concluded in its poetic and religious way that during his hunting days in Sherwood forest, he must have met that ancient spirit of the trees and of Anglo-Saxon nationhood, Robin, and liked him. According to the ballad, Richard had donned the religious habit of a monk for his meeting with the legendary Robin, and this is yet another indication of how deeply rooted the story is in the old unchanging animistic beliefs of the country folk, dressed up – like the king – as those beliefs were in borrowed Christian clothing over older religious beliefs.

After his weekend hunting, Richard moved on to Southwell, there to meet William the Lion, the king of Scotland, who had come to attend his crowning ceremony. They travelled together during Holy Week, spending a night at Melton Mowbray before reaching Northampton on 9 April, where they spent Easter. William's attempt to persuade Richard to cede much of northern England to him, including Northumberland, Cumberland and Westmorland on the grounds that these counties had once formed part of his predecessors' heritage had little success, but his failure does not seem to have affected the friendship between the two men, who reached Winchester together on 15 April. Two days later, on the Sunday after Easter, after making his confession and receiving absolution from the archbishop of Canterbury, Richard was ceremonially robed and crowned in St Swithin's priory in the presence of William of Scotland, Queen Eleanor and a large company of bishops and barons, before proceeding to the cathedral. On arrival, he was led through the nave, crowded with people standing shoulder to shoulder, and on through the choir to the high altar in the sanctuary, where he knelt to receive a blessing from the archbishop of Canterbury. Mass was then said, accompanied by a choir of monks and abbots singing plainsong, and after the final blessing the king was led out of the building and back to the priory in continuing solemnity under a canopy of silk. There, having changed into less formal clothing, he dined in the monks' refectory before repairing to Winchester castle, where he spent the night. The whole thing was a magnificent performance in support of Richard's royal authority; but we shall misunderstand it if we regard it as a mere publicity stunt, however splendidly staged, for those taking part in it believed that what they were doing was a deeply significant piece of work, rooted in the reality of their relationship with God. Konrad Lorenz, in a slightly different context, made an illuminating comment. 'The iconoclast regards the pomp of the ritual as an inessential superficiality, but I believe he is entirely wrong . . . Fidelity to the symbol implies fidelity to everything it signifies.' Medieval men and women seem to have known this instinctively, and if we are to understand them, the things they did, and their motives for doing them, we would do well to remember this aspect of their understanding of life and of their own nature.

On 22 April, Richard left Winchester for Portsmouth, where a fleet of a hundred small ships had been gathered to transport a large army to Normandy; but the weather was against him, the sea continuously whipped up by late spring gales blowing in from the Atlantic, and he was forced to delay sailing. He tried to curb his impatience by spending some of his time hunting, but in his absence trouble broke out between some Welsh mercenaries and some Brabançons; men on both sides were killed, and he was forced to return to the city to restore order and punish the culprits. For three days, while the gale showed no sign of blowing itself out, and the skies looked more like those of mid-winter than those of the first week in May, Richard fretted, swearing that Portsmouth was the most tedious and boring place on earth, and on 2 May he could bear it no longer; he ordered the army to embark, and told the sailors to set sail. When they advised him not to do so, he told them to take their advice elsewhere; but the sailors were right, and having spent a hideously uncomfortable night with both men and horses being sick as they pitched about in the dark, airless and appallingly crowded lower decks of the storm-tossed ships in the Solent and off the Isle of Wight, even Richard had to admit defeat, and the fleet was ordered to return to port. For another week there was hardly a break in the clouds as they scudded in from the Atlantic and the gale continued, making any thought of putting to sea impossible; but on 11 May the wind abated, and early the next day the whole fleet set sail for Normandy. It had been a frustrating time, but now that at last it was over, Richard's temper improved. He did not know that he would never set foot in England again.

On landing at Barfleur, Richard received a tumultuous welcome from crowds so dense that 'you could not throw an apple in the air without it dropping on someone's head;' or so it was said at the time. The people were genuinely thrilled to see him, cheering and singing,

'God has come again in his strength.
Soon now the king of France will go.'

They did not like Philip Augustus. They were Normans, not Frenchmen, and the French king had no business in their land. So Richard was greeted everywhere with rapturous enthusiasm by cheering crowds as he made his way from Barfleur to Caen, where he stayed for a few days before moving on to Lisieux. There, his brother, John, arrived, having decided to desert the French king and throw himself upon his brother's mercy; he did not even dare approach his brother, but sent a message to say that he was in town. Richard bade him come to see him and not to be afraid, and when he did so, greeted him with a mixture of contemptuous indulgence and remarkable generosity. He was not to fear, Richard told him; he was little more than a child (he was twenty-six!) and he had been misled by others. They were the true culprits, who deserved punishment, and they would receive it. But if Richard was generous to him, John of Alençon, in whose house the king was staying, was less so; he told John bluntly that he was a lucky man to get off so lightly: far more lightly than he deserved or than Richard would have fared, if John had been in his brother's shoes and their roles had been reversed. How John took this rebuke is not recorded, but it is unlikely that he took it well; he was not the most estimable of men, as he demonstrated only too clearly immediately after his reconciliation to his brother. For the manner in which he chose to show his gratitude to Richard was to be as unscrupulously treacherous to Philip Augustus as he had just ceased to be to Richard. The French king had recently made him governor of Evreux, having invaded eastern Normandy and captured the place before Richard could return to defend his lands, and John now returned there, entering it as governor in the name of the king of France, while carefully refraining from telling the garrison that he had changed sides overnight. Once inside, however, he had the unsuspecting French massacred, and proudly declared the town returned to its rightful lord, namely his brother, King Richard.

Evreux was not the only Norman city to be captured by Philip of France during Richard's captivity in Germany; he had besieged and taken two or three dozen other towns and fortresses in Normandy alone, some by force and some as a result of the surrender of their garrisons, which had given up hope of ever seeing Richard alive again after so long an absence, and it was to recapture these strongholds from the French king that Richard now set himself. His most urgent task, however, was to prevent Philip's making any further gains. The French king was in the process of laying siege to Verneuil, a key fortress on the approaches to Rouen from the south, and Richard was determined to relieve the place before it could fall to him. Under the command of a certain William de Mortemer, the garrison had greeted the arrival of Philip and his army with something very like *insouciance* born of the fact that they had been besieged a year previously without succumbing: a feat they were confident of repeating. They had greeted the French by throwing open the gate of the city, and shouting from the walls a derisive invitation to their king to be their guest; they would give him the warmest of welcomes, they promised, if only he would be good enough to step inside. When there was no response, hooting with irreverent laughter, they slammed the city gate, having painted an extremely rude and unflattering portrait of Philip on it for the edification of his troops. Philip had not been amused. He had prosecuted the siege with anger and determination to teach the garrison manners, and by the time that Richard was ready to come to their assistance, they were in considerable distress; the French siege engines had demolished part of the city wall, and while the defenders' resolution to resist Philip's attack was unimpaired, their self-confidence was not what it had been in the early days of the siege. Somehow, however, they managed to smuggle a knight out of the city and through the French lines to bring the news of their straits to Richard, whom he met a few miles west of Verneuil. Richard immediately ordered a mixed force of knights, crossbowmen and foot soldiers to go to the city's relief, fighting their way into it if necessary, but with any luck taking the French by surprise and entering the place unopposed; whatever happened, the garrison must be reinforced. Meanwhile, others were sent east on a forced march with orders to cut the French supply lines and to harass them from the rear.

Both parties were successful, and the position of the French army under the walls of Verneuil was transformed almost overnight; from being on the point of victory they suddenly found themselves facing a garrison whose morale had been raised to new heights by the arrival of reinforcements and the news of Richard's approach, while their line of retreat was threatened by other English troops. To make matters worse, news of John's apostasy and the fate of the French garrison of Evreux reached Philip Augustus at about the same time as Richard's men succeeded in reinforcing Verneuil, and he was so angry that he led a detachment of his men away from the siege to punish John and the citizens of Evreux for their compliance in the slaughter of his men, even though the townsfolk could not possibly have had any chance of preventing it. On hearing news of the approach of the French king, John fled, leaving the citizens of the place to pay the price of his crime: a price duly exacted by Philip Augustus, who sacked the city and massacred most of its inhabitants. Meanwhile, however, the French troops which he had left behind under the walls of Verneuil had had enough. Seeing Philip depart for Evreux and aware that Richard was on his way, they waited only one day after Philip's departure before deciding to retreat before the hero of the recent Crusade could arrive. It was a sensible move on their part, for Richard was far stronger than they were; but they had left their retreat too late to make good their escape unscathed. Richard chased them for a day or two, capturing much of their equipment and arms, and killing stragglers and a few men of the rearguard, before he entered Verneuil in triumph on 30 May to a tremendous welcome from garrison and citizens alike. It is said that he was so delighted with the way in which they had fought during the siege that he kissed every one of them in token of his gratitude.

He was right to be grateful to the people of Verneuil; their courage and endurance had given him a victory over Philip Augustus which was to prove a turning-point in the war. Hitherto, the French king, aided and abetted by Richard's brother John, had had his own way in almost all things, but now with Richard's arrival on the scene with a large new army from England, he was about to lose many of the castles and fortified towns he had captured during Richard's absence, even though the war was to drag on for years with the normal ups and downs of fortune being experienced by both sides at different times. It was the usual kind of medieval warfare of siege and counter-siege, of the capture of castles and towns, the burning of crops, the laying waste of enemy lands, the sacking of cities, of march and chase and counter-march and very few pitched battles. To follow it in detail, listing the various places gained or lost – Neufmarché, Aumâle, Eu, Mortemer, Arques, Illiers-l'Evêque, Gaillon, Marcilly-sur-Eure, Pacy, Tillières-sur-Avre to mention but a very few – would be tedious in the extreme and comprehensible only to someone with a first class knowledge of medieval French geography. However, no such daunting task is necessary, a much less detailed account of the general course of the war is sufficient to gain an understanding of the last few years of Richard's life; and this is fortunate, not only for the reader, but also for the historian, for the records of this particular period leave much to be desired. One of the most reliable sources of information about Richard's life up to this point has been Roger of Howden, thought to be a Yorkshire cleric; he had been on Crusade with him, and he wrote two valuable accounts of the events of his time, the *Gesta*

Henricii II et Ricardi I and the *Chronica*. But now Roger had returned to his native Yorkshire, and was forced to rely on second-hand reports and hearsay for his account of Richard's last few years. Other sources are patchy, confusing and sometimes mutually contradictory when it comes to describing the details of any particular event, its exact date, and who did what to whom, although the overall course of the war with its main happenings and occasional periods of truce is clear enough most of the time.

Although Richard's most important losses during the years of his absence on Crusade and in captivity had been in Normandy, his Angevin domain had not escaped, and after the relief of Verneuil he led his army south into Aquitaine in a bid to recapture some of the castles of the Loire which his brother John had surrendered to Philip Augustus. On his way through Tours, he ejected the canons of St Martin, the patron saint of France and at one time bishop of Tours, from their houses and confiscated their rents, though what they had done to incur his wrath is not known. The citizens of Tours must also have been in his bad books, for they made him a present of two thousand marks in compensation for an unspecified fault before he moved on to join his brother-in-law, Sancho of Navarre, under the formidable walls of the huge and forbidding fortress of Loches on the river Indre. He found the Navarrese together with a few Brabantine mercenaries in the lowest of spirits, convinced that they would never take the place, impregnable as it both looked and was reputed to be. But the word 'impregnable' was not to be found in Richard's vocabulary, and after he had assaulted the place for three days and nights with siege engines, on 13 June the garrison surrendered: not surprisingly, as it turned out, for it consisted of only five knights and two dozen men-at-arms – or so one authority asserts, while another speaks of 'a large garrison', which seems less likely to be true.

In the space of a month, Richard had inflicted a number of stinging defeats on the king of France, while the most that Philip had managed to do in return had been to sack Evreux, demolish a small and unimportant castle a few miles from Rouen, and capture the earl of Leicester, who had ventured out without an escort. It had been a bad month for Philip, and he now proposed a truce. Richard was not averse to the idea in principle, for his own troops needed a rest, but after several days of increasingly angry debate he refused to agree to the terms suggested by the French king, and the two sides parted in an atmosphere of mutual recrimination and bitterness to resume hostilities. Since Richard had been so successful in Aquitaine, Philip now marched south to prevent his making any further gains in the Loire valley, and one of the more dramatic events of the war began to take shape. Hearing of Philip's approach, Richard led his army northwards to take up position below the walls of Vendôme on the upper reaches of the Loire, blocking the road which Philip needed to take if he was to have any effect in the rich wine-growing country farther downstream. There, Richard hoped that at last he would be able to bring the French army to battle, and the prospects of a decisive engagement looked even brighter a day or so later when Philip, having been told by his scouts that Richard and his army lay just ahead of him, sent a bombastic message to announce that he intended to attack in the morning. But Philip and the truth were infrequent bedfellows, and having delivered his martial challenge, he turned and fled in the opposite direction. It was not long before Richard discovered the deception and gave chase, catching up with the retreating French army in the woods near Fréteval, where their retreat was turned into a rout. Determined to have his revenge on Philip Augustus, Richard pursued him until his horse was so tired that it could carry him no further, whereupon, according to Roger of Howden, he was immediately supplied with another. But even with a fresh horse, he failed to overtake the French king, who, according to another account, had deserted his army and was hearing Mass in a church some distance from the road on which his army was being harried by Richard's men; but if Philip escaped capture, many of his men, their horses, tents, siege engines and equipment did not. Worse still, in the days before banks and credit cards, kings had to carry much of their treasure with them, if their men were to be paid, and this too fell into Richard's hands together with some papers in which he found the names of those of his own subjects who had been prepared to join the French king during his absence on Crusade and in captivity in Germany.

It was a humiliating defeat for Philip of France; twice within the space of little over a month since Richard's return to France he had lost an army, a wagon train, some artillery, and much treasure, once at Verneuil and now again in the woods near Fréteval, and the effect on the morale of his supporters was devastating, while Richard's reputation for invincibility reached new heights. It was a reputation which sent shudders down the backs of those of his subjects who had sided with the French king while Richard had been abroad, and he now turned south to re-establish his authority there, armed with a list of their names. That he did so re-establish it, we know, but of the details of how he did so during the next few weeks we know nothing except what he himself said in a letter to the archbishop of Canterbury, Hubert Walter. 'Know that, by the grace of God,' he wrote, 'who in all things supports the right, we have taken Taillebourg and Marsillac, and all the castles and lands of Geoffrey de Rancon, as well as the cities of Angoulême, Neufchatel, Montignac, Lachaise and all the other castles and lands of the count of Angoulême. We captured the city of Angoulême and its citadel in a single evening, and in the course of the whole campaign we have taken fully three hundred knights and forty thousand men.' However he may have achieved all this, it was another remarkable feat of arms, for, as one contemporary observed, he had 'established his authority from the castle of Verneuil to the Pyrenees, and no one could stand out against him'; and all this in a matter of weeks.

But however well Richard might be restoring his authority in his southern lands, in Normandy things were not going so well for him. There, John and the earl of Arundel were taken by surprise by the king of France, still smarting from his defeat near Fréteval, and roundly defeated near the town of Vaudreuil. This left the field wide open to Philip to make further gains there but, having recently lost the bulk of two armies, he needed time before he could exploit his success; as a result, once again he proposed a truce, this time speaking from a position of some strength, and since by now Richard's men were even more in need of a rest than they had been previously, after the usual arguments and angry exchanges, on 23 July 1194, representatives of the two sides signed a truce at the little town of Tillières on the river Avre half way between Nonancourt and Verneuil. It was to last until November of the next year, and although like all medieval truces it was honoured more in the breach than the observance, at least it provided a respite from war for those engaged in the fighting; for a time at least they could enjoy their private lives in something like peace.

But what was Richard's private life like? In spite of the fact that the lives of medieval kings were lived more publicly than privately, we know very little of how Richard spent his time. Like others in his position and with his background, he loved hunting, and there is evidence that he was something of a *bon viveur*; he enjoyed a good feast from time to time, although, as already briefly mentioned, it is easy to forget how limited the pleasures of the table were, even for kings, throughout the Middle Ages and beyond, when more than half the fruits and vegetables we find in every supermarket virtually every day of the year, either tinned, frozen or freshly imported by air from somewhere oceans away, were totally unknown, while everything else was available only in season and almost entirely absent throughout the winter months. Wine was abundant for the nobility and even for some humbler folk, and Richard seems to have enjoyed it, as no doubt he did over Christmas 1194, which he spent at Rouen resting from his military exertions. Whether Berengaria was with him or not is not known, however, and this is perhaps the most intriguing mystery of his private life; for what was their relation-ship like? Their marriage, like all royal marriages at that time, had been primarily a political arrangement, and in this respect it had paid handsome dividends in Richard's alliance with his father-in-law, Sancho of Navarre, who had backed him nobly in his wars with Philip Augustus, both during his absence and also on his return from captivity; but the marriage had produced no children, and this it had certainly been designed to do, for kings needed heirs to ensure the continuing stability of their realms when they died, and the failure of Berengaria to have a child was both serious and worrying. No one knows, and presumably no one ever will know, just why she never had a child. She may have been that wretched creature, so much dreaded by all her sex throughout most of history, a barren woman, and this would go some way to explain why, after the first months of their marriage, Richard spent so little time with her; for what was the point of continuing to sleep with a woman if she was barren: a woman whom one had married, not because of any physical attraction or desire, but for political reasons in order to produce an heir? A mistress was different; the fewer children she had, the more one could enjoy her favours. On the other hand the fruitlessness of the marriage may have been caused by Richard. It is possible that he was infertile or perhaps impotent; but while this is possible, it does not seem very likely. He had at least one illegitimate child, a son named Philip of Cognac, which makes any idea that he was infertile difficult to accept; while the suggestion that he may have been impotent cannot be true if there is any substance in the numerous charges brought against him by his contemporaries that, on the contrary, he was grossly over-sexed and filled with intemperate lust for women: charges which may well have been the cause of the hermit's celebrated warning to him to avoid 'illicit acts', if he did not want to bring the wrath of God down on his head; and thus we are left no wiser as to the cause of Berengaria's childlessness.

In fact, Richard's encounter with the censorious old anchorite took place round about Christmas time 1194, while he was at Rouen, and the old man's dark apocalyptic threats had little effect; Richard remained unimpressed, and presumably therefore continued to indulge in whatever 'illicit acts' he may have been enjoying before the pious old harbinger of woe took it upon him to warn him of his coming fate; and whatever those acts may have been, fire and brimstone did not descend upon him from above as the old man had prophesied: a fact which may have reinforced Richard's somewhat cynical attitude to those who tried to correct his morals from time to time. This attitude was made very clear on another occasion, when yet another self-appointed Jeremiah, a celebrated preacher named Fulk of Neuilly, taxed him with some of his other vices. 'I warn you,' he said, 'that unless you see to it that your three shameless daughters are married soon, God will punish you for their sins.' Richard replied that he had no daughters, as Fulk knew perfectly well; he should therefore stop talking nonsense. 'I am not talking nonsense,' Fulk retorted unabashed. 'You do indeed have three shameless daughters, and their names are Pride, Avarice and Lust.' 'Listen to this hypocrite!' Richard expostulated, turning to the assembled company. 'He accuses me of having three shameless daughters, Pride, Avarice and Lust, and urges me to arrange marriages for them. Very well! I will do as he requests. I give Pride to the Knights Templar, Avarice to the Cistercian Order, and Lust to the bishops and archbishops of the Church.' But Roger of Howden, who tells this particular story, adds rather piously that the king should have been ashamed to raise a laugh at the expense of so holy a man as Fulk, and goes on to relate how Richard became gravely ill at Easter 1195, and was so shaken with remorse for his past sins that he swore to amend his life, if only he was spared. 'He was not ashamed to confess the guiltiness of his life,' Roger continues, 'and after receiving absolution, he took back his wife, whom he had not known for a long time and, putting aside all illicit intercourse, he remained faithful to her, and they became one flesh, and the Lord gave them health of body and soul.' But splendidly generous as the Lord thus proved himself to be, he still refrained from giving poor Berengaria a child or Richard an heir.

This picture of a reformed Richard living faithfully and respectably in peace with his wife at Rouen during a welcome respite from war, going hunting and occasionally wining and dining with his friends, and presumably enjoying himself in other equally innocent ways too, may conjure up a charming vision of the royal couple at home on holiday, rather like an English royal couple enjoying an idyllic few days at Windsor; but if it does so, it would be a pity, for nothing could be farther from the truth. The truce of Tillières may have temporarily outlawed open warfare, but a good deal of minor military skulduggery went on most of the time on both sides, unimpeded by any finicky fidelity to the letter of the terms of the truce, and however thoroughly Richard may have amended his life and become one flesh with Berengaria, he would not have been the man he was if he had not been fairly frequently away from Rouen, overseeing or even conducting the covert military operations against Philip of France which are known to have taken place during the year which followed the signing of the truce. Records are sparse almost to the point of non-existence, so that very few details are known; but the situation of the two sides when the truce was signed in July 1194 is known, when negotiations for a possible peace treaty were begun. By that time Richard was in a far stronger position than he had been a year or so earlier, having somehow recaptured various castles, forced Philip to abandon certain places as being no longer tenable, and rebuilt other strongholds to his own advantage and the disadvantage of the French king. One incident during this time, however, has escaped the general oblivion, and is worth describing, since it is typical of the way in which each side tried to mislead the other without the smallest reference to the terms of the truce.

Vaudreuil was a key Norman fortress which Philip had acquired while Richard was in Germany. Since then, he had defeated John and the earl of Arundel when they had tried to retake the place, and as a result he still held it; but as Richard's forces had crept forward during the truce, Philip's whole position in Normandy had become more and more untenable, and he had begun to realize that eventually he would have to relinquish Vaudreuil. So a conference was held with the ostensible purpose of making the necessary arrangements for a French withdrawal. However, unknown to Richard and contrary to the terms of the truce, Philip had begun to undermine the walls of Vaudreuil, determined to demolish it rather than allow it to fall back intact into Richard's hands, and the conference had no other purpose from his point of view than to gain enough time for his men to complete their work of demolition before the king of England could re-enter such an important strategic fortress. Consequently, while the two sides were discussing the cession of the castle, suddenly there was an immense rumbling crash as the great walls fell down, and only then did Richard realize that Philip had tricked him once again. Furious, he ordered an attack, swearing by God's legs that he would take his revenge on the French king for his duplicity; but Philip was a master of the art of deceit and a past-master of the more important art of avoiding the consequences of his perfidy, and he had already begun to make good his escape across the Seine, having ordered his men to break down the bridge at Portjoie behind him. So, once again, Richard was cheated of his revenge; but if Philip escaped, Vaudreuil did not. Richard took what was left of it together with what was left of the French army which had been abandoned to its fate by Philip as he ensured his own safety.

Philip was not the only one to cheat during the truce. Richard, too, did not miss an opportunity to further his own cause by ignoring its terms whenever he could do so with impunity; and on the whole he gained a good deal more than did the French king. Medieval truces were like that. Even after a peace treaty was signed by the two sides at Louviers over Christmas 1195, both behaved as though they knew perfectly well that peace would not last. Indeed, it was at this time that Richard began to build the great complex of fortified buildings – castle, palace, and fortifications – on the Seine at Les Andelys known under the portmanteau name of Château-Gaillard, which has usually been rendered into English as Saucy Castle, though 'Defiant' might be nearer to what Richard meant when he named it 'Gaillard'. However that may have been, it remains a military masterpiece, proof of Richard's many talents; for its site is a proof of his vision as a strategist, commanding as it does the approaches to Rouen and the heart of his Norman duchy, while its design is a proof of his genius as a military engineer with its many original and innovative features. In a letter written in 1907, T.E. Lawrence, who was making a study of crusader castles at the time, was deeply impressed. 'Its plan is marvellous,' he wrote, 'the execution wonderful, and the situation perfect. The whole construction bears the stamp of genius. Richard I must have been a far greater man than we usually consider him.' Incidentally, it also cost an enormous sum of money, more than most of his other building projects put together, which is an indication of how important Richard took it to be and of how little trust he put in the peace treaty with Philip.

After its construction, Richard tended to spend much of his time there; indeed, it became his favourite place of residence, and it was while he was there that he had a meeting – an encounter might be a better word – with Bishop Hugh of Lincoln, who was canonized in 1220 to become St Hugh of Lincoln. It was a significant meeting during which not only did both men appear at their best, but in a very real sense they also personified two dominant and sometimes opposing forces in twelfth-century society. For Hugh personified the early medieval church at its absolute best, while on this particular occasion Richard came very near to personifying the early medieval monarchy at its best too; for while many medieval kings could behave abominably, some could also put modern dictators, presidents and ruling politicians to shame with sudden gestures of great generosity, humility and sheer humanity. The reason for this encounter between Hugh and Richard was a dispute between the bishop and some of Richard's tax collectors. As part of a fund-raising campaign to pay for the war in France, it had been decreed that certain church property should be sequestrated; but Hugh had refused to allow this to happen in his diocese of Lincoln. He admitted that the church was in duty bound to come to the assistance of the king when he was at war within his realm of England itself, but it was under no such obligation to help him wage war abroad. Richard was told of Hugh's recalcitrance, and duly ordered the seizure of the property in question, whether Hugh agreed or not; but the bishop's reputation for sanctity was so great that no one could be found to carry out the royal command, much to Richard's increased annoyance. Much the same happened when he sent some men of higher rank than the normal tax collectors to enforce his will upon the obstinate prelate; on arrival in Lincoln, they proved to be so obviously embarrassed by their task and uncomfortable at the thought of using force to prevail over so saintly a man as the bishop that Hugh had pity on them, and decided to go to France and explain himself to Richard in person. On arrival at Château-Gaillard, he found Richard at Mass in the chapel as the choir sang the anthem, *Ave, inclyte praesul Christi, flos pulcherime!* – Hail, renowned priest of Christ, blossom of great beauty! – and his chaplains, worried by the possible outcome of his encounter with the king, took it to be a good omen. Richard was in his stall near the entrance of the chapel, facing the altar, surrounded by courtiers, a couple of archbishops and two bishops, and as Hugh approached, he frowned and turned his head away. Undaunted, Hugh continued on his way until he faced Richard. 'My Lord King, kiss me,' he said. But Richard was not to be so easily mollified; he turned his head even farther away without deigning to reply. Still undaunted, Hugh grasped Richard's tunic and shook it gently, saying, 'Come on! You owe me a kiss. I have come a long way to see you.' This time Richard replied. 'You deserve no kiss from me.' But Hugh shook him more vigorously, this time by his cloak, and said, 'Yes, I do! I have every right to one. Kiss me!' shaking the king backwards and forwards until Richard laughed in spite of himself at the sheer courage of the man, and kissed him. It is easy to imagine how everyone else in the chapel had been holding their breath, as they had watched this little drama unfold, while the priest at the altar went on mumbling the words of the Mass and, as it finished, they moved aside to make room for Hugh to take his place among them after Richard had kissed him; but Hugh smiled, shook his head, and went and knelt in front of the altar with his head lowered in prayer. Then, as the choir began to sing the *Agnus Dei*, Richard got up from his stall, and went and knelt by Hugh's side, where, at the appropriate liturgical moment, he turned and gave him the kiss of peace. Later, after the service and a long conversation with Hugh, Richard is said to have remarked, 'Truly, if all the bishops and archbishops were like him, there is not a prince in Christendom who would dare to raise his head in their presence.'

But to return to the peace treaty signed at Louviers at Christmas, Richard was wise not to trust it. It lasted less than six months before hostilities broke out again, and the war, inter-rupted occasionally by yet another truce and even less frequently by short periods of peace, dragged on its dreary and destructive way. It was fought in Normandy, in the Seine valley, in Berry, and on the borders of Anjou, and although records of the fighting are sparse, it seems that most of the time things went Richard's way, though he suffered a reverse from time to time. Meanwhile, behind the military scenes an equally important – indeed, perhaps an even more important – diplomatic war was being waged between the two sides, and this, too, went largely in Richard's favour. It has been customary for many years to say that, while Richard was a much better soldier than the French King, as a politician and diplomat Philip was by far the more able man. If diplomatic talent is measured by the lengths to which a man is prepared to go in dishonesty, breaking his word, and general deceit – and even the most cursory study of history lends some support to such a conclusion – then Philip was undoubtedly a better diplomat than Richard. Moreover, in the end he achieved his political objective in the overthrow of the Angevin power in France, and since nothing succeeds like success, a chorus of historians have sung Philip's diplomatic and political praises. This has been true especially of French historians, who have every reason to regard the man who brought unity to their country with favour, while judging Richard to have been a failure for losing his Angevin inheritance in France; but that is precisely what Richard did not do, and might never have done, had he not been killed by a random shot from a crossbow below the walls of the little castle at Châlus in the Limousin. It was John who lost both the Angevin domains in France and the war with Philip, not Richard, whose last years were marked by some remarkable triumphs, both in the military field and in that of diplomacy, and perhaps especially in the latter.

In the summer of 1196, to the consternation of the French king and the astonishment of the diplomatic world, after the death of Count Raymond V of Toulouse, Richard quietly approached Raymond's son, Raymond VI, and suggested that an alliance between himself as duke of Aquitaine and Raymond as count of Toulouse and his nearest neighbour might well be beneficial to both parties; the two had been at daggers drawn, fighting each other for the best part of forty years – a fact which had suited Philip down to the ground – but was it not now time to settle their differences in peace? Richard was prepared to renounce his claim to Toulouse, and to give the hand of his sister Joan to the count in marriage with a suitably appealing dowry in return for a close and friendly alliance. Raymond VI was delighted to make peace with Richard, thus escaping from the melancholy, repetitive and appallingly costly business of war and counter-war with the dukes of Aquitaine, while gaining most of the objectives for which his father had fought; and so to the world's shocked surprise he travelled to Rouen, and there became Richard's brother-in-law.

With his southern flank now free from threat, Richard turned northwards to Flanders, one of the smallest, but also one of the most densely populated and richest countries in Europe. Geographically, it was in a difficult position; it was obviously essential for it to maintain good relations with its large neighbour, France, to the south, and Count Baldwin of Flanders and Hainault, to give him his full title, had always tried to do so, taking Philip's side during his recent ascendancy while Richard was captive in Germany; but his country was equally dependent in many ways upon its other great neighbour across the narrow sea, with whom it was in an even closer economic relationship than it was with France. Cut off its trade with England, and not only would its prosperity be undermined, but it would very soon be desperately short of food, especially grain imported from East Anglia, which it needed to feed the people of cities like Lille and Bruges, where woollen cloth was made, much of it from English wool. Richard's first move in an attempt to persuade Baldwin to stop supporting the king of France was to impose a trade embargo; no more food and no more wool was to be exported to Flanders, and any Englishmen caught doing so would have their goods seized, while they themselves would be hanged. But having applied the stick, Richard now dangled a carrot before Baldwin's nose, promising him a large cash payment, a number of other gifts, and a splendid consignment of wine from Aquitaine, if he would cease to support the king of France and support Richard instead. Since the war with France was going Richard's way more often than not – a fact which must have been known to Baldwin, or he would never have acted as he did – in July 1197 he signed a formal treaty with Richard. The embargo on trade was immediately lifted, Baldwin was handsomely rewarded, and the king of France's nose was put most thoroughly out of joint.

These two diplomatic triumphs, one in Toulouse and the other in Flanders, changed the balance of power in western Europe decisively in Richard's favour; and they were not his only successes in the diplomatic field. Having conquered Sicily, the Emperor Henry VI of Hohenstaufen died of a fever at Messina at about this time, having managed in his thirty-two short years of life to gain a reputation for insatiable ambition, treachery and unspeakable cruelty, and his death plunged Germany into confusion over who was to be his heir. Needless to say, Richard and Philip supported rival contestants for the vacant imperial throne, and while the details of the ensuing struggle, extremely complicated and tedious as they are, happily need not concern us, the fact that Richard's allies and kinsmen amongst the princes of the Lower Rhine received his support for their own pet candidate, Henry the Lion's son, Otto of Brunswick, served to strengthen their allegiance to him and their support for him in his war with Philip Augustus. It was yet another diplomatic success.

But these diplomatic moves and counter-moves, important as they were, formed no more than the background to the main military contest, which continued as before; and despite his military ascendancy, time was beginning to run out for Richard. Before it actually did so, however, he enjoyed one more military triumph over Philip Augustus which is worth describing, if only because the word 'enjoy' is almost certainly the right one to describe Richard's feelings on this particular occasion. It happened in September 1198. Baldwin of Flanders, true to his new treaty obligations to Richard, invaded Artois and laid siege to the city of St Omer, whose citizens called urgently for help from Philip; but Philip could do little for them, for he was getting the worst of the war in Normandy against Richard, who had forced him to flee when he had attempted a raid into the Norman Vexin. Richard had retaliated by raiding the French Vexin and capturing a number of small border fortresses, including that at Courcelles. When told of Richard's advance, the French king had set out to bring relief to the beleaguered garrison of the place, not knowing that Courcelles had already fallen; but as he and his army marched to its relief, they were spotted by one of Richard's patrols, accompanied by Richard himself. Realizing that to summon his main force before attacking the French army would give Philip Augustus time to escape and jeopardize the element of surprise, Richard decided to attack while the French were wholly unprepared, even though his own force was greatly inferior in numbers. As usual, he led the attack himself, according to one contemporary writer 'like a hungry lion which catches sight of its prey', and for the second time within a few days Philip Augustus was forced to take to flight. While his men were being either killed or captured, Philip galloped at breakneck speed for the castle at Gisors, the one sanctuary in which he hoped that he might find refuge, if he could reach it in time. If he had failed to do so, as very nearly happened, the history of Europe would have been very different; as it was, however, the French king escaped, even though Richard's pursuit was so hot that the drawbridge at the gate of the great castle at Gisors collapsed under the weight of French knights struggling to reach safety; twenty were drowned in the moat below the drawbridge, and it was said at the time that Philip himself was one of those who had to be dragged from the water to safety. Several hundred other French knights were captured before they could reach the sanctuary of the castle, and apart from the hair's breadth escape of the French king Richard's victory was complete. But it was destined to be his last.

By the winter of 1198, both Philip Augustus and Richard came under pressure from the pope to settle their differences, and once again to go to the aid of their fellow Christians in the Holy Land; but Richard refused to make peace with the French king while he still held any Norman territory. When the papal legate chided him for putting his own quarrel with Philip above the pressing needs of the people of Outremer, Richard was furious. 'You forget that if it had not been for his determination to leave me in the Holy Land to shoulder the whole burden of the war while he returned to vent his malice upon my inheritance, I would have recovered Jerusalem long ago. And when I did return, what did the church do to help me?' Chastened, the papal legate departed. Richard simmered down and, as the weeks passed, was persuaded to agree reluctantly to a limited truce with Philip. It proved to be fragile in the extreme, each side eyeing the other with the utmost suspicion, and there were frequent small breaches of its terms, while certain areas of conflict were specifically excluded from its embrace. One of these was the rebellion of some of Richard's subjects in Angoulême and Limousin, encouraged in the first place by Philip Augustus and thereafter supported by him, but now abandoned to their fate by the French king. Once again, however, really reliable records are more noticeable by their absence than by their profusion, and the progress of this particular little war, including as it does the story of Richard's death, has been so largely appropriated by the creators of historical propaganda, romantic legend, and something very like fiction that it is difficult to sort out fact from fable.

The romantic story, laced with propaganda vilifying Richard, begins in March 1199, when news of a magnificent golden treasure, turned up by a plough near the little town of Châlus not far from Limoges, is said to have reached the king. It consisted of 'an Emperor and his wife, sons and daughters, all of pure gold, seated round a golden table', according to one account, and was almost certainly of Roman origin. Another version of the story turns the treasure into a hoard of golden coins, while yet another relates how Count Ademar of Angoulême, one of the rebels against Richard supported by the French king, in surprisingly dutiful mood sent most of a great hoard of gold and silver found on his land to Richard as his liege lord, but that Richard, evil man that he was and consumed with greed, demanded the lot, and when it was refused, attacked his subject's castle at Châlus. Meanwhile, other versions of the story of Richard's attack on the castle at Châlus make no mention of treasure trove, which may never have existed except in the imagination of those who wished to blacken Richard's memory, presenting him as one who, at the sweet smell of treasure, immediately began to behave like a beast with the smell of blood in its nostrils. In fact, it is much more likely that his attack on Châlus was merely the first move in his campaign to punish Ademar of Angoulême and Aimar of Limoges, whose rebellion in Aquitaine in support of the French king had constituted a blow against the heart of the Angevin empire. It has often been said that all his life Richard thought of himself first and foremost as the duke of Aquitaine and only after that as king of England, and a rebellion in Aquitaine was something which he never found it possible to tolerate or lightly to forgive; the two men had to be punished, and having temporarily settled matters with Philip Augustus, he turned south to deal with them. His plan seems to have been to attack and subdue their castles one by one, Châlus being the first on the list, while the fortress at Nontron is known to have been his next objective. The little castle was not a formidable obstacle, and it was defended by no more than two, possibly three, knights and a handful of mercenaries: a garrison of perhaps forty men in all. Probably they could have been starved into submission with no trouble, but as always Richard was impatient; there were other rebel fortresses to be subdued, and time was never on the side of the hesitant.

The siege had been going on for three days when, in the late afternoon of 26 March 1199, Richard urged his men to redouble their efforts; the bombardment by his crossbowmen and archers was immediately intensified to give cover to those working below improvised shelters at the foot of the castle wall, where they were laboriously undermining it in the hope that the inevitability of its eventual collapse would encourage the defenders to give up the unequal struggle and surrender. This renewed attack did not induce them to surrender, but it did encourage all of them except one man to keep their heads well down. Deserted by everyone else, however, this one solitary defender continued to fight, protecting himself from the bolts and arrows of the besiegers by wielding a frying pan as a makeshift shield against the incoming missiles. When Richard arrived on the scene, the first thing he saw was this one stalwart and indomitable figure battling away on the top of the castle tower, wielding his frying pan like a champion tennis player, and he was so delighted by the sheer courage of the man that he burst out laughing and began to applaud. He was wearing a helmet and carrying a shield, but he had not bothered to don body armour, and as he applauded this latter-day Horatius, the man, spotting his arrival at the scene of the battle, fired his crossbow at him, though whether he knew that his target was the king of England, we shall never know. If Richard had not been momentarily off his guard while applauding the man, he would probably have been able to raise his shield and protect himself in time, but as it was the bolt hit him where his neck met his left shoulder, deeply embedding itself there.

After he had been hit, Richard returned to his tent, where he tried to pull out the bolt. He failed. It was too deeply embedded in his flesh; but in his efforts to remove it, he broke off the wooden shaft, leaving the iron bolt, about as long as a man's hand, firmly stuck. He called for his doctor, who was forced to cut it out with a knife. Having done so, he bandaged the wound, and told Richard to stay in his tent and rest, an order which Richard obeyed only in part; he remained in his tent, but he had no intention of resting, instead following his usual way of life as though nothing untoward had happened. As the days passed, however, his wound became septic, gangrene set in and began to spread. Richard had seen too many men die from putrefaction spreading from wounds more trivial than his own to be under any misapprehension as to what was happening to him. He sent a message to his mother, and Eleanor came as quickly as she could. By the time of her arrival, Châlus had fallen, and Richard had asked to see the man who had shot him. As defiant as he had been with his frying pan on the castle tower, perhaps to hide his fear even from himself, the man faced Richard without apology or plea for mercy. Richard in his turn, perhaps out of admiration for the man's indomitable spirit, or perhaps because, as a religious man in the process of dying, he was forcibly reminded of the words in the Lord's prayer, 'Forgive us our trespasses, as we forgive those who trespass against us,' forgave him, commanding that he should go free. A little later, he made his confession, and received the sacrament of Extreme Unction. At the time of Vespers on 7 April, Richard died.

XIII

Richard was buried in the Abbey Church at Fontevraud on Palm Sunday by Hugh of Lincoln and the bishops of Poitiers and Angers. He was laid in a tomb at the feet of his father, Henry II, and a few years later an effigy of him was placed on it. His heart was sent to Rouen Cathedral in a metal casket, where it remained until the time of the French revolution, when the casket was rifled, and its contents thrown away as mere rubbish: an unconsciously prophetic and symbolic gesture, for although the honour paid to Richard by this world took a very long time to pass away, in recent years the immense renown in which he was held for centuries, rather like his heart, has been thrown away as rubbish, and replaced by criticism, contumely and condemnation. The celebrated little Latin aphorism of St Thomas à Kempis, *Sic transit gloria mundi*, though hackneyed, is nevertheless so apt as to be irresistible in this context. Moreover, it is worth quoting, for inevitably it poses the question as to why Richard was held in almost idolatrous regard for so many years, only to be thoroughly reassessed and condemned in the past century and a half.

The answer to the first half of that question is easily given, for in many ways Richard was the incarnation of Chaucer's 'verray parfit gentil knight', even though 'gentil' would not be the word chosen by most people today to describe him; but when Chaucer was writing about a century after Richard's time, the word did not mean the same as 'gentle' means today: that is to say, kind, considerate, 'wouldn't-hurt-a-fly'. In Chaucer's day, it meant 'well born', 'having the right to bear arms' with the secondary connotation of 'honourable, generous, noble and courteous', and to most people alive in the Middle Ages Richard was all those things. He was the *preux chevalier par excellence*, handsome, strong, courageous, Christian, and royal to his finger-tips. Inheriting the dukedom of Aquitaine while still in his teens, he had fought to preserve the peace of his huge domain and to suppress the bellicosity of the perpetually quarrelsome barons there, who did not seem to have changed much since the worst days of the Dark Ages from which Europe was emerging at last; the fact that he met their violence with equal violence − or, indeed, superior violence − and their brutality with ruthless determination not to allow it to triumph, far from alienating most of the people of medieval Europe, made them thank God that at last they were ruled by someone with the courage and determination to control these latter-day barbarians in high places. After Stephen's disastrous reign, Richard's father had enforced the rule of law in England with much the same determination to meet violence with violence when necessary, rather than to allow it to prevail. Stephen had been a 'gentle' man in the modern sense of that adjective, and if Richard had been like him, people would have despaired; but he was not, and they rejoiced. Indeed, even his enemies respected him for his toughness.

But, of course, his efforts to make law prevail over lawlessness in Aquitaine would not, by themselves, have won him the esteem in which the whole medieval western world held him for so long. Two other things contributed to the growth of his legendary renown: the romance of his Crusade against Saladin, and the way in which he led his men from the front rather than from the rear, fighting alongside them and sharing their dangers, and almost invariably leading them to victory. To many people today the Crusades are examples of some of the worst fruits of religious bigotry and intransigence that the world has ever seen: a judgement with which many dedicated Christians would agree; but such a description would have been regarded as both ludicrous and very nearly blasphemous by everyone without exception in Richard's day. To recover the holy places where the Son of God had been born, lived and worked his miracles: the garden where he had been delivered into the hands of wicked men: the city in which he had been tried, condemned and crucified for the sins of the whole world and the salvation of all men, and to be able to pray again on that mount with its olive trees, from which he had ascended into heaven: to take part in all that was the most sacred duty to which any Christian man could be called. After all, it was the pope who called men to go on Crusade for God's sake and that of their fellow Christians, so how could such an enterprise be anything but holy? Thus the people despised and condemned by the twelfth century were not the crusaders for their religious bigotry and violence, but those faithless and craven creatures who failed to respond to the pope's call to rally to Christ's banner. Many of the kings had dragged their feet; even Henry II had procrastinated again and again, and Philip Augustus had not only done his best to avoid joining the Crusade in the first place, but had scuttled home like a rat at the first opportunity, when at last he got to Outremer. But Richard had not hesitated, taking the Cross immediately when he heard of the disastrous defeat of the Christian forces by Saladin on the Horns of Hattin; and this, too, had contributed to his renown. Here at last was a Christian prince who took his duty to Christ and his fellow Christians seriously enough to risk his life in their service, and not to hesitate to do so.

But perhaps the most potent ingredients in the making of Richard into a legendary hero were his extraordinary feats of courage in battle and his equally extraordinary relationship of mutual respect, admiration and courtesy with Saladin. Those feats of courage have already been described, and need not be described again, but their rarity in the annals of history must not be forgotten. For which other kings or great military commanders have ever behaved as Richard did as his ship arrived off Jaffa only to discover that the city was on the point of capitulation, whereupon he immediately beached his galley, thus effectively destroying his only means of retreat, and, leaping into the sea, waded ashore, and personally led a charge up the beach against an enemy, whose strength he could not possibly have known?

And how often has history recorded such a gesture as that made by Saladin, when, seeing Richard unhorsed in the midst of the battle outside Jaffa, he sent him a splendid Arab stallion as a gift and a token of his admiration? It is possible that the story is apocryphal, but the fact that Richard and Saladin held each other in the kind of chivalrous esteem that might have given birth to such an act of immortal generosity is true enough and, taken together with stories of Richard's heroic deeds, it is the stuff of which romantic legends are made; and those legends, though faded and banished nowadays from the historian's study, were very much still alive in the 1950s in the school playgrounds of Kent, where children used regularly to play games involving 'being' Richard the Lionheart, the greatest hero of them all.

The other half of the question posed at the beginning of this chapter was, 'Why has Richard been so thoroughly reassessed and condemned in the past century and a half?' Various factors contributing to his deconsecration are obvious enough, and some of the criticisms levelled at him have already been noticed in the course of this book. But there have been others, and perhaps the most influential were those made by Bishop William Stubbs, the great nineteenth-century historian. Adopting the high moral tone of that august century, he described Richard as 'a man of blood, whose crimes were those of one whom long use of warfare had made too familiar with slaughter: a bad son, a bad husband, a selfish ruler, and a vicious man.' These criticisms lie at the root of today's reassessment of Richard and the rejection of the romantic legend attached to his name. They set the fashion, which has been followed ever since; but how valid are they? Plainly, Richard was indeed 'a man of blood . . . familiar with slaughter'. That is undeniable; but what else could he have been, given that he was Henry II's son born in 1157 to inherit over half of a France peopled by bellicose barons like Bertrand de Born, who revelled in warfare? War was forced on Richard by his rank, his social position and his duty as duke of Aquitaine, while he was still in his teens. How would the bishop have had him respond to the call made a little later by that episcopal *primus inter pares*, the pope, to go and become familiar with the slaughter of infidels in the Holy Land, an enterprise held to be godly even by such a saint as Hugh of Lincoln? A very large number of people born in the last decades of the nineteenth century became all too familiar with slaughter between 1914 and 1918, and so did most of their sons including the author of this book between 1939 and 1945, but that hardly lays them open to the accusation of being men of blood with all the odium latent in that heavily loaded phrase. But perhaps the bishop's criticisms were levelled not so much at Richard's participation in the wars of his day, but at the manner in which he waged them; and this is more likely, for in two respects that manner was, if not unique, very rare. Unlike other kings of his day – or, indeed, of almost any day – Richard was both a brilliant soldier and also one who fought in the front rank of battle rather than directing operations from the rear: two rare characteristics. Brilliant soldiers probably cause more blood to be spilled than such men as the grand old duke of York with his *penchant* for marching his ten thousand men up and down hill in the celebrated lampoon, and plainly men who fight in the front rank of a battle do more personal blood spilling than those safely tucked away in the rear; and so it seems highly probable that it was these two characteristics of Richard which incurred the bishop's censure. If so, this is fascinating, for it was also precisely this combination of his brilliance as a commander, with his courage and his willingness to share the dangers of battle with his men that won him the admiration of the world in his own day: even indeed the admiration of his enemies. Thus, what made the twelfth century dub him *coeur de lion* made William Stubbs in the nineteenth call him a man of blood too familiar with slaughter. Richard was essentially a man of his own time, and to judge him by the standards and criteria of the nineteenth century or those of our own age, though very difficult to avoid and perhaps impossible to eschew altogether, however hard the historian may try, is hopelessly unjust. Indeed, it is worse than unjust; it is silly: almost as silly as submitting a great nineteenth-century figure such as Charles Darwin to the judgement of the twelfth century, attempting to get in touch with St Hugh of Lincoln on some celestial telephone to ask his considered opinion of the man and his doctrine of natural selection.

Richard is in such need of an advocate willing to speak in his defence that, at the risk of labouring the point, it is worth looking for a moment at the bishop's other strictures: 'a bad son, a bad husband, a selfish ruler, and a vicious man'; for once again many subsequent historians have followed the bishop's lead, agreeing with him and adding a few enjoyably venomous little jibes of their own. Taking these accusations in order, he certainly was not a bad son to his mother, Eleanor; he adored her all his life, and she adored him. Indeed, he was her favourite son, and he tended to be guided by her more than by anyone else. As to his relationship with his father, Henry, it could be argued that it was never likely to be an easy one; in one respect they were too alike to be able to get on together without friction. Henry was a tremendous personality, larger than life, dominant by nature and accident of birth, accustomed to getting his own way for much the same reasons, and though loving and generous to a fault with his children, determined, perhaps only partly consciously, never to let them forget that he was the king, the master, the boss. Richard was not so very different; very much a dominant personality in his own right, he was no man's lackey, and as a result his relationship with his father was never an easy one; but despite being made duke of Aquitaine when ridiculously young and being encouraged by his mother from time to time to revolt against Henry, again and again, he 'came to heel', as they say, when recalled to his filial duty. In the end, pushed too far by an ageing Henry, he refused to obey, and the final drama of the old man's lonely and embittered death was enacted like a scene from some ancient Greek tragedy, in which the human characters are mere pawns in a game played by the vengeful and immortal gods; but if this makes Richard a bad son in the august opinion of an eminent Victorian bishop, there may well be others who believe that, all things considered, it is astonishing that he was such a comparatively dutiful and forbearing son to his father, given their respective temperaments and the provocation to rebellion under which Richard so often lived.

Plainly, however, the bishop was on much stronger ground when he accused Richard of being a bad husband; for although all accounts agree that he appeared to be genuinely pleased to marry Berengaria in Cyprus, thereafter he spent little time with her, they had no children, and many of his contemporaries accused him of promiscuity with other women. It was even said that, after he had been mortally wounded at Châlus and told by his doctor to take things quietly, he insisted on continuing to enjoy the services of a number of *filles de joie*, to borrow a polite French euphemism, whom he summoned to his bed from the nearby city of Poitiers. In typically volatile twelfth-century fashion, his occasional outbursts of self-abasement and repentance tend to support the idea that he was something of a sexual athlete subject to bouts of revulsion and crises of self-recrimination, and by Victorian standards this would certainly make him a thoroughly bad husband and a vicious man – another of the bishop's charges against him. Indeed, by any standards such behaviour would hardly make him a wife's idea of the perfect spouse; but even if these accusations are true – and they may be nothing of the kind – how badly do they reflect upon Richard by the standards of his own day? As made abundantly clear already in the course of this story, royal marriages were never contracted because the parties to them happened to love each other; on the contrary, they were contracted for political motives and political motives alone. Indeed, one of the 'in' jokes in circles frequented by historians of the Middle Ages is that royal wives were the diplomatic bags of their day. Thus, marriage was one thing, love another, and sexual satisfaction yet another again; and if Richard played fast and loose with women other than his wife, he was doing no more than what was commonplace for most other medieval kings. His great grandfather, Henry I, had at least nineteen illegitimate children, and no one seems to have thought much the worse of him for it. Henry II, Richard's father, was more temperate, though he, too, had more than one mistress over and above Rosamund de Clifford, with whom he enjoyed his celebrated love affair. So if Richard did transgress sexually, he was doing little more than following in the footsteps of his forefathers and conforming to the accepted customs of the day, customs which included occasional bouts of genuine emotional repentance; and the reader must decide for himself or herself whether that makes him 'a bad husband and a vicious man'. No one is likely to conclude that it makes him a particularly good husband, and in the judgement of the nineteenth century it undoubtedly made him a very bad one indeed; but whether Richard's own century would have been quite so sweeping in its condemnation is another matter.

It would be unmannerly not to offer some justification for

singling out Bishop Stubbs from all Richard's other latter-day critics for special attention and disagreement, but there is a sense in which to have done so is to have paid him a compliment; for he was one of the first and most influential of Richard's critics. He set the fashion which other men have followed. Moreover, there is another respect in which he was eminently suitable for special mention; for as Richard was typical of his own century, on the whole conforming to its manners and customs, although in many ways transcending them, so Bishop Stubbs was typical of his. He was a great Victorian historian, conforming to Victorian notions of morality and social propriety, while Richard was a great Plantagenet king conforming to the ways and morals of his time. In this respect at least, king and critic were alike.

In conclusion, then, what can be said of Richard? If the legend which presented him for so long as *par excellence* the *preux chevalier sans peur et sans reproche*, bathing his memory in a golden aura of romance and faultless splendour, was a distortion of the truth, the picture of him as a brutal oaf, bloodthirsty, barbarous and a bugger is a far greater distortion. He had his faults. He could be ruthless to the point of brutality, when he considered that the situation called for ruthlessness; but neither brutality nor ruthlessness for their own sakes were amongst his vices, as they were, for instance, amongst those of the Emperor Henry VI of Hohenstaufen. Like his father and most Plantagenets, he could also be tempestuous, erupting from time to time with terrifying passion as if possessed by a demon, while at other times of real crisis, when lesser men might understandably have panicked and lost control of themselves, Richard remained entirely calm and unruffled, his judgement unimpaired. The unchanging background to his life was his Christian faith, which expressed itself most obviously in his immediate response to the pope's call for a new Crusade against Saladin after the disastrous defeat of the Christians in the Holy Land, in his regular attendance at Mass, and in his occasional bouts of self-recrimination and repentance for his misdoings. His love of music was as deep and genuine as his religion, and although only two of his poems have survived, they are enough to confirm the reputation he gained in his lifetime for real poetic talent. Thus he was a cultured, sophisticated man with a variety of interests and talents. But above all it was his courage and his brilliance as a soldier which impressed his contemporaries, and for which he was remembered with unstinting admiration by succeeding generations.

In the twelfth century, faith and courage were admired above all other virtues; today neither are fashionable, and the ages of faith are so very different from our own – remote, strange, in many ways fascinating but in others abhorrent – that men like Richard, a supremely twelfth-century man, baffle and antagonize many people. But even if he does so, no one should be so lacking in grace or historical imagination as to deny that he was one of that century's greatest children and entirely worthy of the title bestowed on him by an admiring posterity: Richard the Lionheart.

SELECT BIBLIOGRAPHY

SOURCES

Ambroise, *L'Estoire de la Guerre Sainte*, ed. Gaston Paris, Paris 1897

Gervase of Canterbury, *Historical Works*, ed. W.Stubbs, Rolls Series 1879

Ralph of Coggeshall, *Chronicon Anglicanum*, ed. J.Stevenson, Rolls Series 1875

Giraldus Cambrensis, *Concerning the Instruction of Princes*, trans. J. Stevenson, Church Historians of England, 1858

Richard of Devizes, *Chronicon*, ed. J.T. Appleby, London 1963

Ralph of Diss, *Radulfi de Diceto Decani Londiniensis Opera Historica*, ed. W. Stubbs, Rolls Series 1876

Roger of Howden, *Chronica*, ed. W. Stubbs, Rolls Series 1871

Roger of Howden, *Gesta Henrici II et Ricardi I*, ed. W. Stubbs, 1867

William of Newburgh, *Historia Rerum Anglicanum* in *Chronicles of the Reigns of Stephen, Henry II and Richard I*, ed. R. Howlett, Rolls Series 1884

Beha ed-Din ibn Shedad, *Life of Saladin*, ed. C.W. Wilson, London 1897

Guillaume le Breton, *Oeuvres de Rigord et Guillaume le Breton*, ed. H.F. Delaborde, Société de l'Histoire de France, Paris 1882

Guillaume le Breton, *La Philippide*, Paris 1825

Histoire de Guillaume le Maréchal, ed. P. Meyer, Société de l'Histoire de France, Paris 1891

Itinerarium Peregrinorum et Gesta Regis Ricardi, ed. W. Stubbs, Rolls Series 1864

Lives of the Troubadours, trans. and ed. by Ida Farnell, 1896

(Most of these sources are available in translation.)

MODERN WORKS

For general background the following works are good:

J Boussard, *Le Comté d'Anjou sous Henri Plantagenêt et ses fils, 1151–1204*, Paris 1938

A. Bridge, *The Crusades*, London 1980

Joan Evans, *Life in Medieval France*, London 1957

The Oxford History of England, vol III, From Domesday Book to Magna Carta, 1087-1216, by Austin Poole, Oxford, 2nd edition 1955

S. Runciman, *A History of the Crusades*, 3 vols, Cambridge 1968

R.C. Smail, *The Crusaders in Syria and the Holy Land*, London 1973

The following more detailed works are also good:

J. Gillingham, *Richard the Lionheart*, London 1978

A. Kell, *Eleanor of Aquitaine and the Four Kings*, London 1952

K. Norgate, *Richard the Lion Heart*, London 1924

W.L. Warren, *Henry II*, London 1973

PICTURE CREDITS

A twelfth-century church in the village of
Matha near Angoulême
Antony Bridge

The tympanum of the south door of the
Church of St Peter at Aulnay
Antony Bridge

A memorial carving to the Knights of St
John on the wall of the city of Rhodes
Antony Bridge

Crusader walls at Acre
Britain/Israel Public Affairs Centre

Acre and the Sea Gate
Antony Bridge

The Crypt of St John at Acre
Britain/Israel Public Affairs Centre

Crusaders greeting Arabs, from a
fouteenth-century manuscript
Mansell Collection

A portrait of Saladin by an Egyptian artist of
the Fatimid school
Mansell Collection

The crusader castle 'Krak des Chevaliers',
Syria
Sonia Halliday

A plan of Jerusalem, *circa* 1150
Ancient Art & Architecture/Ronald Sheridan

The Dome of the Rock, Jerusalem
Robert Harding Picture Library

The east end of the Abbey of Fontevraud
Ancient Art & Architecture/Ronald Sheridan

An effigy of Richard on his tomb at
Fontevraud
Ancient Art & Architecture/Ronald Sheridan

INDEX